Second Editon

Great Jobs

for

Liberal Arts
Majors

Blythe Camenson

Series Developers and Contributing Authors
Stephen E. Lambert
Julie Ann DeGalan

VGM Career Books

Chicago New York San Francisco Lisbon London Madrid Mexico City
Milan New Delhi San Juan Seoul Singapore Sydney Toronto

Library of Congress Cataloging-in-Publication Data

Camenson, Blythe.
    Great jobs for liberal arts majors / Blythe Camenson.—2nd ed.
        p.   cm. (Great jobs for—)
        Includes index.
        ISBN 0-658-01766-7
        1. Vocational guidance—United States.   2. College graduates—
Employment—United States.   3. Bachelor of arts degree—United States.
4. Master of arts degree—United States.   I. Title.   II. Series.

    HF5382.5.U5 C252   2001
    331.7′0235—dc21   2001035813

VGM Career Books

A Division of The McGraw·Hill Companies

1 2 3 4 5 6 7 8 9 0   LBM/LBM   0 9 8 7 6 5 4 3 2 1

ISBN 0-658-01766-7

This book was set in Adobe Garamond
Printed and bound by Lake Book Manufacturing

McGraw-Hill books are available at special quantity discounts to use as premiums and
sales promotions, or for use in corporate training programs. For more information, please
write to the Director of Special Sales, Professional Publishing, McGraw-Hill, Two Penn
Plaza, New York, NY 10121-2298. Or contact your local bookstore.

This book is printed on acid-free paper.

To all my professors at the University of Massachusetts, Boston, who
guided me carefully down the path of a liberal arts education

CONTENTS

ACKNOWLEDGMENTS

I would like to thank the following professionals for providing insights into the world of liberal arts careers: Carol Behan, high school English teacher; M. Allen Broyles, residential counselor; Marshall J. Cook, university professor and author; Gist Fleshman, attorney; Chris Fuller, marketing and sales general manager; M. J. Goodwin, attorney; Marcia Harris, career services director and author; Betsy Lancefield, editor; and Gerald D. Oster, clinical psychologist and author.

INVESTIGATE THE OPPORTUNITIES

Y ou've heard this before (most likely from engineering majors or students in some other "techie" field): "Oh, liberal arts. You'll certainly be well educated—but unemployable." Or, "There's absolutely nothing you can do with a B.A. in philosophy—except maybe teach." Ditto for English, sociology, anthropology, French, history, women's studies, and the scores of other majors that fall into the general category of liberal arts.

As many students do, you might be progressing through your liberal arts program, semester after semester, year after year, taking your major courses, and signing up for your electives; not really sure *where* you'll be on graduation day or even five to ten years from now.

Maybe some not-so-savvy friends or family members have given you this advice: "If you want to have a successful career, you need to be in some sort of professional program—nursing, engineering, agriculture, accounting. *Anything* but liberal arts."

And in your gut, you worry that they're right. But those professional programs aren't for you. The fields don't interest you. So, what in the world *are* you going to do with that B.A. in psychology, math, Russian history, German literature, or political science?

Have you been on a dead-end path? Will you graduate with nothing more than the ability to entertain party guests with conversation on a variety of interesting and socially relevant topics? And how will you even be able to *give* a party without an income? One thing you know for sure: intelligent conversation does not pay the bills.

Now is the time to put all those fears aside. With some advanced planning and an acquired understanding of your options, you will find that your career choices are as diverse as the number of liberal arts majors. Even more so.

While it's true that nursing majors become nurses and accounting majors become accountants, an English or philosophy major has more to look forward to than just teaching. (Although for some, teaching is the end goal—and a most rewarding path to follow.) The unsolicited comments and advice circulating through your academic circle have no more merit than old wives' tales from an earlier century.

ADVICE FROM THE EXPERTS

Listen to what a professional in the area has to say. She is Marcia Harris, co-author of *The Parent's Crash Course in Career Planning*. She is also director of University Career Services at the University of North Carolina at Chapel Hill—and she knows her job well.

"We are strong proponents of liberal arts degrees at the university. We think liberal arts gives students the broadest background in communication skills, reasoning ability, and the ability to learn.

"It's true that sometimes employers, especially the first-line hiring managers, tend to be a little short-sighted when it comes to liberal arts skills. They think they want recent graduates who can 'hit the ground running.' But there have been a number of research studies to support the fact that the higher up you go—to the higher-level managers and CEOs—the more these people appreciate the value of a liberal arts degree and look for job candidates who have those broad-based skills.

"It's sort of a good news–bad news situation. It's harder for liberal arts graduates to find a job initially, but in the long run, that degree serves them really well.

"What we try to do to is help our students have the best of both worlds, putting the emphasis on skills as opposed to college major. We also try to reach them as early as freshman or sophomore year and say to them, 'You *can* prepare to enter most career fields with a liberal arts degree, but the degree alone is not going to open the doors. If you want to be a banker, for example, you don't have to be a business major, you could be a philosophy major. However, you'll need to demonstrate to the bank executive you interview with during your senior year that you can handle quantitative skills and have legitimate interest in business.'

"A judicious use of electives, part-time work, and internships in related fields is critical. Involvement with campus organizations is also invaluable. For example, on our campus we have more than three hundred different organizations, such as the investment club, the entrepreneur club, and the business students' association. You don't have to be a business major to belong.

If you're a student majoring in political science but thinking about going into advertising, you can join some of these organizations and acquire leadership roles over a period of years. You are *really* building your portfolio to make your case to an employer. You can say, 'I wanted to get this broad-based education, but I have some skills that you might be interested in that relate to this particular position.'

"We have a whole assortment of majors that make up the liberal arts degree at the University of North Carolina. There are certain jobs such as retailing that are open to *any* major. Then there are jobs such as history teacher or translator that would be open to *some* liberal arts majors but not every liberal arts major. To be a history teacher you don't necessarily have to be an education major, but you would need to be a history major."

"I personally advise math majors. I talk to them about a spectrum of careers. At one end of the spectrum are jobs that are so quantitatively oriented, such as actuary, that you have to be a math major. At the other end are jobs open to any major, such as sales or investment banking.

"Your math degree is not usually a plus or a minus; your French degree isn't a plus or a minus. There are jobs open to any major. It goes back to the skills you have acquired during internships and part-time work, not the actual major."

Here are what some other people have to say on the subject. They are not career counselors or student advisors. They are professionals out in the workforce who started their education with a liberal arts degree.

Marshall J. Cook, Author and Professor at the University of Wisconsin, Madison

"A liberal arts degree prepares you to think. It prepares you to deal with complexity, ambiguity, and contradiction. It helps you distinguish among conflicting points of view and broadens your perspective on life.

"Because it does all that, a liberal arts degree is a wonderful preparation for life and for the world of work, in all its complexity, ambiguity, and contradiction.

"I note with satisfaction that some business people are starting to think so, too. I actually know of liberal arts grads being hired for jobs other than as a writer, and editor, a teacher, or a telephone solicitor working only for commission.

"Sometimes graduate school is necessary. I went because I wasn't ready for a 'career,' and didn't know what I wanted to do. I've never been sorry. A master's degree opened up many doors for me, including the job I have now as a professor in an adult education communications department. If the job you want requires it, if you feel you have more to learn in a structured learning setting, and if you can afford the time and money, go for it." (See Marshall Cook's first-hand account in Chapter 10.)

Betsy Lancefield, Editor at Contemporary Books

"I really wanted the old-fashioned, well-rounded education. I didn't want to know just one subject area. I wanted to be conversant in many different areas. In addition, to be honest, I didn't like any one area enough just to do only that. I have B.A. in general studies with an emphasis in linguistics. At the time I graduated there was a lot of emphasis on the business world. They wanted people who knew how to think, who could write, and who had a diverse knowledge and skills base. You end up with terrific versatility.

"The criticism of such a broad major, of course, is that you haven't really specialized in anything. That could be a valid criticism, but often employers will say that they'll train you to perform the tasks they need. What they want is candidates with a basic literacy and ability to solve problems, think creatively, and communicate with people. As far as the particular skills you'll need for the job, they'll train you.

"I think my job as an editor is a great job for a liberal arts major. I use the writing skills I got in college and my familiarity with a broad spectrum of subjects is very helpful. Right now the books I edit are about careers, an area I've mostly learned about on the job. But if I started working with, say, history books, then I'd draw on the information I learned in my history courses. Or I could work on literature books and have a baseline familiarity with that material.

"I feel that the liberal arts degree has allowed me to get started on a lot of diverse projects. The subject areas aren't completely foreign to me.

"I started with general studies because it was the required degree if you wanted to get into a multiple-subjects teaching program. In California, at that time, you couldn't go into teaching with just an education degree. You needed to major in a subject area. The state was having a problem getting teachers who new their subject areas as well as how to teach. The teachers knew pedagogy, but not content.

"I taught for a while, went overseas for a while, and then spent two years at the graduate school of education at Stanford University earning my master's degree in educational anthropology. I knew I wanted to work with kids, so I went back to the school I had worked at out of college and stayed there until I moved to Chicago.

"I had also enjoyed writing and enjoyed the part of my teaching that was helping kids write papers—teaching them organizational skills and writing skills. And I was always helping other people with their writing. I produced the yearbook and school newspaper, and proofread papers and journal articles for Stanford graduate students and professors.

"When I moved to Chicago I decided to focus on getting a job in publishing. I knew that, with my background, I could always go back to teaching if I wanted to. But I landed an editorial position with an educational publisher. I started out as an assistant editor, which was one rung up the ladder. Most newcomers start out as editorial assistants, but I think because of the related experience I had, I was able to start a little higher. I went to the company and made my case, told them the varied things I'd done.

"I took this position because I thought the books were useful to people, but eventually I'd like to work on books that are more educational in nature. I'd like to be doing more classroom materials. I have been approached about getting into the marketing end of the business, but that's not where my heart is. I really like talking with an author about an idea, then watching the idea turn into a proposal, then into a manuscript, then page proofs, and finally a book. That's very satisfying. I don't want someone to hand me a book and say 'go sell this.' The whole reason I got into this field is that I like the creative process.

"And I enjoy working with a lot of different people—authors, freelancers, designers, production people, and manufacturing people. It's really a group effort."

Gerald D. Oster, Clinical Psychologist

"If you think of learning as a lifelong process, a liberal arts education starts you along this path. You gain broad exposure to history, social systems, art, and culture; you learn to assimilate new possibilities for yourself. You also learn to think and communicate critically, examining others' works with a critical mind, instead of depending on others to interpret things for you.

"You prepare yourself for the adult world of work, family, and community service by gaining deeper appreciation for a variety of areas. You begin to see the world through a larger framework, which can change and define your own likes and dislikes.

"A liberal arts education is broad-based but essential in many forms of work. The workforce is filled with more than just technocrats or specialists. Even these highly trained people need to understand and communicate their efforts to the rest of the world and appreciate their accomplishments within the context of everyday people. The world is vast and interesting for you to explore and a broad-based education allows you that comfort in many arenas." (See Chapter 14 for a closer look at Gerald Oster's job.)

THE ROAD AHEAD

In Part One of this book you will learn many valuable tips on the job search, especially how to prepare yourself and make a case for the ideal job you are seeking.

In Part Two, you will explore a variety of career paths, many that are open to any liberal arts majors, some that are more defined, and still some that require further education or training. Chapter Nine will give you a broad overview of the various paths; the remaining chapters will help you narrow those paths.

One you've found the path you want to follow, you'll realize how important your liberal arts degree is in reaching your ultimate destination.

PART ONE

THE
JOB SEARCH

CHAPTER ONE

THE SELF-ASSESSMENT

elf-assessment is the process by which you begin to acknowledge your own particular blend of education, experiences, values, needs, and goals. It provides the foundation for career planning and the entire job search process. Self-assessment involves looking inward and asking yourself what can sometimes prove to be difficult questions. This self-examination should lead to an intimate understanding of your personal traits, your personal values, your consumption patterns and economic needs, your longer-term goals, your skill base, your preferred skills, and your under-developed skills.

You come to the self-assessment process knowing yourself well in some of these areas, but you may still be uncertain about other aspects. You may be well aware of your consumption patterns, but have you spent much time specifically identifying your longer-term goals or your personal values as they relate to work? No matter what level of self-assessment you have undertaken to date, it is now time to clarify all of these issues and questions as they relate to the job search.

The knowledge you gain in the self-assessment process will guide the rest of your job search. In this book, you will learn about all of the following tasks:

- Writing resumes

- Exploring possible job titles

- Identifying employment sites

- Networking

- Interviewing

- Following up

- Evaluating job offers

In each of these steps, you will rely on and often return to the understanding gained through your self-assessment. Any individual seeking employment must be able and willing to express these facets of his or her personality to recruiters and interviewers throughout the job search. This communication allows you to show the world who you are so that together with employers you can determine whether there will be a workable match with a given job or career path.

HOW TO CONDUCT A SELF-ASSESSMENT

The self-assessment process goes on naturally all the time. People ask you to clarify what you mean, you make a purchasing decision, or you begin a new relationship. You react to the world and the world reacts to you. How you understand these interactions and any changes you might make because of them are part of the natural process of self-discovery. There is, however, a more comprehensive and efficient way to approach self-assessment with regard to employment.

Because self-assessment can become a complex exercise, we have distilled it into a seven-step process that provides an effective basis for undertaking a job search. The seven steps include the following:

1. Understanding your personal traits

2. Identifying your personal values

3. Calculating your economic needs

4. Exploring your longer-term goals

5. Enumerating your skill base

6. Recognizing your preferred skills

7. Assessing skills needing further development

As you work through your self-assessment, you might want to create a worksheet similar to the one shown in Exhibit 1.1 starting on the following page. Or you might want to keep a journal of the thoughts you have as you

Exhibit 1.1

SELF-ASSESSMENT WORKSHEET

STEP 1. Understand Your Personal Traits

The personal traits that describe me are:
(Include all of the words that describe you.)

The ten personal traits that most accurately describe me are:
(List these ten traits.)

STEP 2. Identify Your Personal Values

Working conditions that are important to me include:
(List working conditions that would have to exist for you to accept a position.)

The values that go along with my working conditions are:
(Write down the values that correspond to each working condition.)

Some additional values I've decided to include are:
(List those values you identify as you conduct this job search.)

STEP 3. Calculate Your Economic Needs

My estimated minimum annual salary requirement is:
(Write the salary you have calculated based on your budget.)

Starting salaries for the positions I'm considering are:
(List the name of each job you are considering and the associated starting salary.)

STEP 4. Explore Your Longer-Term Goals

My thoughts on longer-term goals right now are:
(Jot down some of your longer-term goals as you know them right now.)

STEP 5. Enumerate Your Skill Base

The general skills I possess are:
(List the skills that underlie tasks you are able to complete.)

The specific skills I possess are:
(List more technical or specific skills that you possess and indicate your level of expertise.)

General and specific skills that I want to promote to employers for the jobs I'm considering are:
(List general and specific skills for each type of job you are considering.)

STEP 6. Recognize Your Preferred Skills
Skills that I would like to use on the job include:
(List skills that you hope to use on the job, and indicate how often you'd like to use them.)

STEP 7. Assess Skills Needing Further Development
Some skills that I'll need to acquire for the jobs I'm considering include:
(Write down skills listed in job advertisements or job descriptions that you don't currently possess.)

I believe I can build these skills by:
(Describe how you plan to acquire these skills.)

---

undergo this process. There will be many opportunities to revise your self-assessment as you start down the path of seeking a career.

STEP 1   Understanding Your Personal Traits

Each person has a unique personality that he or she brings to the job search process. Gaining a better understanding of your personal traits can help you evaluate job and career choices. Identifying these traits and then finding employment that allows you to draw on at least some of them can create a rewarding and fulfilling work experience. If potential employment doesn't allow you to use these preferred traits, it is important to decide whether you can find other ways to express them or whether you would be better off not considering this type of job. Interests and hobbies pursued outside of work hours can be one way to use personal traits you don't have an opportunity to draw on in your work. For example, if you consider yourself an outgoing person and the kinds of jobs you are examining allow little contact with other people, you may be able to achieve the level of interaction that is comfortable for you outside of your work setting. If such a compromise seems impractical or otherwise unsatisfactory, you probably should explore only jobs that provide the interaction you want and need on the job.

Many young adults who are not very confident about their attractiveness to employers will downplay their need for income. They will say, "Money is not all that important if I love my work." But if you begin to document exactly what you need for housing, transportation, insurance, clothing, food, and utilities, you will begin to understand that some jobs cannot meet your financial needs and it doesn't matter how wonderful the job is. If you have to worry each payday about bills and other financial obligations, you won't be very effective on the job. Begin now to be honest with yourself about your needs.

Inventorying Your Personal Traits. Begin the self-assessment process by creating an inventory of your personal traits. Using the list in Exhibit 1.2, decide which of these personal traits describe you.

Exhibit 1.2

PERSONAL TRAITS

Accurate	Considerate	Fair-minded
Active	Cool	Farsighted
Adaptable	Cooperative	Feeling
Adventurous	Courageous	Firm
Affectionate	Critical	Flexible
Aggressive	Curious	Formal
Ambitious	Daring	Friendly
Analytical	Decisive	Future-oriented
Appreciative	Deliberate	Generous
Artistic	Detail-oriented	Gentle
Brave	Determined	Good-natured
Businesslike	Discreet	Helpful
Calm	Dominant	Honest
Capable	Eager	Humorous
Caring	Easygoing	Idealistic
Cautious	Efficient	Imaginative
Cheerful	Emotional	Impersonal
Clean	Empathetic	Independent
Competent	Energetic	Individualistic
Confident	Excitable	Industrious
Conscientious	Expressive	Informal
Conservative	Extroverted	Innovative

Intellectual	Peaceable	Self-disciplined
Intelligent	Personable	Sensible
Introverted	Persuasive	Sensitive
Intuitive	Pleasant	Serious
Inventive	Poised	Sincere
Jovial	Polite	Sociable
Just	Practical	Spontaneous
Kind	Precise	Strong
Liberal	Principled	Strong-minded
Likable	Private	Structured
Logical	Productive	Subjective
Loyal	Progressive	Tactful
Mature	Quick	Thorough
Methodical	Quiet	Thoughtful
Meticulous	Rational	Tolerant
Mistrustful	Realistic	Trusting
Modest	Receptive	Trustworthy
Motivated	Reflective	Truthful
Objective	Relaxed	Understanding
Observant	Reliable	Unexcitable
Open-minded	Reserved	Uninhibited
Opportunistic	Resourceful	Verbal
Optimistic	Responsible	Versatile
Organized	Reverent	Wholesome
Original	Sedentary	Wise
Outgoing	Self-confident	
Patient	Self-controlled	

Focusing on Selected Personal Traits. Of all the traits you identified from the list in Exhibit 1.2, select the ten you believe most accurately describe you. If you are having a difficult time deciding, think about which words people who know you well would use to describe you. Keep track of these ten traits.

Considering Your Personal Traits in the Job Search Process. As you begin exploring jobs and careers, watch for matches between your personal traits and the job descriptions you read. Some jobs will require many personal traits you know you possess, and others will not seem to match those traits.

••••••••••••••••••••••••••••••••••••

An editor's job, for example, requires an individual who can work as part of a team, often coordinating schedules and activities with writers, typesetters, proofreaders, printers, and advertising and promotion departments. Excellent organizational and interpersonal skills are essential qualities. Freelance writers, on the other hand, usually work alone, with limited opportunities for interaction with others. Both have deadlines to meet, but the writer usually has far fewer people to answer to and must be able to work independently.

••••••••••••••••••••••••••••••••••••

Your ability to respond to changing conditions, your decision-making ability, productivity, creativity, and verbal skills all have a bearing on your success in and enjoyment of your work life. To better guarantee success, be sure to take the time needed to understand these traits in yourself.

STEP 2　Identifying Your Personal Values

Your personal values affect every aspect of your life, including employment, and they develop and change as you move through life. Values can be defined as principles that we hold in high regard, qualities that are important and desirable to us. Some values aren't ordinarily connected to work (love, beauty, color, light, relationships, family, or religion), and others are (autonomy, cooperation, effectiveness, achievement, knowledge, and security). Our values determine, in part, the level of satisfaction we feel in a particular job.

Defining Acceptable Working Conditions. One facet of employment is the set of working conditions that must exist for someone to consider taking a job.

Each of us would probably create a unique list of acceptable working conditions, but items that might be included on many people's lists are the amount of money you would need to be paid, how far you are willing to drive or travel, the amount of freedom you want in determining your own schedule, whether you would be working with people or data or things, and the types of tasks you would be willing to do. Your conditions might include statements of working conditions you will *not* accept; for example, you might not be willing to work at night or on weekends or holidays.

If you were offered a job tomorrow, what conditions would have to exist for you to realistically consider accepting the position? Take some time and make a list of these conditions.

Exhibit 1.3

WORK VALUES

Achievement	Development	Physical activity
Advancement	Effectiveness	Power
Adventure	Excitement	Precision
Attainment	Fast pace	Prestige
Authority	Financial gain	Privacy
Autonomy	Helping	Profit
Belonging	Humor	Recognition
Challenge	Improvisation	Risk
Change	Independence	Security
Communication	Influencing others	Self-expression
Community	Intellectual stimulation	Solitude
Competition	Interaction	Stability
Completion	Knowledge	Status
Contribution	Leading	Structure
Control	Mastery	Supervision
Cooperation	Mobility	Surroundings
Creativity	Moral fulfillment	Time freedom
Decision making	Organization	Variety

Realizing Associated Values. Your list of working conditions can be used to create an inventory of your values relating to jobs and careers you are exploring. For example, if one of your conditions stated that you wanted to earn at least $30,000 per year, the associated value would be financial gain. If another condition was that you wanted to work with a friendly group of people, the value that went along with that might be belonging or interaction with people. Exhibit 1.3 provides a list of commonly held values that relate to the work environment; use it to create your own list of personal values.

Relating Your Values to the World of Work. As you read the job descriptions in this book and in other suggested resources, think about the values associated with each position.

· ·

For example, the duties of a reporter would include researching, investigating, conducting interviews, organizing the information in a logical format, and writing and editing articles and profiles. Associated values are intellectual stimulation, organization, communication, and creativity.

· ·

If you were thinking about a career in this field, or any other field you're exploring, at least some of the associated values should match those you extracted from your list of working conditions. Take a second look at any values that don't match up. How important are they to you? What will happen if they are not satisfied on the job? Can you incorporate those personal values elsewhere? Your answers need to be brutally honest. As you continue your exploration, be sure to add to your list any additional values that occur to you.

STEP 3   Calculating Your Economic Needs

Each of us grew up in an environment that provided for certain basic needs, such as food and shelter and, to varying degrees, other needs that we now consider basic, such as cable television, E-mail, or an automobile. Needs such as privacy, space, and quiet, which at first glance may not appear to be monetary needs, may add to housing expenses and so should be considered as you examine your economic needs. For example, if you place a high value on a large, open living space for yourself, it would be difficult to satisfy that need without an associated high housing cost, especially in a densely populated city environment.

As you prepare to move into the world of work and become responsible for meeting your own basic needs, it is important to consider the salary you will need to be able to afford a satisfying standard of living. The three-step process outlined here will help you plan a budget, which in turn will allow you to evaluate the various career choices and geographic locations you are considering. The steps include (1) developing a realistic budget, (2) examining starting salaries, and (3) using a cost-of-living index.

Developing a Realistic Budget. Each of us has certain expectations for the kind of lifestyle we want to maintain. To begin the process of defining your economic needs, it will be helpful to determine what you expect to spend on routine monthly expenses. These expenses include housing, food, transportation, entertainment, utilities, loan repayments, and revolving charge accounts. A worksheet that details many of these expenses is shown in Exhibit 1.4. You may not currently spend anything for certain items, but you probably will have to once you begin supporting yourself. As you develop

Exhibit 1.4

ESTIMATED MONTHLY EXPENSES WORKSHEET

		Could Reduce Spending? (Yes/No)
Cable	$	
Child care		
Clothing		
Educational loan repayment		
Entertainment		
Food		
At home		
Meals out		
Gifts		
Housing		
Rent/mortgage		
Insurance		
Property taxes		
Medical insurance		
Reading materials		
Newspapers		
Magazines		
Books		
Revolving loans/charges		
Savings		
Telephone		
Transportation		
Auto payment		
Insurance		
Parking		
Gasoline		
or		
Cab/train/bus fare		
Utilities		
Electric		
Gas		
Water/sewer		
Vacations		

	Could Reduce Spending? (Yes/No)	
Miscellaneous expense 1	_____	_____
Expense: _____		
Miscellaneous expense 2	_____	_____
Expense: _____		
Miscellaneous expense 3	_____	_____
Expense: _____		

TOTAL MONTHLY EXPENSES: _____

YEARLY EXPENSES (Monthly expenses × 12): _____ _____

INCREASE TO INCLUDE TAXES (Yearly expenses × 1.35): _____ _____ =

MINIMUM ANNUAL SALARY REQUIREMENT: _____ _____

this budget, be generous in your estimates, but keep in mind any items that could be reduced or eliminated. If you are not sure about the cost of a certain item, talk with family or friends who would be able to give you a realistic estimate.

If this is new or difficult for you, start to keep a log of expenses right now. You may be surprised at how much you actually spend each month for food or stamps or magazines. Household expenses and personal grooming items can often loom very large in a budget, as can auto repairs or home maintenance.

Income taxes must also be taken into consideration when examining salary requirements. State and local taxes vary, so it is difficult to calculate exactly the effect of taxes on the amount of income you need to generate. To roughly estimate the gross income necessary to generate your minimum annual salary requirement, multiply the minimum salary you have calculated (see Exhibit 1.4) by a factor of 1.35. The resulting figure will be an approximation of what your gross income would need to be, given your estimated expenses.

Examining Starting Salaries. Starting salaries for each of the career tracks are provided throughout this book. These salary figures can be used in conjunction with the cost-of-living index (discussed in the next section) to determine whether you would be able to meet your basic economic needs in a given geographic location.

Using a Cost-of-Living Index. If you are thinking about trying to get a job in a geographic region other than the one where you now live, understanding differences in the cost of living will help you come to a more informed decision about making a move. By using a cost-of-living index, you can compare salaries offered and the cost of living in different locations with what you know about the salaries offered and the cost of living in your present location.

Many variables are used to calculate the cost-of-living index. Often included are housing, groceries, utilities, transportation, health care, clothing, and entertainment expenses. Right now you do not need to worry about the details associated with calculating a given index. The main purpose of this exercise is to help you understand that pay ranges for entry-level positions may not vary greatly, but the cost of living in different locations *can* vary tremendously.

Newspaper	Annual Salary	Salary Equivalent to Ohio	Change in Buying Power
New York Times	$60,266	$49,720	+ $10,546
Los Angeles Daily News	$24,700	$29,044	– $4,344
Minneapolis Star Tribune	$23,244	$24,382	– $1,138
Cleveland Plain Dealer	$26,643	—	—

If you moved to New York City and secured employment as an assistant editor at the *New York Times*, you would be able to maintain a lifestyle similar to the one you led in Cleveland; in fact, you would even be able to enhance your lifestyle, given the increase in buying power. The same would not be true for a move to Los Angeles or Minneapolis. You would decrease your buying power, given the rate of pay and cost of living in these cities.

Many websites, such as Yahoo!'s (http://verticals.yahoo.com/cities/salary.html), can assist you as you undertake this research. Using any search engine, enter the keywords *cost-of-living index*. Several choices will appear. Choose one site, and look for options such as cost-of-living analysis or cost-of-living comparator. Some sites will ask you to register and/or pay for the information, but most sites are free.

••••••••••••••••••••••••••••••••••••

You can work through a similar exercise for any type of job you are considering and for many locations when current salary information is available. It will be worth your time to undertake this analysis if you are seriously considering a relocation. By doing so you will be able to make an informed choice.

STEP 4 Exploring Your Longer-Term Goals

There is no question that when we first begin working, our goals are to use our skills and education in a job that will reward us with employment, income, and status relative to the preparation we brought with us to this position. If we are not being paid as much as we feel we should for our level of education or if job demands don't provide the intellectual stimulation we had hoped for, we experience unhappiness and as a result often seek other employment.

Most jobs we consider "good" are those that fulfill our basic "lower-level" needs of security, food, clothing, shelter, income, and productive work. But even when our basic needs are met and our jobs are secure and productive, we as individuals are constantly changing. As we change, the demands and expectations we place on our jobs may change. Fortunately, some jobs grow and change with us, and this explains why some people are happy throughout many years in a job.

But more often people are bigger than the jobs they fill. We have more goals and needs than any job could satisfy. These are "higher-level" needs of self-esteem, companionship, affection, and an increasing desire to feel we are employing ourselves in the most effective way possible. Not all of these higher-level needs can be met through employment, but for as long as we are employed, we increasingly demand that our jobs play their part in moving us along the path to fulfillment.

Another obvious but important fact is that we change as we mature. Although our jobs also have the potential for change, they may not change as frequently or as markedly as we do. There are increasingly fewer one-job, one-employer careers; we must think about a work future that may involve voluntary or forced moves from employer to employer. Because of that very real possibility, we need to take advantage of the opportunities in each position we hold to acquire skills and competencies that will keep us viable and attractive as employees in a job market that not only is technology/computer dependent, but also is populated with more and more small, self-transforming organizations rather than the large, seemingly stable organizations of the past.

It may be difficult in the early stages of the job search to determine whether the path you are considering can meet these longer-term goals. Reading about career paths and individual career histories in your field can be very helpful in this regard. Meeting and talking with individuals further along in their careers can be enlightening as well. Older workers can provide valuable guidance on "self-managing" your career, which will become an increasingly valuable skill in the future. Some of these ideas may seem remote as you read this now, but you should be able to appreciate the need to ensure that you are growing, developing valuable new skills, and researching other employers who might be interested in your particular skills package.

· ·

If you are considering a position as an editor at a newspaper, you would gain a better perspective on this career if you talked to an entry-level editorial assistant; a more experienced assistant or full editor; and, finally, a senior editor, managing editor, or editor-in-chief who has a considerable work history in the newspaper field. Each will have a different perspective, unique concerns, and an individual set of values and priorities.

· ·

STEP 5 Enumerating Your Skill Base

In terms of the job search, skills can be thought of as capabilities that can be developed in school, at work, or by volunteering and then used in specific job settings. Many studies have documented the kinds of skills that employers seek in entry-level applicants. For example, some of the most desired skills for individuals interested in the teaching profession are the ability to interact effectively with students one-on-one, to manage a classroom, to adapt to varying situations as necessary, and to get involved in school activities. Business employers have also identified important qualities, including enthusiasm for the employer's product or service, a businesslike mind, the ability to follow written or oral instructions, the ability to demonstrate self-control, the confidence to suggest new ideas, the ability to communicate with all members of a group, an awareness of cultural differences, and loyalty, to name just a few. You will find that many of these skills are also in the repertoire of qualities demanded in your college major.

To be successful in obtaining any given job, you must be able to demonstrate that you possess a certain mix of skills that will allow you to carry out the duties required by that job. This skill mix will vary a great deal from job to job; to determine the skills necessary for the jobs you are seeking, you can read job advertisements or more generic job descriptions, such as those found later in this book. If you want to be effective in the job search, you must directly show employers that you possess the skills needed to be successful in filling the position. These skills will initially be described on your resume and then discussed again during the interview process.

Skills are either general or specific. General skills are those that are developed throughout your college years by taking classes, being employed, and getting involved in other related activities such as volunteer work or campus organizations. General skills include the ability to read and write, to perform computations, to think critically, and to communicate effectively. Specific skills are also acquired on the job and in the classroom, but they allow you to complete tasks that require specialized knowledge. Computer programming, drafting, language translating, and copyediting are just a few examples of specific skills that may relate to a given job.

To develop a list of skills relevant to employers, you must first identify the general skills you possess, then list specific skills you have to offer, and, finally, examine which of these skills employers are seeking.

Identifying Your General Skills. Because you possess or will possess a college degree, employers will assume that you can read and write, perform certain basic computations, think critically, and communicate effectively. Employers will want to see that you have acquired these skills, and they will want to know which additional general skills you possess.

One way to begin identifying skills is to write an experiential diary. An experiential diary lists all the tasks you were responsible for completing for each job you've held and then outlines the skills required to do those tasks. You may list several skills for any given task. This diary allows you to distinguish between the tasks you performed and the underlying skills required to complete those tasks. Here's an example:

Tasks	Skills
Answering telephone	Effective use of language, clear diction, ability to direct inquiries, ability to solve problems
Waiting on tables	Poise under conditions of time and pressure, speed, accuracy, good memory, simultaneous completion of tasks, sales skills

For each job or experience you have participated in, develop a worksheet based on the example shown here. On a resume, you may want to describe these skills rather than simply listing tasks. Skills are easier for the employer to appreciate, especially when your experience is very different from the employment you are seeking. In addition to helping you identify general skills, this experiential diary will prepare you to speak more effectively in an interview about the qualifications you possess.

Identifying Your Specific Skills. It may be easier to identify your specific skills because you can definitely say whether you can speak other languages, program a computer, draft a map or diagram, or edit a document using appropriate symbols and terminology.

Using your experiential diary, identify the points in your history where you learned how to do something very specific, and decide whether you have a beginning, intermediate, or advanced knowledge of how to use that particular skill. Right now, be sure to list *every* specific skill you have, and don't consider whether you like using the skill. Write down a list of specific skills you have acquired and the level of competence you possess—beginning, intermediate, or advanced.

Relating Your Skills to Employers. You probably have thought about a couple of different jobs you might be interested in obtaining, and one way to begin relating the general and specific skills you possess to a potential employer's needs is to read actual advertisements for these types of positions (see Part Two for resources listing actual job openings).

· ·

For example, you might be interested in a career as a senior editor for a magazine. A typical job listing might read, "Requires 2–5 years experience, organizational and interpersonal skills, imagination, drive, and the ability to work under pressure." If you then used any one of a number of general sources of information that describe the job of senior editor, you would find additional information. Senior editors also develop story ideas, make assignments, work with staff and freelance writers, edit articles, and coordinate tasks with other magazine departments.

Begin building a comprehensive list of required skills with the first job description you read. Exploring advertisements for and descriptions of several types of related positions will reveal an important core of skills necessary for obtaining the type of work you're interested in. In building this list, include both general and specific skills.

The following is a sample list of skills needed to be successful as a senior editor for a magazine. These items were extracted from general resources and actual job listings.

JOB: SENIOR EDITOR

General Skills	Specific Skills
Disseminate information	Write editorials
Gather information	Take notes
Conduct research	Write letters
Work in hectic environment	Write memos
Meet deadlines	Use tape recorder
Work in noisy environment	Develop story ideas
Work long hours near deadline	Assign articles
Work well with other people	Edit articles
Exhibit creativity	Schedule articles
Exhibit drive	Proofread
Be able to work under	Familiar with word
pressure	processing
Be organized	Layout pages
Be able to supervise the	Select illustrations
work of others	
Have excellent written and	
verbal skills	
Be able to conduct meetings	

On separate sheets of paper, try to generate a comprehensive list of required skills for at least one job you are considering.

The list of general skills that you develop for a given career path would be valuable for any number of jobs you might apply for. Many of the specific skills would also be transferable to other types of positions. For example, developing story ideas is a required skill for senior eidtors working on a newspaper.

•••

Now review the list of skills that are required for jobs you are considering, and check off those skills that *you know you possess*. You should refer to these specific skills on the resume that you write for this type of job. See Chapter 2 for details on resume writing.

STEP 6 Recognizing Your Preferred Skills

In the previous section you developed a comprehensive list of skills that relate to particular career paths that are of interest to you. You can now relate these to skills that you prefer to use. We all use a wide range of skills (some researchers say individuals have a repertoire of about five hundred skills), but we may not particularly be interested in using all of them in our work. There may be some skills that come to us more naturally or that we use successfully time and time again and that we want to continue to use; these are best described as our preferred skills. For this exercise use the list of skills that you created for the previous section, and decide which of them you are *most interested in using* in future work and how often you would like to use them. You might be interested in using some skills only occasionally, while others you would like to use more regularly. You probably also have skills that you hope you can use constantly.

As you examine job announcements, look for matches between this list of preferred skills and the qualifications described in the advertisements. These skills should be highlighted on your resume and discussed in job interviews.

STEP 7 Assessing Skills Needing Further Development

Previously you compiled a list of general and specific skills required for given positions. You already possess some of these skills; those that remain to be developed are your underdeveloped skills.

If you are just beginning the job search, there may be gaps between the qualifications required for some of the jobs you're considering and skills you possess. The thought of having to admit to and talk about these underdeveloped skills, especially in a job interview, is a frightening one. One way to put a healthy perspective on this subject is to target and relate your exploration of underdeveloped skills to the types of positions you are seeking. Recognizing these shortcomings and planning to overcome them with either on-the-job training or additional formal education can be a positive way to address the concept of underdeveloped skills.

On your worksheet or in your journal, make a list of up to five general or specific skills required for the positions you're interested in that you *don't currently possess*. For each item list an idea you have for specific action you could take to acquire that skill. Do some brainstorming to come up with possible actions. If you have a hard time generating ideas, talk to people currently working in this type of position, professionals in your college career services office, trusted friends, family members, or members of related professional associations.

If, for example, you are interested in a job for which you don't have some specific required experience, you could locate training opportunities such as classes or workshops offered through a local college or university, community college, or club or association that would help you build the level of expertise you need for the job.

You will notice in this book that many excellent positions for your major demand computer skills. While basic word processing has been something you've done all through college, you may be surprised at the additional computer skills required by employers. Many positions for college graduates will ask for some familiarity with spreadsheet programming, and frequently some database-management software familiarity is a job demand as well. Desktop publishing software, graphics programs, and basic Web-page design also pop up frequently in job ads for college graduates. If your degree program hasn't introduced you to a wide variety of computer applications, what are your options? If you're still in college, take what computer courses you can before you graduate. If you've already graduated, look at evening programs, continuing education courses, or tutorial programs that may be available commercially. Developing a modest level of expertise will encourage you to be more confident in suggesting to potential employers that you can continue to add to your skill base on the job.

In Chapter 5 on interviewing, we will discuss in detail how to effectively address questions about underdeveloped skills. Generally speaking, though, employers want genuine answers to these types of questions. They want you to reveal "the real you," and they also want to see how you answer difficult questions. In taking the positive, targeted approach discussed above, you show the employer that you are willing to continue to learn and that you have a plan for strengthening your job qualifications.

USING YOUR SELF-ASSESSMENT

Exploring entry-level career options can be an exciting experience if you have good resources available and will take the time to use them. Can you effectively complete the following tasks?

1. Understand your personality traits and relate them to career choices

2. Define your personal values

3. Determine your economic needs

4. Explore longer-term goals

5. Understand your skill base

6. Recognize your preferred skills

7. Express a willingness to improve on your underdeveloped skills

If so, then you can more meaningfully participate in the job search process by writing a more effective resume, finding job titles that represent work you are interested in doing, locating job sites that will provide the opportunity for you to use your strengths and skills, networking in an informed way, participating in focused interviews, getting the most out of follow-up contacts, and evaluating job offers to find those that create a good match between you and the employer. The remaining chapters in Part One guide you through these next steps in the job search process. For many job seekers, this process can take anywhere from three months to a year to implement. The time you will need to put into your job search will depend on the type of job you want and the geographic location where you'd like to work. Think of your effort as a job in itself, requiring you to set aside time each week to complete the needed work. Carefully undertaken efforts may reduce the time you need for your job search.

CHAPTER TWO

THE RESUME AND COVER LETTER

The task of writing a resume may seem overwhelming if you are unfamiliar with this type of document, but there are some easily understood techniques that can and should be used. This section was written to help you understand the purpose of the resume, the different types of resume formats available, and how to write the sections of information traditionally found on a resume. We will present examples and explanations that address questions frequently posed by people writing their first resume or updating an old resume.

Even within the formats and suggestions given, however, there are infinite variations. True, most resumes follow one of the outlines suggested, but you should feel free to adjust the resume to suit your needs and make it expressive of your life and experience.

WHY WRITE A RESUME?

The purpose of a resume is to convince an employer that you should be interviewed. Whether you're mailing, faxing, or E-mailing this document, you'll want to present enough information to show that you can make an immediate and valuable contribution to an organization. A resume is not an in-depth historical or legal document; later in the job search process you may be asked to document your entire work history on an application form and attest to its validity. The resume should, instead, highlight relevant information pertaining directly to the organization that will receive the document or to the type of position you are seeking.

We will discuss four types of resumes in this chapter: chronological, functional, targeted, and digital. The reasons for using one type of resume over another and the typical format for each are addressed in the following sections.

THE CHRONOLOGICAL RESUME

The chronological resume is the most common of the various resume formats and therefore the format that employers are most used to receiving. This type of resume is easy to read and understand because it details the chronological progression of jobs you have held. (See Exhibit 2.1.) It begins with your most recent employment and works back in time. If you have a solid work history or have experience that provided growth and development in your duties and responsibilities, a chronological resume will highlight these achievements. The typical elements of a chronological resume include the heading, a career objective, educational background, employment experience, activities, and references.

The Heading

The heading consists of your name, address, telephone number, and other means of contact. This may include a fax number, E-mail address, and your home-page address. If you are using a shared E-mail account or a parent's business fax, be sure to let others who use these systems know that you may receive important professional correspondence. You wouldn't want to miss a vital E-mail or fax! If your resume directs readers to a personal home page on the Web, be certain it's a professional personal home page designed to be viewed by a prospective employer. This may mean making substantial changes in the home page you currently mount on the Web.

We suggest that you spell out your full name in your resume heading and type it in all capital letters in bold type. After all, you are the focus of the resume! If you have a current as well as a permanent address and you include both in the heading, be sure to indicate until what date your current address will be valid. The two-letter state abbreviation should be the only abbreviation that appears in your heading. Don't forget to include the zip code with your address and the area code with your telephone number.

Exhibit 2.1

CHRONOLOGICAL RESUME

BARBARA O'NEIL

Mungovan Hall	14 Fleming Street
University of Massachusetts–Lowell	Apartment 26A
Lowell, MA 01851	Key West, FL 98766
(603) 555-5555	(723) 555-5555
boneil@xxx.com	
(until May 2002)	

OBJECTIVE
To obtain a position in publishing, initially as an editor and ultimately as a managing editor.

EDUCATION
Bachelor of Arts in English
University of Massachusetts–Lowell
May 2002
Minor: Human Relations

HONORS/AWARDS
Chancellor's Scholar, Spring/Fall Semesters, 2001
Who's Who Among Universities and Colleges, 2001–2002
Greater Lowell Rotary Award—Student of the Year, 2000

RELATED COURSES
Intellectual Property Law	Media and the Marketplace
Ethics in Publishing	Creative Writing

EXPERIENCE
Staff Assistant Intern. Boston Herald. Boston, MA, 2001–present. One of five assistants for a major newspaper. Assist travel editor in screening freelance submissions and press releases. Performs editing and proofreading duties.

Staff Assistant. Campbell and Hall, Boston, MA, summers, 1999–2001. Editorial department, trade hardcover division. Proofread and edited manuscripts for publication.

Tutor. Academic Support Services, University of Massachusetts, Lowell, MA, part-time, 1999–2000. Taught students basic composition, organizatinal, and writing skills.

ACTIVITIES
Yearbook Editor, University of Massachusetts, 2000–present.
Speakers Bureau Volunteer (Escorted guest speakers; coordinated accommodations and transportation).

REFERENCES
Available upon request.

The Objective

As you formulate the wording for this part of your resume, keep the following points in mind.

The Objective Focuses the Resume. Without a doubt this is the most challenging part of the resume for most resume writers. Even for individuals who have decided on a career path, it can be difficult to encapsulate all they want to say in one or two brief sentences. For job seekers who are unfocused or unclear about their intentions, trying to write this section can inhibit the entire resume writing process.

Recruiters tell us time and time again that the objective creates a frame of reference for them. It helps them see how you express your goals and career focus. In addition, the statement may indicate in what ways you can immediately benefit an organization. Given the importance of the objective, every point covered in the resume should relate to it. If information doesn't relate, it should be omitted. You'll file a number of resume variations in your computer. There's no excuse for not being able to tailor a resume to individual employers or specific positions.

Choose an Appropriate Length. Because of the brevity necessary for a resume, you should keep the objective as short as possible. Although objectives of only four or five words often don't show much direction, objectives that take three full lines could be viewed as too wordy and might possibly be ignored.

Consider Which Type of Objective Statement You Will Use. There are many ways to state an objective, but generally there are four forms this statement can take: (1) a very general statement; (2) a statement focused on a specific position; (3) a statement focused on a specific industry; or (4) a summary of your qualifications. In our contacts with employers, we often hear that many resumes don't exhibit any direction or career goals, so we suggest avoiding general statements when possible.

1. General Objective Statement. General objective statements look like the following:

- An entry-level educational programming coordinator position

- An entry-level marketing position

This type of objective would be useful if you know what type of job you want but you're not sure which industries interest you.

2. Position-Focused Objective. Following are examples of objectives focusing on a specific position:

- To obtain the position of conference coordinator at State College

- To obtain a position as assistant editor at *Time* magazine

When a student applies for an advertised job opening, this type of focus can be very effective. The employer knows that the applicant has taken the time to tailor the resume specifically for this position.

3. Industry-Focused Objective. Focusing on a particular industry in an objective could be stated as follows:

- To begin a career as a sales representative in the cruise line industry

4. Summary of Qualifications Statement. The summary of qualifications can be used instead of an objective or in conjunction with an objective. The purpose of this type of statement is to highlight relevant qualifications gained through a variety of experiences. This type of statement is often used by individuals with extensive and diversified work experience. An example of a qualifications statement follows:

••

A degree in general studies and four years of progressively increasing job responsibility in several different departments within a major publishing house have prepared me to begin a career as an editor with a firm that values hard work and attention to detail.

....

Support Your Objective. A resume that contains any one of these types of objective statements should then go on to demonstrate why you are qualified to get the position. Listing academic degrees can be one way to indicate qualifications. Another demonstration would be in the way previous experiences, both volunteer and paid, are described. Without this kind of documentation in the body of the resume, the objective looks unsupported. Think of the resume as telling a connected story about you. All the elements should work together to form a coherent picture that ideally should relate to your statement of objective.

Education

This section of your resume should indicate the exact name of the degree you will receive or have received, spelled out completely with no abbreviations. The degree is generally listed after the objective, followed by the institution name and location, and then the month and year of graduation. This section could also include your academic minor, grade point average (GPA), and appearance on the Dean's List or President's List.

If you have enough space, you might want to include a section listing courses related to the field in which you are seeking work. The best use of a "related courses" section would be to list some course work that is not traditionally associated with the major. Perhaps you took several computer courses outside your degree that will be helpful and related to the job prospects you are entertaining. Several education section examples are shown here:

....

- Bachelor of Arts Degree in General Studies
  University of Florida, Gainesville, January 2000
  Minor: Creative Writing

- Bachelor of Arts Degree in English
  Tufts University, Medford, MA, May 2000

- Bachelor of Arts Degree in History
  SUNY Buffalo, NY, May 2000
  Minor: English Education

An example of a format for a related courses section follows:

RELATED COURSES

Public Relations	Techincal Writing
Public Speaking	Problem Solving
Educational Psychology	Research Methods

Experience

The experience section of your resume should be the most substantial part and should take up most of the space on the page. Employers want to see what kind of work history you have. They will look at your range of experiences, longevity in jobs, and specific tasks you are able to complete. This section may also be called "work experience," "related experience," "employment history," or "employment." No matter what you call this section, some important points to remember are the following:

1. **Describe your duties** as they relate to the position you are seeking.

2. **Emphasize major responsibilities** and indicate increases in responsibility. Include all relevant employment experiences: summer, part-time, internships, cooperative education, or self-employment.

3. **Emphasize skills**, especially those that transfer from one situation to another. The fact that you coordinated a student organization, chaired meetings, supervised others, and managed a budget leads one to suspect that you could coordinate other things as well.

4. **Use descriptive job titles** that provide information about what you did. A "Student Intern" should be more specifically stated as, for example, "Magazine Operations Intern." "Volunteer" is also too general; a title such as "Peer Writing Tutor" would be more appropriate.

5. **Create word pictures** by using active verbs to start sentences. Describe *results* you have produced in the work you have done.

A limp description would say something such as the following: "My duties included helping with production, proofreading, and editing. I used a word-processing package to alter text." An action statement would be stated as follows: "Coordinated and assisted in the creative marketing of brochures and seminar promotions, becoming proficient in Word."

Remember, an accomplishment is simply a result, a final measurable product that people can relate to. A duty is not a result; it is an obligation— every job holder has duties. For an effective resume, list as many results as you can. To make the most of the limited space you have and to give your description impact, carefully select appropriate and accurate descriptors from the list of action words in Exhibit 2.2.

Exhibit 2.2

RESUME ACTION VERBS

Achieved	Converted	Finalized
Acted	Coordinated	Generated
Administered	Corrected	Handled
Advised	Created	Headed
Analyzed	Decreased	Helped
Assessed	Defined	Identified
Assisted	Demonstrated	Illustrated
Attained	Designed	Implemented
Balanced	Determined	Improved
Budgeted	Developed	Increased
Calculated	Directed	Influenced
Collected	Documented	Informed
Communicated	Drafted	Initiated
Compiled	Edited	Innovated
Completed	Eliminated	Instituted
Composed	Ensured	Instructed
Conceptualized	Established	Integrated
Condensed	Estimated	Interpreted
Conducted	Evaluated	Introduced
Consolidated	Examined	Learned
Constructed	Explained	Lectured
Controlled	Facilitated	Led

Maintained	Produced	Selected
Managed	Projected	Served
Mapped	Proposed	Showed
Marketed	Provided	Simplified
Met	Qualified	Sketched
Modified	Quantified	Sold
Monitored	Questioned	Solved
Negotiated	Realized	Staffed
Observed	Received	Streamlined
Obtained	Recommended	Studied
Operated	Recorded	Submitted
Organized	Reduced	Summarized
Participated	Reinforced	Systematized
Performed	Reported	Tabulated
Planned	Represented	Tested
Predicted	Researched	Transacted
Prepared	Resolved	Updated
Presented	Reviewed	Verified
Processed	Scheduled	

Here are some traits that employers tell us they like to see:

- Teamwork

- Energy and motivation

- Learning and using new skills

- Versatility

- Critical thinking

- Understanding how profits are created

- Organizational acumen

- Communicating directly and clearly, in both writing and speaking

- Risk taking

- Willingness to admit mistakes

- High personal standards

SOLUTIONS TO FREQUENTLY ENCOUNTERED PROBLEMS

Repetitive Employment with the Same Employer

EMPLOYMENT: The Foot Locker, Portland, Oregon. Summer 2001, 2002, 2003. Initially employed in high school as salesclerk. Due to successful performance, asked to return next two summers at higher pay with added responsibility. Ranked as the #2 salesperson the first summer and #1 the next two summers. Assisted in arranging eye-catching retail displays; served as manager of other summer workers during owner's absence.

A Large Number of Jobs

EMPLOYMENT: Recent Hospitality Industry Experience: Affiliated with four upscale hotel/restaurant complexes (September 2001–February 2004), where I worked part- and full-time as a waiter, bartender, disc jockey, and bookkeeper to produce income for college.

Several Positions with the Same Employer

EMPLOYMENT: Coca-Cola Bottling Co., Burlington, Vermont, 2001–2004. In four years, I received three promotions, each with increased pay and responsibility.

Summer Sales Coordinator: Promoted to hire, train, and direct efforts of add-on staff of fifteen college-age route salespeople hired to meet summer peak demand for product.

Sales Administrator: Promoted to run home office sales desk, managing accounts and associated delivery schedules for professional sales force of ten people. Intensive phone work, daily interaction with all personnel, and strong knowledge of product line required.

Route Salesperson: Summer employment to travel and tourism industry sites that use Coke products. Met specific schedule demands, used good communication skills with wide variety of customers, and demonstrated strong selling skills. Named salesperson of the month for July and August of that year.

QUESTIONS RESUME WRITERS OFTEN ASK

How Far Back Should I Go in Terms of Listing Past Jobs?

Usually, listing three or four jobs should suffice. If you did something back in high school that has a bearing on your future aspirations for employment, by all means list the job. As you progress through your college career, high school jobs will be replaced on the resume by college employment.

Should I Differentiate Between Paid and Nonpaid Employment?

Most employers are not initially concerned about how much you were paid. They are anxious to know how much responsibility you held in your past employment. There is no need to specify that your work was as a volunteer if you had significant responsibilities.

How Should I Represent My Accomplishments or Work-Related Responsibilities?

Succinctly, but fully. In other words, give the employer enough information to arouse curiosity but not so much detail that you leave nothing to the imagination. Besides, some jobs merit more lengthy explanations than others. Be sure to convey any information that can give an employer a better understanding of the depth of your involvement at work. Did you supervise others? How many? Did your efforts result in a more efficient operation? How much did you increase efficiency? Did you handle a budget? How much? Were you promoted in a short time? Did you work two jobs at once or fifteen hours per week after high school? Where appropriate, quantify.

Should the Work Section Always Follow the Education Section on the Resume?

Always lead with your strengths. If your education closely relates to the employment you now seek, put this section after the objective. Or, if you are weak on the academic side but have a surplus of good work experiences, consider reversing the order to lead with employment.

How Should I Present My Activities, Honors, Awards, Professional Societies, and Affiliations?

This section of the resume can add valuable information for an employer to consider if used correctly. The rule of thumb for information in this section is to include only those activities that are in some way relevant to the objective stated on your resume. If you can draw a valid connection between your activities and your objective, include them; if not, leave them out.

Granted, this is hard to do. Playing center on the championship basketball team or serving as coordinator of the biggest homecoming parade ever held are roles that have meaning for you and represent personal accomplishments you'd like to share. But the resume is a brief document, and the information you provide on it should help the employer make a decision about your job eligibility. Including personal details can be confusing and could hurt your candidacy. Limiting your activity list to a few significant experiences can be very effective.

If you are applying for a position as a safety officer, your certificate in Red Cross lifesaving skills or CPR would be related and valuable. You would want to include it. If, however, you are applying for a job as a junior account executive in an advertising agency, that information would be unrelated and superfluous. Leave it out.

Professional affiliations and honors should all be listed; especially important are those related to your job objective. Social clubs and activities need not be a part of your resume unless you hold a significant office or you are looking for a position related to your membership. Be aware that most prospective employers' principal concerns are related to your employability, not your social life. If you have any, publications can be included as an addendum to your resume.

The focus of the resume is your experience and education. It is not necessary to describe your involvement in activities. However, if your resume needs to be lengthened, this section provides the freedom either to expand on or mention only briefly the contributions you have made. If you have made significant contributions (e.g., an officer of an organization or a particularly long tenure with a group), you may choose to describe them in more detail. It is not always necessary to include the dates of your memberships with your activities the way you would include job dates.

There are various ways in which to present additional information. You may give this section a number of different titles. Assess what you want to list, and then use an appropriate title. Do not use "extracurricular activities." This terminology is scholastic, not professional, and therefore not appropriate. The following are two examples:

- ACTIVITIES: Society for Technical Communication, Student Senate, Student Admissions Representative, Senior Class Officer

- ACTIVITIES:
  - Society for Technical Communication Member
  - Student Senator
  - Student Admissions Representative
  - Senior Class Officer

The position you are looking for will determine what you should or should not include. *Always* look for a correlation between the activity and the prospective job.

How Should I Handle References?

The use of references is considered a part of the interview process, and they should never be listed on a resume. You would always provide references to a potential employer if requested to, so it is not even necessary to include this section on the resume if space does not permit. If space is available, it is acceptable to include one of the following statements:

- REFERENCES: Furnished upon request.

- REFERENCES: Available upon request.

Individuals used as references must be protected from unnecessary contacts. By including names on your resume, you leave your references unprotected. Overuse and abuse of your references will lead to less-than-supportive comments. Protect your references by giving out their names only when you are being considered seriously as a candidate for a given position.

THE FUNCTIONAL RESUME

The functional resume departs from a chronological resume in that it organizes information by specific accomplishments in various settings: previous jobs, volunteer work, associations, and so forth. This type of resume permits you to stress the substance of your experiences rather than the position titles you have held. (See Exhibit 2.3.) You should consider using a functional resume if you have held a series of similar jobs that relied on the same skills or abilities.

The Objective

A functional resume begins with an objective that can be used to focus the contents of the resume.

Specific Accomplishments

Specific accomplishments are listed on this type of resume. Examples of the types of headings used to describe these capabilities might include research, computer skills, teaching, communication, production, management, marketing, or writing. The headings you choose will directly relate to your experience and the tasks that you carried out. Each accomplishment section contains statements related to your experience in that category, regardless of when or where it occurred. Organize the accomplishments and the related tasks you describe in their order of importance as related to the position you seek.

Exhibit 2.3

FUNCTIONAL RESUME

CARLOS HIDALGO

Student Apartment 12
Michigan State University
Detroit, MI 36754
(216) 555-5555
Fax (216) 555-5556
chidalgo@xxx.com
(until May 2003)

12 Cornwall Street
Rocky River, OH 44116
(212) 555-5555

OBJECTIVE
A position as a multisubject elementary school teacher, for a private school, that allows me to show my initiative and use my teaching and methodology skills.

CAPABILITIES
- Familiarity with K–6 curriculum
- Curriculum design
- Inspiring and motivating children

SELECTED ACCOMPLISHMENTS
Tutoring: Worked with 5- through 11-year-olds in an after-school remedial program. Responsible for reading and math, raising levels to the appropriate grade or beyond. Selected materials, including subject-specific software, developed and implemented study plans, and coordinated assessments.

Team Player: Collaborated with coworkers and professionals in other subject areas. Met with parents and teachers. Participated in staff meetings.

Organizing Activities: Planned and implemented recreational activities for young children including sports events and craft workshops.

AWARDS
Graduated with honors in general studies
Nominated to National Honor Society
Awarded commendation by YMCA for work with disadvantaged youths

EMPLOYMENT HISTORY
YMCA, After-School Program,
Detroit, Michigan 2001–2003
YMCA , Summer Day Camp,
Summers, 1999–Present

EDUCATION
Bachelor of Arts in General Studies
Michigan State University, Detroit, Michigan
May 2003

REFERENCES
Provided upon request.

Experience or Employment History

Your actual work experience is condensed and placed after the specific accomplishments section. It simply lists dates of employment, position titles, and employer names.

Education

The education section of a functional resume is identical to that of the chronological resume, but it does not carry the same visual importance because it is placed near the bottom of the page.

References

Because actual reference names are never listed on a resume, a statement of reference availability is optional.

THE TARGETED RESUME

The targeted resume focuses on specific work-related capabilities you can bring to a given position within an organization. (See Exhibit 2.4.) It should be sent to an individual within the organization who makes hiring decisions about the position you are seeking.

The Objective

The objective on this type of resume should be targeted to a specific career or position. It should be supported by the capabilities, accomplishments, and achievements documented in the resume.

Capabilities

Capabilities should be statements that illustrate tasks you believe you are capable of based on your accomplishments, achievements, and work history. Each should relate to your targeted career or position. You can stress your qualifications rather than your employment history. This approach may require research to obtain an understanding of the nature of the work involved and the capabilities necessary to carry out that work.

Accomplishments/Achievements

This section relates the various activities you have been involved in to the job market. These experiences may include previous jobs, extracurricular activities at school, internships, and part-time summer work.

Experience

Your work history should be listed in abbreviated form and may include position title, employer name, and employment dates.

Education

Because this type of resume is directed toward a specific job target and an individual's related experience, the education section is not prominently located at the top of the resume as is done on the chronological resume.

DIGITAL RESUMES

Today's employers have to manage an enormous number of resumes. One of the most frequent complaints the writers of this series hear from students is the failure of employers to even acknowledge the receipt of a resume and cover letter. Frequently, the reason for this poor response or nonresponse is the volume of applications received for every job. In an attempt to better manage the considerable labor investment involved in processing large numbers of resumes, many employers are requiring digital submission of resumes. There are two types of digital resumes: those that can be E-mailed or posted to a website, called *electronic resumes*, and those that can be "read" by a com-

Exhibit 2.4

TARGETED RESUME

AMANDA BAILEY

Redbud Apartments 223
Middlebury College
Middlebury, VT 09878
(802) 555-5555
Fax (802) 555-5556
manda@xxx.com
(until May 2004)

43 London Street
Rosendale, NY 12472
(914) 555-5555

JOB TARGET
Development Coordinator position within a university alumni or other fund-raising office.

CAPABILITIES
- Comfortable in diverse settings
- Able to communicate effectively to diverse audiences
- Bilingual Spanish/English
- Strong background in community resources
- Skilled writer in a variety of formats

ACHIEVEMENTS
- Several articles published in local newspapers
- Researched fund-raising goal for local Big Brother/Big Sister Chapter
- Reached volunteer recruitment goal
- Maintained a 4.0 grade point average throughout college

WORK HISTORY

2003–present *Assistant Development Officer*, Burlington, VT Big Brother/Big Sister. Organized fund-raising events, developed promotional material, coordinated volunteers.

2001–present *Public Relations Assistant*, Children's Hospital. Part-time community service work.

2001–2002 *Nurse's Aide*, Children's Hospital. Part-time work assisting medical staff.

EDUCATION
Bachelor of Arts in Sociology, 2004
Middlebury College
Middlebury, Vermont

---

puter, commonly called *scannable resumes.* Though the format may be a bit different from the traditional "paper" resume, the goal of both types of digital resumes is the same—to get you an interview! These resumes must be designed to be "technologically friendly." What that basically means to you is that they should be free of graphics and fancy formatting.

Electronic Resumes

Sometimes referred to as plain-text resumes, electronic resumes are designed to be E-mailed to an employer or posted to a commercial Internet database such as CareerMosaic.com, America's Job Bank (www.ajb.dni.us), or Monster.com.

Some technical considerations:

- Electronic resumes must be written in American Standard Code for Information Interchange (ASCII), which is simply a plain-text format. These characters are universally recognized so that every computer can accurately read and understand them. To create an ASCII file of your current resume, open your document, then save it as a text or ASCII file. This will eliminate all formatting. Edit as needed using your computer's text editor application.

- Use a standard-width typeface. Courier is a good choice because it is the font associated with ASCII in most systems.

- Use a font size of 11 to 14 points. A 12-point font is considered standard.

- Your margin should be left-justified.

- Do not exceed sixty-five characters per line because the word-wrap function doesn't operate in ASCII.

- Do not use boldface, italics, underlining, bullets, or various font sizes. Instead, use asterisks, plus signs, or all capital letters when you want to emphasize something.

Exhibit 2.5

DIGITAL RESUME

ANDREW TYLER
117 Stetson Avenue
Small School, NV 02459
508-555-5555
atyler@xxx.com

KEYWORD SUMMARY
B.A. Psychology, 2002
Counseling, School,
Evaluation, Referral Services,
Learning Disabilities

EDUCATION
Bachelor of Arts, Psychology, 2002
Small State College, Small School, Nevada
Minor: Human Behavior
G.P.A.: 3.0/4.0

RELATED COURSES
Social Work
Sociology
Criminology
Brain and Behavior

SKILL TRAINING
Certified EMT, Lifesaving, First Aid,
CPR, Self-Defense, Triathlete

EXPERIENCE
Nevada Counseling Center, 2001–2002
* Numerous assignments over two years
* Provider referral services to clients
* Promoted and increase in salary
* Staff training in assessment

Student Representative to Judicial Council, 1999–2001
* Participated in student conduct hearings
* Drafted sanctions document
* Presented to student groups

House Painting, 2000
* Established business with friends

COLLEGE ATHLETICS
* Played on inter-hall sports teams
* Cocaptain of the football team

REFERENCES
Available upon request.

++ Willing to relocate ++

- Avoid graphics and shading.

- Use as many "keywords" as you possibly can. These are words or phrases usually relating to skills or experience that either are specifically used in the job announcement or are popular buzzwords in the industry.

- Minimize abbreviations.

- Your name should be the first line of text.

- Conduct a "test run" by E-mailing your resume to yourself and a friend before you send it to the employer. See how it transmits, and make any changes you need to. Continue to test it until it's exactly how you want it to look.

- Unless an employer specifically requests that you send the resume in the form of an attachment, don't. Employers can encounter problems opening a document as an attachment, and there are always viruses to consider.

- Don't forget your cover letter. Send it along with your resume as a single message.

Scannable Resumes

Some companies are relying on technology to narrow the candidate pool for available job openings. Electronic Applicant Tracking uses imaging to scan, sort, and store resume elements in a database. Then, through OCR (Optical Character Recognition) software, the computer scans the resumes for keywords and phrases. To have the best chance at getting an interview, you want to increase the number of "hits"—matches of your skills, abilities, experience, and education to those the computer is scanning for—your resume will get. You can see how critical using the right keywords is for this type of resume.

Technical considerations include:

- Again, do not use boldface (newer systems may read this OK, but many older ones won't), italics, underlining, bullets, shading, graphics, or multiple font sizes. Instead, for emphasis, use asterisks, plus signs, or all capital letters. Minimize abbreviations.

- Use a popular typeface such as Courier, Helvetica, Ariel, or Palatino. Avoid decorative fonts.

- Font size should be between 11 and 14 points.

- Do not compress the spacing between letters.

- Use horizontal and vertical lines sparingly; the computer may misread them as the letters L or I.

- Left-justify the text.

- Do not use parentheses or brackets around telephone numbers, and be sure your phone number is on its own line of text.

- Your name should be the first line of text and on its own line. If your resume is longer than one page, be sure to put your name on the top of all pages.

- Use a traditional resume structure. The chronological format may work best.

- Use nouns that are skill-focused, such as *management, writer,* and *programming.* This is different from traditional paper resumes, which use action-oriented verbs.

- Laser printers produce the finest copies. Avoid dot-matrix printers.

- Use standard, light-colored paper with text on one side only. Since the higher the contrast, the better, your best choice is black ink on white paper.

- Always send original copies. If you must fax, set the fax on fine mode, not standard.

- Do not staple or fold your resume. This can confuse the computer.

- Before you send your scannable resume, be certain the employer uses this technology. If you can't determine this, you may want to send two versions (scannable and traditional) to be sure your resume gets considered.

RESUME PRODUCTION AND OTHER TIPS

An ink-jet printer is the preferred option for printing your resume. Begin by printing just a few copies. You may find a small error or you may simply want to make some changes, and it is less frustrating and less expensive if you print in small batches.

Resume paper color should be carefully chosen. You should consider the types of employers who will receive your resume and the types of positions for which you are applying. Use white or ivory paper for traditional or conservative employers or for higher-level positions.

Black ink on sharp, white paper can be harsh on the reader's eyes. Think about an ivory or cream paper that will provide less contrast and be easier to read. Pink, green, and blue tints should generally be avoided.

Many resume writers buy packages of matching envelopes and cover sheet stationery that, although not absolutely necessary, help convey a professional impression.

If you'll be producing many cover letters at home, be sure you have high-quality printing equipment. Learn standard envelope formats for business, and retain a copy of every cover letter you send out. You can use the copies to take notes of any telephone conversations that may occur.

If attending a job fair, either carry a briefcase or place your resume in a nicely covered legal-size pad holder.

THE COVER LETTER

The cover letter provides you with the opportunity to tailor your resume by telling the prospective employer how you can be a benefit to the organization. It allows you to highlight aspects of your background that are not already discussed in your resume and that might be especially relevant to the organization you are contacting or to the position you are seeking. Every resume should have a cover letter enclosed when you send it out. Unlike the resume, which may be mass-produced, a cover letter is most effective when it is individually prepared and focused on the particular requirements of the organization in question.

A good cover letter should supplement the resume and motivate the reader to review the resume. The format shown in Exhibit 2.6 is only a suggestion to help you decide what information to include in writing a cover letter.

Begin the cover letter with your street address twelve lines down from the top. Leave three to five lines between the date and the name of the person to whom you are addressing the cover letter. Make sure you leave one blank line between the salutation and the body of the letter and between paragraphs. After typing "Sincerely," leave four blank lines and type your name. This should leave plenty of room for your signature. A sample cover letter is shown in Exhibit 2.7.

The following guidelines will help you write good cover letters:

1. Be sure to type your letter neatly; ensure there are no misspellings.

2. Avoid unusual typefaces, such as script.

3. Address the letter to an individual, using the person's name and title. To obtain this information, call the company. If answering a blind newspaper advertisement, address the letter "To Whom It May Concern" or omit the salutation.

4. Be sure your cover letter directly indicates the position you are applying for and tells why you are qualified to fill it.

5. Send the original letter, not a photocopy, with your resume. Keep a copy for your records.

6. Make your cover letter no more than one page.

7. Include a phone number where you can be reached.

8. Avoid trite language and have someone read the letter over to react to its tone, content, and mechanics.

9. For your own information, record the date you send out each letter and resume.

Exhibit 2.6

COVER LETTER FORMAT

Your Street Address
Your Town, State, Zip
Phone Number
Fax Number
E-mail

Date

Name
Title
Organization
Address

Dear _____:

First Paragraph. In this paragraph state the reason for the letter, name the specific position or type of work you are applying for, and indicate from which resource (career services office, website, newspaper, contact, employment service) you learned of this opening. The first paragraph can also be used to inquire about future openings.

Second Paragraph. Indicate why you are interested in this position, the company, or its products or services, and what you can do for the employer. If you are a recent graduate, explain how your academic background makes you a qualified candidate. Try not to repeat the same information found in the resume.

Third Paragraph. Refer the reader to the enclosed resume for more detailed information.

Fourth Paragraph. In this paragraph say what you will do to follow up on your letter. For example, state that you will call by a certain date to set up an interview or to find out if the company will be recruiting in your area. Finish by indicating your willingness to answer any questions they may have. Be sure you have provided your phone number.

Sincerely,

Type your name
Enclosure

Exhibit 2.7

SAMPLE COVER LETTER

P.O. Box 435
Plymouth, MA 02360
(508) 555-4434
April 25, 2003

Arlene Tierney
Director of Personnel
Colonial Williamsburg Foundation
P.O. Drawer T
Williamsburg, VA 23185

Dear Ms. Tierney:

In May of 2003, I will graduate from Tufts University with a bachelor of arts degree in history. I read of your opening for an assistant researcher in *The Herald* on Sunday, April 24, 2003, and I am very interested in the possibilities it offers. I am writing to explore the opportunity for employment with the Foundation.

The ad indicated you were looking for creative individuals with an interest in U.S. history and good communication skills. I believe I possess those qualities. During the summers while in college, I worked at Plimoth Plantation in several capacities, including character interpreter and as an assistant in the costume department. Through my work there, I learned the importance of good research skills and maintaining a positive attitude with coworkers and visitors.

In addition to the various history courses in my academic program, I felt it important to enroll in some anthropology, psychology, and computer courses, particularly intro and advanced Internet classes.

These courses helped me become comfortable with understanding eighteenth-century American culture, as well as honing my researching skills. I believe these accomplishments will help me to represent the Colonial Williamsburg Foundation in a professional and enthusiastic manner.

I would like to meet with you to discuss how my education and experience would be consistent with your needs. I will contact your office next week to discuss the possibility of an interview. In the meantime, if you have any questions or require additional information, please contact me at my home, (508) 555-4434.

Sincerely,

James Ponti
Enclosure

CHAPTER THREE

RESEARCHING CAREERS

One common question a career counselor encounters is "What can I do with my degree?" Liberal arts majors often struggle with this problem because, unlike their fellow students in more applied fields, such as accounting, computer science, or health and physical education, there is real confusion about just what kinds of jobs they can get with their degree and what kinds of organizations will hire them. Accounting majors become accountants, computer science majors can work as data analysts. What jobs are open to liberal arts majors?

WHAT DO THEY CALL THE JOB YOU WANT?

There is every reason to be unaware. One reason for confusion is perhaps a mistaken assumption that a college education provides job training. In most cases it does not. Of course, applied fields such as engineering, management, or education provide specific skills for the workplace, whereas most liberal arts degrees simply provide an education. A liberal arts education exposes you to numerous fields of study and teaches you quantitative reasoning, critical thinking, writing, and speaking, all of which can be successfully applied to a number of different job fields. But it still remains up to you to choose a job field and to learn how to articulate the benefits of your education in a way the employer will appreciate.

As indicated in Chapter 1 on self-assessment, your first task is to understand and value what parts of that education you enjoyed and were good at and would continue to enjoy in your life's work. Did your writing courses encourage you in your ability to express yourself in writing? Did you enjoy the research process, and did you find that your work was well received? Did you enjoy any of your required quantitative subjects such as algebra or calculus?

The answers to questions such as these provide clues to skills and interests you bring to the employment market over and above the credential of your degree. In fact, it is not an overstatement to suggest that most employers who demand a college degree immediately look beyond that degree to you as a person and your own individual expression of what you like to do and think you can do for them, regardless of your major.

Collecting Job Titles

The world of employment is a big place, and even seasoned veterans of the job hunt can be surprised about what jobs are to be found in what organizations. You need to become a bit of an explorer and adventurer and be willing to try a variety of techniques to begin a list of possible occupations that might use your talents and education. Once you have a list of possibilities that you are interested in and qualified for, you can move on to find out what kinds of organizations have these job titles.

· ·

Not every employer seeking to hire a liberal arts major may be equally desirable to you. Some employment environments may be more attractive to you than others. A modern languages major with fluency in more than one language, for example, might expect to do interpreting or translation work. But somone with those skills could also find work in a variety of social service agencies—for the government, for corporations with overseas concerns, for large advertising firms, for financial institutions, or even in hospital settings. Each of these environments presents a different "culture" with associated norms in the pace of work, the subject matter of interest, and the backgrounds of its employees. Although the job titles may be the same, not all locations may present the same "fit" for you.

If you majored in another liberal arts area, economics, for example, and you have also developed some strong communications skills, you might naturally think about a

career in banking or business. But economics majors with
these skills and interests might go on to teach others their
skills or work for the foreign service or a variety of other
government or nonprofit agencies, in fund-raising, or for
insurance companies. Each of these job titles can also be
found in a number of different settings.

....

Take training, for example. Trainers write policy and procedural manu-
als and actively teach to assist all levels of employees in mastering various
tasks and work-related systems. Trainers exist in all large corporations, banks,
consumer goods manufacturers, medical diagnostic equipment firms, sales
organizations, and any organization that has processes or materials that need
to be presented to and learned by the staff.

In reading job descriptions or want ads for any of these positions, you
would find your four-year degree a "must." However, the academic major
might be less important than your own individual skills in critical thinking,
analysis, report writing, public presentations, and interpersonal communication. Even more important than thinking or knowing you have certain skills
are your ability to express those skills concretely and the examples you use
to illustrate them to an employer.

The best beginning to a job search is to create a list of job titles you might
want to pursue, learn more about the nature of the jobs behind those titles,
and then discover what kinds of employers hire for those positions. In the
following section we'll teach you how to build a job title directory to use in
your job search.

Developing a Job Title Directory That Works for You

A job title directory is simply a complete list of all the job titles you are interested in, are intrigued by, or think you are qualified for. After combining the
understanding gained through self-assessment with your own individual interests and the skills and talents you've acquired with your degree, you'll soon
start to read and recognize a number of occupational titles that seem right
for you. There are several resources you can use to develop your list, including computer searches, books, and want ads.

Computerized Interest Inventories. One way to begin your search is to identify a number of jobs that call for your degree and the particular skills and
interests you identified as part of the self-assessment process. There are
excellent interactive career-guidance programs on the market to help you
produce such selected lists of possible job titles. Most of these are available

at high schools and colleges and at some larger town and city libraries. Two of the industry leaders are *CHOICES* and *DISCOVER*. Both allow you to enter interests, values, educational background, and other information to produce lists of possible occupations and industries. Each of the resources listed here will produce different job title lists. Some job titles will appear again and again, while others will be unique to a particular source. Investigate all of them!

Reference Sources. Books on the market that may be available through your local library or career counseling office also suggest various occupations related to specific majors. The following are only a few of the many good books on the market: *The College Board Guide to 150 Popular College Majors, College Majors and Careers: A Resource Guide for Effective Life Planning* both by Paul Phifer, and *Kaplan's What to Study: 101 Fields in a Flash*. All of these books list possible job titles within the academic major. The *Occupational Outlook Handbook* (*OOH*) describes many of the job titles in the criminal justice employment fields under broad categories such as Service, Professional and Technical, and Managerial and Administrative Occupations and also identifies those jobs by their *Dictionary of Occupational Titles* (*DOT*) code. (See the following discussion.)

••

Many college and university career office Web pages offer some great information on what you can do with specific majors. Several of the best we've seen are from Florida State University (www.fsu.edu/ccis/matchmajor/match menu.html), Georgia Southern University (www2.gasou .edu/sta/career), and the University of North Carolina at Wilmington (www.uncwil.edu/staff/careers/majors.html). In addition to potential job titles and/or employers, these sites provide you with further related resources to explore, including websites.

••

Each job title deserves your consideration. Like removing the layers of an onion, the search for job titles can go on and on! As you spend time doing this activity, you are actually learning more about the value of your degree. What's important in your search at this point is not to become critical or selective but rather to develop as long a list of possibilities as you can. Every source used will help you add new and potentially exciting jobs to your growing list.

Want Ads. It has been well publicized that newspaper want ads represent only about 10 to 15 percent of the current job market. However, with the current high state of employment as this book goes to press, the percentage of jobs advertised in the newspapers and on-line is rising dramatically, so don't ignore this source.

If you are able to be mobile in your job search, you may want to search the classified sections of newspapers in other cities. This is now possible on-line. A good source for this search is the site called www.looksmart.com. Using the keywords *newspaper classifieds* will lead you to a site where you can search by state alphabetically. It's an excellent source for want ads.

Remember, because want ads are written for what an organization *hopes* to find, you don't have to meet absolutely every criterion. However, if certain requirements are stated as absolute minimums and you cannot meet them, it's best not to waste your time.

A recent examination of the *Boston Sunday Globe* (www.boston.com) reveals the following possible occupations for a liberal arts major with some computer skills and limited work experience. (This is only a partial list of what was available.)

- Admissions representative
- Salesperson
- Compliance director
- Assistant principal gifts writer
- Public relations officer

- Technical writer
- Personnel trainee
- G.E.D. examiner
- Direct mail researcher
- Associate publicist

After performing this exercise for a few Sundays, you'll find you have collected a new library of job titles.

The Sunday want ads exercise is important because these jobs are out in the marketplace. They truly exist, and people with your qualifications are being sought to apply. What's more, many of these advertisements describe the duties and responsibilities of the job advertised and give you a beginning sense of the challenges and opportunities such a position presents. Some will indicate salary, and that will be helpful as well. This information will better define the jobs for you and provide some good material for possible interviews in that field.

Exploring Job Descriptions

Once you've arrived at a solid list of possible job titles that interest you and for which you believe you are somewhat qualified, it's a good idea to do some research on each of these jobs. The preeminent source for such job information is the *Dictionary of Occupational Titles*, or *DOT* (www.wave.net /upg/immigration/dot_index.html). This directory lists every conceivable job and provides excellent up-to-date information on duties and responsibilities, interactions with associates, and day-to-day assignments and tasks. These descriptions provide a thorough job analysis, but they do not consider the possible employers or the environments in which a job may be performed. So, although a position as public relations officer may be well defined in terms of duties and responsibilities, it does not explain the differences in doing public relations work in a college or a hospital or a factory or a bank. You will need to look somewhere else for work settings.

Learning More About Possible Work Settings

After reading some job descriptions, you may choose to edit and revise your list of job titles once again, discarding those you feel are not suitable and keeping those that continue to hold your interest. Or you may wish to keep your list intact and see where these jobs may be located. For example, if you are interested in public relations and you appear to have those skills and the requisite education, you'll want to know what organizations do public relations. How can you find that out? How much income does someone in public relations make a year and what is the employment potential for the field of public relations?

To answer these and many other questions about your list of job titles, we recommend you try any of the following resources: *Careers Encyclopedia;* a career information center site such as that provided by the American Marketing Association at www.amaboston.org/jobs.htm; *College to Career: The Guide to Job Opportunities;* and the *Occupational Outlook Handbook* (http://stats.bls.gov/ocohome.htm). Each of these resources, in a different way, will help to put the job titles you have selected into an employer context. Perhaps the most extensive discussion is found in the *Occupational Outlook Handbook*, which gives a thorough presentation of the nature of the work, the working conditions, employment statistics, training, other qualifications, and advancement possibilities as well as job outlook and earnings. Related occupations are also detailed, and a select bibliography is provided to help you find additional information.

Continuing with our public relations example, your search through these reference materials would teach you that the public relations jobs you find attractive are available in larger hospitals, financial institutions, most corporations (both consumer goods and industrial goods), media organizations, and colleges and universities.

Networking to Get the Complete Story

You now have not only a list of job titles but also, for each of these job titles, a description of the work involved and a general list of possible employment settings in which to work. You'll want to do some reading and keep talking to friends, colleagues, teachers, and others about the possibilities. Don't neglect to ask if the career office at your college maintains some kind of alumni network. Often such alumni networks will connect you with another graduate from the college who is working in the job title or industry you are seeking information about. These career networkers offer what assistance they can. For some it is a full day "shadowing" the alumnus as he or she goes about the job. Others offer partial-day visits, tours, informational interviews, resume reviews, job postings, or, if distance prevents a visit, telephone interviews. As fellow graduates, they'll be frank and informative about their own jobs and prospects in their field.

Take them up on their offer and continue to learn all you can about your own personal list of job titles, descriptions, and employment settings. You'll probably continue to edit and refine this list as you learn more about the realities of the job, the possible salary, advancement opportunities, and supply and demand statistics.

In the next section we'll describe how to find the specific organizations that represent these industries and employers so that you can begin to make contact.

WHERE ARE THESE JOBS, ANYWAY?

Having a list of job titles that you've designed around your own career interests and skills is an excellent beginning. It means you've really thought about who you are and what you are presenting to the employment market. It has caused you to think seriously about the most appealing environments to work in, and you have identified some employer types that represent these environments.

The research and the thinking that you've done thus far will be used again and again. They will be helpful in writing your resume and cover letters, in talking about yourself on the telephone to prospective employers, and in answering interview questions.

Now is a good time to begin to narrow the field of job titles and employment sites down to some specific employers to initiate the employment contact.

Finding Out Which Employers Hire People Like You

This section will provide tips, techniques, and specific resources for developing an actual list of specific employers that can be used to make contacts. It is only an outline that you must be prepared to tailor to your own particular needs and according to what you bring to the job search. Once again, it is important to communicate with others along the way exactly what you're looking for and what your goals are for the research you're doing. Librarians, employers, career counselors, friends, friends of friends, business contacts, and bookstore staff will all have helpful information on geographically specific and new resources to aid you in locating employers who'll hire you.

Identifying Information Resources

Your interview wardrobe and your new resume might have put a dent in your wallet, but the resources you'll need to pursue your job search are available for free (although you may choose to copy materials on a machine instead of taking notes by hand). The categories of information detailed here are not hard to find and are yours for the browsing.

Numerous resources described in this section will help you identify actual employers. Use all of them or any others that you identify as available in your geographic area. As you become experienced in this process, you'll quickly figure out which information sources are helpful and which are not. If you live in a rural area, a well-planned day trip to a major city that includes a college career office, a large college or city library, state and federal employment centers, a chamber of commerce office, and a well-stocked bookstore can produce valuable results.

There are many excellent resources available to help you identify actual job sites. They are categorized into employer directories (usually indexed by product lines and geographic location), geographically based directories (designed to highlight particular cities, regions, or states), career-specific directories (e.g., *Sports MarketPlace*, which lists tens of thousands of firms involved with sports), periodicals and newspapers, targeted job posting publications, and videos. This is by no means meant to be a complete treatment of resources but rather a starting point for identifying useful resources.

Working from the more general references to highly specific resources, we provide a basic list to help you begin your search. Many of these you'll find easily available. In some cases reference librarians and others will suggest even better materials for your particular situation. Start to create your own customized bibliography of job search references. Use copying services to save time and to allow you to carry away information about organizations' missions, locations, company officers, phone numbers, and addresses.

Geographically Based Directories. The Job Bank series published by Bob Adams, Inc. (www.aip.com) contains detailed entries on each area's major employers, including business activity, address, phone number, and hiring contact name. Many listings specify educational backgrounds being sought in potential employees. Each volume contains a solid discussion of each city's or state's major employment sectors. Organizations are also indexed by industry. Job Bank volumes are available for the following places: Atlanta, Boston, Chicago, Dallas–Ft. Worth, Denver, Detroit, Florida, Houston, Los Angeles, Minneapolis, New York, Ohio, Philadelphia, San Francisco, Seattle, St. Louis, Washington, D.C., and other cities throughout the Northwest.

National Job Bank (www.careercity.com) lists employers in every state, along with contact names and commonly hired job categories. Included are many small companies often overlooked by other directories. Companies are also indexed by industry. This publication provides information on educational backgrounds sought and lists company benefits.

Periodicals and Newspapers. Several sources are available to help you locate which journals or magazines carry job advertisements in your field. Other resources help you identify opportunities in other parts of the country.

- *www.looksmart.com*
  If you want to search the classified sections of newspapers in other cities, a good source is this site. Using the keyword *newspaper classifieds* will lead you to where you can search alphabetically by state.

- *www.careerpath.com*
  Connects to classified job ads from newspapers around the country. Select the job title and then select the state or region of the state.

Targeted Job Posting Publications. Although the resources that follow are national in scope, they are either targeted to one medium of contact (telephone), focused on specific types of jobs, or less comprehensive than the sources previously listed.

- *Job Hotlines USA* (www.careers.org/topic/01_002.html)
  Pinpoints more than 1,000 hard-to-find telephone numbers for companies and government agencies that use prerecorded job messages and listings. Very few of the telephone numbers listed are toll-free, and sometimes recordings are long, so—callers, beware!

- *The Job Hunter* (www.jobhunter.com)
  A national biweekly newspaper listing business, arts, media, government, human services, health, community-related, and student services job openings.

- *Current Jobs for Graduates* (www.graduatejobs.com)
  A national employment listing for liberal arts professions, including editorial positions, management opportunities, museum work, teaching, and nonprofit work.

- *Environmental Opportunities* (www.ecojobs.com)
  Serves environmental job interests nationwide by listing administrative, marketing, and human resources positions along with education-related jobs and positions directly related to a degree in an environmental field.

- *Y National Vacancy List*
  (www.ymcahrm.ns.ca/employed/jobleads.html) Shows YMCA professional vacancies, including development, administration, programming, membership, and recreation postings.

- *ARTSearch*
  A national employment service bulletin for the arts, including administration, managerial, marketing, and financial management jobs.

- *Community Jobs*
  An employment newspaper for the nonprofit sector that provides a variety of listings, including project manager, canvas director, government relations specialist, community organizer, and program instructor.

- *College Placement Council Annual: A Guide to Employment Opportunities for College Graduates*
  An annual guide containing solid job-hunting information and, more important, displaying ads from large corporations actively seeking recent college graduates in all majors. Company profiles provide brief descriptions and available employment opportunities. Contact names and addresses are given. Profiles are indexed by organization name, geographic location, and occupation.

Videos. You may be one of the many job seekers who likes to get information via a medium other than paper. Many career libraries, public libraries, and career centers in libraries carry an assortment of videos that will help you learn new techniques and get information helpful in the job search.

Locating Information Resources

Throughout these introductory chapters, we have continually referred you to various websites for information on everything from job listings to career information. These same resources remain our best advice for your general research on career information. Using the Web gives you a mobility at your computer that you don't enjoy if you rely solely on books or newspapers or printed journals. Moreover, material on the Web, if the site is maintained, can be up-to-date, which may be crucial if you are looking at a cutting-edge career, in which technology changes almost daily. Federal government sites offer the option in some cases of downloading application materials, and many will accept your resume on-line.

You'll eventually identify the information resources that work best for you, but make certain you've covered the full range of resources before you begin to rely on a smaller list. Here's a short list of informational sites that many liberal arts job seekers find helpful:

- Public and college libraries

- College career centers

- Bookstores

- Internet

- Local and state government personnel offices

Each one of these sites offers a collection of resources that will help you get the information you need.

As you meet and talk with service professionals at all these sites, be sure to let them know what you're doing. Inform them of your job search, what you've already accomplished, and what you're looking for. The more people who know you're job seeking, the greater the possibility that someone will have information or know someone who can help you along your way.

Public and College Libraries. Large city libraries, college and university libraries, and even well-supported town library collections contain a variety of resources to help you conduct a job search. It is not uncommon for libraries to have separate "vocational choices" sections with books, tapes, computer terminals, and associated materials relating to job search and selection. Some are now even making resume-creation software available for use by patrons.

Some of the publications we name throughout this book are expensive reference items that are rarely purchased by individuals. In addition, libraries carry a wide range of newspapers and telephone yellow pages as well as the usual array of books. If resources are not immediately available, many libraries have loan arrangements with other facilities and can make information available to you relatively quickly.

Take advantage not only of the reference collections but also of the skilled and informed staff. Let them know exactly what you are looking for, and they'll have their own suggestions. You'll be visiting the library frequently, and the reference staff will soon come to know who you are and what you're working on. They'll be part of your job search network!

College Career Centers. Career libraries, which are found in career centers at colleges and universities and sometimes within large public libraries, contain a unique blend of the job search resources housed in other settings. In addition, career libraries often purchase a number of job listing publications, each of which targets a specific industry or type of job. You may find job listings specifically for entry-level positions for your major. Ask about job posting newsletters or newspapers focused on careers in the area that most interests you. Each center will be unique, but you are certain to discover some good sources of jobs.

Most college career libraries now hold growing collections of video material on specific industries and on aspects of your job search process, including dress and appearance, how to manage the luncheon or dinner interview, how to be effective at a job fair, and many other titles. Some larger corporations produce handsome video materials detailing the variety of career paths and opportunities available in their organizations.

Some career libraries also house computer-based career planning and information systems. These interactive computer programs help you to clarify your values and interests and will combine them with your education to provide possible job titles and industry locations. Some even contain extensive lists of graduate school programs.

One specific kind of service a career library will be able to direct you to is computerized job search services. These services, of which there are many, are run by private companies, individual colleges, or consortiums of colleges. They attempt to match qualified job candidates with potential employers. The candidate submits a resume (or an application) to the service. This information (which can be categorized into hundreds of separate fields of data) is entered into a computer database. Your information is then compared with the information from employers about what they desire in a prospective employee. If there is a match between what they want and what you have indicated you can offer, the job search service or the employer will contact you directly to continue the process.

Computerized job search services can complement an otherwise complete job search program. They are *not*, however, a substitute for the kinds of activities described in this book. They are essentially passive operations that are random in nature. If you have not listed skills, abilities, traits, experiences, or education *exactly* as an employer has listed its needs, there is simply no match.

Consult with the staff members at the career libraries you use. These professionals have been specifically trained to meet the unique needs you present. Often you can just drop in and receive help with general questions, or you may want to set up an appointment to speak one-on-one with a career counselor to gain special assistance.

Every career library is different in size and content, but each can provide valuable information for the job search. Some may even provide limited counseling. If you have not visited the career library at your college or alma mater, call and ask if these collections are still available for your use. Be sure to ask about other services that you can use as well.

If you are not near your own college as you work on your job search, call the career office and inquire about reciprocal agreements with other colleges that are closer to where you live. Very often, your own alma mater can arrange for you to use a limited menu of services at another school. This typically would include access to a career library and job posting information and might include limited counseling.

Bookstores. Any well-stocked bookstore will carry some job search books that are worth buying. Some major stores will even have an extensive section devoted to materials, including excellent videos, related to the job search process. You will also find copies of local newspapers and business magazines. The one advantage that is provided by resources purchased at a bookstore is that you can read and work with the information in the comfort of your own home and do not have to conform to the hours of operation of a library, which can present real difficulties if you are working full-time as you seek employment. A few minutes spent browsing in a bookstore might be a beneficial break from your job search activities and turn up valuable resources.

Internet. There's no doubt about it, the Web is a job hunter's best friend. But the Web can also be an overwhelmingly abundant source of information—so much information that it becomes difficult to identify what's important and what is not. A simple search under the phrase *liberal arts* can bring up sites that will be very meaningful for you and sites whose information is trivial and irrelevant to your job search. You need a strategy to master the Web, just as we advise a strategy to master the job search. Here are some suggestions:

1. Thoroughly utilize the websites identified throughout this guide. They've been chosen with you in mind, and many of them will be very helpful to you.

2. Begin to build your own portfolio of websites on your computer. Use the "bookmarking" function on your Web browser to build a series of bookmark folders for individual categories of good websites. You may have a folder for "entry-level job ad" sites and another folder for "professional associations," and so on. Start your folders with the sites in this book that seem most helpful to you.

3. Visit your college career center (or ask for reciprocity consideration at a local college) and your nearby local and/or state and university libraries. All of these places have staff who are skilled researchers and can help you locate and identify more sites that are more closely targeted to your growing sense of job direction.

4. Use the E-mail function or Webmaster address that you'll find on many sites. Some sites encourage questions via E-mail. We have found that the response time to E-mail questions for website mailboxes can vary considerably, but more often than not, replies are quite prompt. Sometimes a website will list the E-mail of the "Webmaster" or "Webguru," and we have contacted those individuals with good success as well. So, if you have a question about a website, use these options to get satisfaction.

Local and State Government Personnel Offices. You'll learn that it's most efficient to establish a routine for checking job postings. Searching for a job is a full-time job (or should be!), and you don't want to waste time or feel that you're going around in circles. So, establish a routine by which each week, on the most appropriate day, you check out that day's resources. For example, if you live in a midsize city with a daily paper, you'll probably give the want ads a once-over every morning so that you can act immediately on any good job opening.

The same strategy applies to your local and state government personnel offices. Find out when and how they post jobs, and put those offices on your weekly checklist, so that you don't miss any reasonable openings. Your local municipality's personnel office may simply use a bulletin board in the town hall or a clipboard on a counter in the office. Make these stops part of your weekly routine, and you'll find that people begin to recognize you and become aware of your job search, which could prove to be very helpful. Most local governmental units are required to post jobs in public places for a stated period before the hiring process begins. It should be easy to find out where and how they do this. Keep a close eye on those sites.

State personnel offices are larger, less casual operations, but the principles are the same. State jobs are advertised, and the office can tell you what advertising mechanisms they use—which newspapers, what websites, and when jobs are posted. The personnel offices themselves are worth a visit, if you are close enough. In addition to all the current job postings, many state personnel offices have "spec sheets," which are detailed job specifications of all the positions they are apt to advertise. You could pick up a spec sheet for every job related to law enforcement or criminal justice and keep them in a file for later reference when such a job is advertised.

Many state personnel offices also publish a weekly or biweekly "open recruitment" listing of career opportunities that have not yet been filled. These listings are categorized by job title as well as by branch of government, and often by whether a test is needed to qualify for the position or not. An increasing number of state personnel or human resources offices are on-line and offer many services on the Web. A fine general website that can help you locate your state personnel office is www.piperinfo.com/state/index.cfm. While each state's site is different, you can count on access to the state human resources office and sometimes even the human resources offices of many of the state's larger cities. For example, the State of Connecticut lists an additional twenty-seven city sites that each have human resources departmental listings. So, you could search the State of Connecticut Human Resource Office and then jump to the City of Stamford and review city jobs on its site.

CHAPTER FOUR

NETWORKING

etworking is the process of deliberately establishing relationships to get career-related information or to alert potential employers that you are available for work. Networking is critically important to today's job seeker for two reasons: it will help you get the information you need, and it can help you find out about *all* of the available jobs.

GETTING THE INFORMATION YOU NEED

Networkers will review your resume and give you feedback on its effectiveness. They will talk about the job you are looking for and give you a candid appraisal of how they see your strengths and weaknesses. If they have a good sense of the industry or the employment sector for that job, you'll get their feelings on future trends in the industry as well. Some networkers will be very forthcoming about salaries, job-hunting techniques, and suggestions for your job search strategy. Many have been known to place calls right from the interview desk to friends and associates who might be interested in you. Each networker will make his or her own contribution, and each will be valuable.

Because organizations must evolve to adapt to current global market needs, the information provided by decision makers within various organizations will be critical to your success as a new job market entrant. For example, you might learn about the concept of virtual organizations from a networker. Virtual organizations coordinate economic activity to deliver value to customers by using resources outside the traditional boundaries of the organization. This concept is being discussed and implemented by chief executive officers of many organizations, including Ford Motor, Dell, and IBM. Networking can help you find out about this and other trends currently affecting the industries under your consideration.

FINDING OUT ABOUT ALL OF THE AVAILABLE JOBS

Not every job that is available at this very moment is advertised for potential applicants to see. This is called the *hidden job market*. Only 15 to 20 percent of all jobs are formally advertised, which means that 80 to 85 percent of available jobs do not appear in published channels. Networking will help you become more knowledgeable about all the employment opportunities available during your job search period.

Although someone you might talk to today doesn't know of any openings within his or her organization, tomorrow or next week or next month an opening may occur. If you've taken the time to show an interest in and knowledge of their organization, if you've shown the company representative how you can help achieve organizational goals and that you can fit into the organization, you'll be one of the first candidates considered for the position.

NETWORKING: A PROACTIVE APPROACH

Networking is a proactive rather than a reactive approach. You, as a job seeker, are expected to initiate a certain level of activity on your own behalf; you cannot afford to simply respond to jobs listed in the newspaper. Being proactive means building a network of contacts that includes informed and interested decision makers who will provide you with up-to-date knowledge of the current job market and increase your chances of finding out about employment opportunities appropriate for your interests, experience, and level of education.

An old axiom of networking says, "You are only two phone calls away from the information you need." In other words, by talking to enough people, you will quickly come across someone who can offer you help. Start with your professors. Each of them probably has a wide circle of contacts. In their work and travel they might have met someone who can help you or direct you to someone who can.

CONTROL AND THE NETWORKING PROCESS

In deliberately establishing relationships, the process of networking begins with you in control—*you* are contacting specific individuals. As your network expands and you establish a set of professional relationships, your search for information or jobs will begin to move outside of your total control. A part of the networking process involves others assisting you by gathering information for you or recommending you as a possible job candidate. As additional people become a part of your networking system, you will have less knowledge about activities undertaken on your behalf; you will undoubtedly be contacted by individuals whom you did not initially approach. If you want to function effectively in surprise situations, you must be prepared at all times to talk with strangers about the informational or employment needs that motivated you to become involved in the networking process.

PREPARING TO NETWORK

In deliberately establishing relationships, maximize your efforts by organizing your approach. Five specific areas in which you can organize your efforts include reviewing your self-assessment, reviewing your research on job sites and organizations, deciding who it is you want to talk to, keeping track of all your efforts, and creating your self-promotion tools.

Review Your Self-Assessment

Your self-assessment is as important a tool in preparing to network as it has been in other aspects of your job search. You have carefully evaluated your personal traits, personal values, economic needs, longer-term goals, skill base, preferred skills, and underdeveloped skills. During the networking process you will be called upon to communicate what you know about yourself and relate it to the information or job you seek. Be sure to review the exercises that you completed in the self-assessment section of this book in preparation for networking. We've explained that you need to assess what skills you have acquired from your major that are of general value to an employer and to be ready to express those in ways employers can appreciate as useful in their own organizations.

Review Research on Job Sites and Organizations

In addition, individuals assisting you will expect that you'll have at least some background information on the occupation or industry of interest to you.

Refer to the appropriate sections of this book and other relevant publications to acquire the background information necessary for effective networking. They'll explain how to identify not only the job titles that might be of interest to you but also what kinds of organizations employ people to do that job. You will develop some sense of working conditions and expectations about duties and responsibilities—all of which will be of help in your networking interviews.

Decide Who It Is You Want to Talk To

Networking cannot begin until you decide whom it is that you want to talk to and, in general, what type of information you hope to gain from your contacts. Once you know this, it's time to begin developing a list of contacts. Five useful sources for locating contacts are described here.

College Alumni Network. Most colleges and universities have created a formal network of alumni and friends of the institution who are particularly interested in helping currently enrolled students and graduates of their alma mater gain employment-related information.

· ·

> Because liberal arts is such a broad-based degree program, you'll find an abundance of graduates spanning the full spectrum of possible employment. Just the diversity alone, as evidenced by an alumni list from your college or university, should be encouraging and informative to the liberal arts graduate. Among such a diversified group, there are likely to be scores you would enjoy talking with and perhaps could meet.

· ·

It is usually a simple process to make use of an alumni network. Visit your college's website and locate the alumni office and/or your career center. Either or both sites will have information about your school's alumni network. You'll be provided with information on shadowing experiences, geographic information, or those alumni offering job referrals. If you don't find what you're looking for, don't hesitate to phone or E-mail your career center and ask what they can do to help you connect with an alum.

Alumni networkers may provide some combination of the following services: day-long shadowing experiences, telephone interviews, in-person interviews, information on relocating to given geographic areas, internship information, suggestions on graduate school study, and job vacancy notices.

....

What a valuable experience. Perhaps you are interested in law but don't think your major will be acceptable to law school. Spending a day with an attorney alumnus and asking numerous questions about his or her own undergraduate preparation will be a far better decision criterion for you than any reading on the subject could possibly provide.

In addition to your own observations, the alumnus will have his or her own perspective on the importance of different majors to a law career and which branches might suit you and which may not. The law professional will give you realistic and honest feedback on your job search concerns.

....

Present and Former Supervisors. If you believe you are on good terms with present or former job supervisors, they may be an excellent resource for providing information or directing you to appropriate resources that would have information related to your current interests and needs. Additionally, these supervisors probably belong to professional organizations that they might be willing to utilize to get information for you.

....

If, for example, you were interested in working for a magazine publisher and you are currently working in an independent bookstore, talk with your supervisor or the owner. He or she may belong to the Chamber of Commerce, whose director would have information on local publishers that are in need of editorial help. You would be able to obtain the names and telephone numbers of these people, thus enabling you to begin the networking process.

....

Employers in Your Area. Although you may be interested in working in a geographic location different from the one where you currently reside, don't overlook the value of the knowledge and contacts those around you are able to provide. Use the local telephone directory and newspaper to identify the types of organizations you are thinking of working for or professionals who have the kinds of jobs you are interested in. Recently, a call made to a local hospital's financial administrator for information on working in health care financial administration yielded more pertinent information on training seminars, regional professional organizations, and potential employment sites than a national organization was willing to provide.

Employers in Geographic Areas Where You Hope to Work. If you are thinking about relocating, identifying prospective employers or informational contacts in the new location will be critical to your success. Here are some tips for on-line searching. First, use a "metasearch" engine to get the most out of your search. Metasearch engines combine several engines into one powerful tool. We frequently use www.dogpile.com and www.metasearch.com for this purpose. Try using the city and state as your keywords in a search. *New Haven, Connecticut* will bring you to the city's website with links to the chamber of commerce, member businesses, and other valuable resources. By using www.looksmart.com you can locate newspapers in any area, and they, too, can provide valuable insight before you relocate. Of course, both dogpile and metasearch can lead you to yellow and white page directories in areas you are considering.

Professional Associations and Organizations. Professional associations and organizations can provide valuable information in several areas: career paths that you might not have considered, qualifications relating to those career choices, publications that list current job openings, and workshops or seminars that will enhance your professional knowledge and skills. They can also be excellent sources for background information on given industries: their health, current problems, and future challenges.

There are several excellent resources available to help you locate professional associations and organizations that would have information to meet your needs. Two especially useful publications are the *Encyclopedia of Associations* and *National Trade and Professional Associations of the United States*.

Keep Track of All Your Efforts

It can be difficult, almost impossible, to remember all the details related to each contact you make during the networking process, so you will want to develop a record-keeping system that works for you. Formalize this process by using your computer to keep a record of the people and organizations you want to contact. You can simply record the contact's name, address, and telephone number, and what information you hope to gain. Each entry might look something like this:

Contact Name	Address	Phone #	Purpose
Mr. Lee Perkins Osaka Branch	13 Muromachi Osaka-shi	73-8906	Local market information

You could record this as a simple Word document and you could still use the "Find" function if you were trying to locate some data and could only recall the firm's name or the contact's name. If you're comfortable with database management and you have some database software on your computer, then you can put information at your fingertips even if you have only the zip code! The point here is not technological sophistication but good record keeping.

Once you have created this initial list, it will be helpful to keep more detailed information as you begin to actually make the contacts. Using the Network Contact Record form in Exhibit 4.1 will help you keep good information on all your network contacts. They'll appreciate your recall of details of your meetings and conversations, and the information will help you to focus your networking efforts.

Create Your Self-Promotion Tools

There are two types of promotional tools that are used in the networking process. The first is a resume and cover letter, and the second is a one-minute "infomercial," which may be given over the telephone or in person.

Techniques for writing an effective resume and cover letter are discussed in Chapter 2. Once you have reviewed that material and prepared these important documents, you will have created one of your self-promotion tools.

The one-minute infomercial will demand that you begin tying your interests, abilities, and skills to the people or organizations you want to network with. Think about your goal for making the contact to help you understand what you should say about yourself. You should be able to express yourself easily and convincingly. If, for example, you are contacting an alumnus of your institution to obtain the names of possible employment sites in a distant city, be prepared to discuss why you are interested in moving to that location, the types of jobs you are interested in, and the skills and abilities you possess that will make you a qualified candidate.

To create a meaningful one-minute infomercial, write it out, practice it as if it will be a spoken presentation, rewrite it, and practice it again if necessary until expressing yourself comes easily and is convincing.

Exhibit 4.1

NETWORK CONTACT RECORD

Name: (Be certain your spelling is correct.)

Title: (Pick up a business card to be certain of the correct title.)

Employing organization: (Note any parent company or subsidiaries.)

Business mailing address: (This is often different from the street address.)

Business E-mail address: _____

Business telephone number: (Include area code and alternative numbers.)

Business fax number: _____

Source for this contact: (Who referred you, and what is their relationship to

the contact?)

Date of call or letter: (Use plenty of space here to record multiple phone calls or

visits, other employees you may have met, names of

secretaries/receptionists, and so forth.)

Content of discussion: (Keep enough notes here to remind you of the substance of

your visits and telephone conversations in case some time

elapses between contacts.)

Follow-up necessary to continue working with this contact: (Your contact may request

that you send him or her some materials or direct you to

contact an associate. Note any such instructions or

assignments in this space.)

Name of additional networker: (Here you would record the names and phone numbers of

Address: additional contacts met at this employer's site. Often you will

be introduced to many people, some of whom may indicate

E-mail: a willingness to help in your job search.)

Phone: _____

Fax: _____

Name of additional networker: _____

Address: _____

E-mail: _____

Phone: _____

Fax: _____

Name of additional networker: _____

Address: _____

E-mail: _____

Phone: _____

Fax: _____

Date thank-you note written: (May help to date your next contact.)

Follow-up action taken: (Phone calls, visits, additional notes.)

Other miscellaneous notes: (Record any other additional interaction you think may be

important to remember in working with this networking client.

You will want this form in front of you when telephoning or

just before and after a visit.)

Here's a simplified example of an infomercial for use over the telephone:

· ·

Hello, Mrs. Jones? My name is John Anderson. I am a recent graduate of East Coast College, and I wish to enter the advertising field. I was an English major and feel confident that I have many of the skills I understand are valued in advertising, such as writing, creativity, speaking, and delivering effective presentations. What's more, I work well under pressure. I have read that can be a real advantage in your business!

Mrs. Jones, I'm calling you because I still need more information about the advertising field. I'm hoping you'll have the time to sit down with me for about half an hour and discuss your perspective on advertising careers. There are so many possible places to get into advertising, and I am seeking some advice on which of those settings might be the best bet for my particular combination of skills and experience.

Would you be willing to do that for me? I would greatly appreciate it. I am available most mornings, if that's convenient for you.

· ·

It very well may happen that your employer contact wishes you to communicate by E-mail. The infomercial quoted above could easily be rewritten for an E-mail message. You should "cut and paste" your resume right into the E-mail text itself.

Other effective self-promotion tools include portfolios for those in the arts, writing professions, or teaching. Portfolios show examples of work, photographs of projects or classroom activities, or certificates and credentials that are job related. There may not be an opportunity to use the portfolio during an interview, and it is not something that should be left with the organization. It is designed to be explained and displayed by the creator. However, during some networking meetings, there may be an opportunity to illustrate a point or strengthen a qualification by exhibiting the portfolio.

BEGINNING THE NETWORKING PROCESS

Set the Tone for Your Communications

It can be useful to establish "tone words" for any communications you embark upon. Before making your first telephone call or writing your first letter, decide what you want the person to think of you. If you are networking to try to obtain a job, your tone words might include descriptors such as *genuine, informed,* and *self-knowledgeable.* When you're trying to acquire information, your tone words may have a slightly different focus, such as *courteous, organized, focused,* and *well-spoken.* Use the tone words you establish for your contacts to guide you through the networking process.

Honestly Express Your Intentions

When contacting individuals, it is important to be honest about your reasons for making the contact. Establish your purpose in your own mind and be able and ready to articulate it concisely. Determine an initial agenda, whether it be informational questioning or self-promotion, present it to your contact, and be ready to respond immediately. If you don't adequately prepare before initiating your overture, you may find yourself at a disadvantage if you're asked to immediately begin your informational interview or self-promotion during the first phone conversation or visit.

Start Networking Within Your Circle of Confidence

Once you have organized your approach—by utilizing specific researching methods, creating a system for keeping track of the people you will contact, and developing effective self-promotion tools—you are ready to begin networking. The best way to begin networking is by talking with a group of people you trust and feel comfortable with. This group is usually made up of your family, friends, and career counselors. No matter who is in this inner circle, they will have a special interest in seeing you succeed in your job search. In addition, because they will be easy to talk to, you should try taking some risks in terms of practicing your information-seeking approach. Gain confidence in talking about the strengths you bring to an organization and the underdeveloped skills you feel hinder your candidacy. Be sure to review the section on self-assessment for tips on approaching each of these areas. Ask for critical but constructive feedback from the people in your circle of confidence on the letters you write and the one-minute infomercial you have developed. Evaluate whether you want to make the changes they suggest, then practice the changes on others within this circle.

Stretch the Boundaries of Your Networking Circle of Confidence

Once you have refined the promotional tools you will use to accomplish your networking goals, you will want to make additional contacts. Because you will not know most of these people, it will be a less comfortable activity to undertake. The practice that you gained with your inner circle of trusted friends should have prepared you to now move outside of that comfort zone.

It is said that any information a person needs is only two phone calls away, but the information cannot be gained until you (1) make a reasonable guess about who might have the information you need and (2) pick up the telephone to make the call. Using your network list that includes alumni, instructors, supervisors, employers, and associations, you can begin preparing your list of questions that will allow you to get the information you need. Review the question list that follows and then develop a list of your own.

Questions You Might Want to Ask

1. In the position you now hold, what do you do on a typical day?

2. What are the most interesting aspects of your job?

3. What part of your work do you consider dull or repetitive?

4. What were the jobs you had that led to your present position?

5. How long does it usually take to move from one step to the next in this career path?

6. What is the top position to which you can aspire in this career path?

7. What is the next step in *your* career path?

8. Are there positions in this field that are similar to your position?

9. What are the required qualifications and training for entry-level positions in this field?

10. Are there specific courses a student should take to be qualified to work in this field?

11. What are the entry-level jobs in this field?

12. What types of training are provided to persons entering this field?

13. What are the salary ranges your organization typically offers to entry-level candidates for positions in this field?

14. What special advice would you give a person entering this field?

15. Do you see this field as a growing one?

16. How do you see the content of the entry-level jobs in this field changing over the next two years?

17. What can I do to prepare myself for these changes?

18. What is the best way to obtain a position that will start me on a career in this field?

19. Do you have any information on job specifications and descriptions that I may have?

20. What related occupational fields would you suggest I explore?

21. How could I improve my resume for a career in this field?

22. Who else would you suggest I talk to, both in your organization and in other organizations?

Questions You Might Have to Answer

To communicate effectively, you must anticipate questions that will be asked of you by the networkers you contact. Review the following list and see if you can easily answer each of these questions. If you cannot, it may be time to revisit the self-assessment process.

1. Where did you get my name, or how did you find out about this organization?

2. What are your career goals?

3. What kind of job are you interested in?

4. What do you know about this organization and this industry?

5. How do you know you're prepared to undertake an entry-level position in this industry?

6. What course work have you done that is related to your career interests?

7. What are your short-term career goals?

8. What are your long-term career goals?

9. Do you plan to obtain additional formal education?

10. What contributions have you made to previous employers?

11. Which of your previous jobs have you enjoyed the most and why?

12. What are you particularly good at doing?

13. What shortcomings have you had to face in previous employment?

14. What are your three greatest strengths?

15. Describe how comfortable you feel with your communication style.

General Networking Tips

Make Every Contact Count. Setting the tone for each interaction is critical. Approaches that will help you communicate in an effective way include politeness, being appreciative of time provided to you, and being prepared and thorough. Remember, *everyone* within an organization has a circle of influence, so be prepared to interact effectively with each person you encounter in the networking process, including secretarial and support staff. Many information or job seekers have thwarted their own efforts by being rude to some individuals they encountered as they networked because they made the incorrect assumption that certain persons were unimportant.

Sometimes your contacts may be surprised at their ability to help you. After meeting and talking with you, they might think they have not offered much in the way of help. A day or two later, however, they may make a contact that would be useful to you and refer you to that person.

With Each Contact, Widen Your Circle of Networkers. Always leave an informational interview with the names of at least two more people who can help you get the information or job that you are seeking. Don't be shy about asking for additional contacts; networking is all about increasing the number of people you can interact with to achieve your goals.

Make Your Own Decisions. As you talk with different people and get answers to the questions you pose, you may hear conflicting information or get conflicting suggestions. Your job is to listen to these "experts" and decide what information and which suggestions will help you achieve *your* goals. Only implement those suggestions that you believe will work for you.

SHUTTING DOWN YOUR NETWORK

As you achieve the goals that motivated your networking activity—getting the information you need or the job you want—the time will come to inactivate all or parts of your network. As you do, be sure to tell your primary supporters about your change in status. Call or write to each one of them and give them as many details about your new status as you feel is necessary to maintain a positive relationship.

Because a network takes on a life of its own, activity undertaken on your behalf will continue even after you cease your efforts. As you get calls or are contacted in some fashion, be sure to inform these networkers about your change in status, and thank them for assistance they have provided.

Information on the latest employment trends indicates that workers will change jobs or careers several times in their lifetime. Networking, then, will be a critical aspect in the span of your professional life. If you carefully and thoughtfully conduct your networking activities during your job search, you will have a solid foundation of experience when you need to network the next time around.

CHAPTER FIVE

INTERVIEWING

C ertainly, there can be no one part of the job search process more fraught with anxiety and worry than the interview. Yet seasoned job seekers welcome the interview and will often say, "Just get me an interview and I'm on my way!" They understand that the interview is crucial to the hiring process and equally crucial for them, as job candidates, to have the opportunity of a personal dialogue to add to what the employer may already have learned from the resume, cover letter, and telephone conversations.

Believe it or not, the interview is to be welcomed, and even enjoyed! It is a perfect opportunity for you, the candidate, to sit down with an employer and express yourself and display who you are and what you want. Of course, it takes thought and planning and a little strategy; after all, it *is* a job interview! But it can be a positive, if not pleasant, experience and one you can look back on and feel confident about your performance and effort.

For many new job seekers, a job, any job, seems a wonderful thing. But seasoned interview veterans know that the job interview is an important step for both sides—the employer and the candidate—to see what each has to offer and whether there is going to be a "fit" of personalities, work styles, and attitudes. And it is this concept of balance in the interview, that both sides have important parts to play, that holds the key to success in mastering this aspect of the job search strategy.

Try to think of the interview as a conversation between two interested and equal partners. You both have important, even vital, information to deliver and to learn. Of course, there's no denying the employer has some leverage, especially in the initial interview for recruitment or any interview scheduled by the candidate and not the recruiter. That should not prevent the interviewee from seeking to play an equal part in what should be a fair exchange of information. Too often the untutored candidate allows the interview to become one-sided. The employer asks all the questions and the candidate simply responds. The ideal would be for two mutually interested parties to sit down and discuss possibilities for each. This is a conversation of significance, and it requires preparation, thought about the tone of the interview, and planning of the nature and details of the information to be exchanged.

PREPARING FOR THE INTERVIEW

The length of most initial interviews is about thirty minutes. Given the brevity, the information that is exchanged ought to be important. The candidate should be delivering material that the employer cannot discover on the resume, and in turn, the candidate should be learning things about the employer that he or she could not otherwise find out. After all, if you have only thirty minutes, why waste time on information that is already published? The information exchanged is more than just factual, and both sides will learn much from what they see of each other, as well. How the candidate looks, speaks, and acts are important to the employer. The employer's attention to the interview and awareness of the candidate's resume, the setting, and the quality of information presented are important to the candidate.

Just as the employer has every right to be disappointed when a prospect is late for the interview, looks unkempt, and seems ill-prepared to answer fairly standard questions, the candidate may be disappointed with an interviewer who isn't ready for the meeting, hasn't learned the basic resume facts, and is constantly interrupted by telephone calls. In either situation there's good reason to feel let down.

There are many elements to a successful interview, and some of them are not easy to describe or prepare for. Sometimes there is just a chemistry between interviewer and interviewee that brings out the best in both, and a good exchange takes place. But there is much the candidate can do to pave the way for success in terms of his or her resume, personal appearance, goals, and interview strategy—each of which we will discuss. However, none of this preparation is as important as the time and thought the candidate gives to personal self-assessment.

Self-Assessment

Neither a stunning resume nor an expensive, well-tailored suit can compensate for candidates who do not know what they want, where they are going, or why they are interviewing with a particular employer. Self-assessment, the process by which we begin to know and acknowledge our own particular blend of education, experiences, needs, and goals, is not something that can be sorted out the weekend before a major interview. Of all the elements of interview preparation, this one requires the longest lead time and cannot be faked.

Because the time allotted for most interviews is brief, it is all the more important for job candidates to understand and express succinctly why they are there and what they have to offer. This is not a time for undue modesty (or for braggadocio either); it is a time for a compelling, reasoned statement of why you feel that you and this employer might make a good match. It means you have to have thought about your skills, interests, and attributes; related those to your life experiences and your own history of challenges and opportunities; and determined what that indicates about your strengths, preferences, values, and areas needing further development.

A common complaint of employers is that many candidates didn't take advantage of the interview time; they didn't seem to know why they were there or what they wanted. When candidates are asked to talk about themselves and their work-related skills and attributes, employers don't want to be faced with shyness or embarrassed laughter; they need to know about you so they can make a fair determination of you and your competition. If you don't take advantage of the opportunity to make a case for your employability, you can be certain the person ahead of you has or the person after you will, and it will be on the strength of those impressions that the employer will hire.

If you need some assistance with self-assessment issues, refer to Chapter 1. Included are suggested exercises that can be done as needed, such as making up an experiential diary and extracting obvious strengths and weaknesses from past experiences. These simple assignments will help you look at past activities as collections of tasks with accompanying skills and responsibilities. Don't overlook your high school or college career office. Many offer personal counseling on self-assessment issues and may provide testing instruments such as the *Myers-Briggs Type Indicator* (*MBTI*), the *Harrington-O'Shea Career Decision-Making System* (*CDM*), the *Strong Interest Inventory* (*SII*), or any other of a wide selection of assessment tools that can help you clarify some of these issues prior to the interview stage of your job search.

The Resume

Resume preparation has been discussed in detail, and some basic examples of various types were provided. In this section we want to concentrate on how best to use your resume in the interview. In most cases the employer will have seen the resume prior to the interview, and, in fact, it may well have been the quality of that resume that secured the interview opportunity.

An interview is a conversation, however, and not an exercise in reading. So, if the employer hasn't seen your resume and you have brought it along to the interview, wait until asked or until the end of the interview to offer it. Otherwise, you may find yourself staring at the back of your resume and simply answering "yes" and "no" to a series of questions drawn from that document.

Sometimes an interviewer is not prepared and does not know or recall the contents of the resume and may use the resume to a greater or lesser degree as a "prompt" during the interview. It is for you to judge what that may indicate about the individual performing the interview or the employer. If your interviewer seems surprised by the scheduled meeting, relies on the resume to an inordinate degree, and seems otherwise unfamiliar with your background, this lack of preparation for the hiring process could well be a symptom of general management disorganization or may simply be the result of poor planning on the part of one individual. It is your responsibility as a potential employee to be aware of these signals and make your decisions accordingly.

• •

In any event, it is perfectly acceptable for you to get the conversation back to a more interpersonal style by saying something like, "Mr. Smith, you might be interested in some recent writing experience I gained in an internship that is not detailed on my resume. May I tell you about it?" This can return the interview to two people talking to each other, not one reading and the other responding.

• •

By all means, bring at least one copy of your resume to the interview. Occasionally, at the close of an interview, an interviewer will express an interest in circulating a resume to several departments, and you could then offer the copy you brought. Sometimes, an interview appointment provides an opportunity to meet others in the organization who may express an interest in you and your background, and it may be helpful to follow up with a copy of your resume. Our best advice, however, is to keep it out of sight until needed or requested.

Appearance

Although many of the absolute rules that once dominated the advice offered to job candidates about appearance have now been moderated significantly, conservative is still the watchword unless you are interviewing in a fashion-related industry. For men, conservative translates into a well-cut dark suit with appropriate tie, hosiery, and dress shirt. A wise strategy for the male job seeker looking for a good but not expensive suit would be to try the men's department of a major department store. They usually carry a good range of sizes, fabrics, and prices; offer professional sales help; provide free tailoring; and have associated departments for putting together a professional look.

For women, there is more latitude. Business suits are still popular, but they have become more feminine in color and styling with a variety of jacket and skirt lengths. In addition to suits, better-quality dresses are now worn in many environments and, with the correct accessories, can be most appropriate. Company literature, professional magazines, the business section of major newspapers, and television interviews can all give clues about what is being worn in different employer environments.

Both men and women need to pay attention to issues such as hair, jewelry, and makeup; these are often what separates the candidate in appearance from the professional workforce. It seems particularly difficult for the young job seeker to give up certain hairstyles, eyeglass fashions, and jewelry habits, yet those can be important to the employer who is concerned with your ability to successfully make the transition into the organization. Candidates often find the best strategy is to dress conservatively until they find employment. Once employed and familiar with the norms within your organization, you can begin to determine a look that you enjoy, works for you, and fits your organization.

Choose clothes that suit your body type, fit well, and flatter you. Feel good about the way you look! The interview day is not the best time for a new hairdo, a new pair of shoes, or any other change that will distract you or cause you to be self-conscious. Arrive a bit early to avoid being rushed, and ask the receptionist to direct you to a restroom for any last-minute adjustments of hair and clothes.

Employer Information

Whether your interview is for graduate school admission, an overseas corporate position, or a reporter position with a local newspaper, it is important to know something about the employer or the organization. Keeping in mind that the interview is relatively brief and that you will hopefully have other interviews with other organizations, it is important to keep your research in proportion. If secondary interviews are called for, you will have additional time to do further research. For the first interview, it is helpful to know the organization's mission, goals, size, scope of operations, and so forth. Your research may uncover recent areas of challenge or particular successes that may help to fuel the interview. Use the "What Do They Call the Job You

Want?" section of Chapter 3, your library, and your career or guidance office to help you locate this information in the most efficient way possible. Don't be shy in asking advice of these counseling and guidance professionals on how best to spend your preparation time. With some practice, you'll soon learn how much information is enough and which kinds of information are most useful to you.

INTERVIEW CONTENT

We've already discussed how it can help to think of the interview as an important conversation—one that, as with any conversation, you want to find pleasant and interesting and to leave you with a good feeling. But because this conversation is especially important, the information that's exchanged is critical to its success. What do you want them to know about you? What do you need to know about them? What interview technique do you need to particularly pay attention to? How do you want to manage the close of the interview? What steps will follow in the hiring process?

Except for the professional interviewer, most of us find interviewing stressful and anxiety-provoking. Developing a strategy before you begin interviewing will help you relieve some stress and anxiety. One particular strategy that has worked for many and may work for you is interviewing by objective. Before you interview, write down three to five goals you would like to achieve for that interview. They may be technique goals: smile a little more, have a firmer handshake, be sure to ask about the next stage in the interview process before leaving. They may be content-oriented goals: find out about the company's current challenges and opportunities; be sure to speak of your recent research, writing experiences, or foreign travel. Whatever your goals, jot down a few of them as goals for each interview.

Most people find that in trying to achieve these few goals, their interviewing technique becomes more organized and focused. After the interview, the most common question friends and family ask is "How did it go?" With this technique, you have an indication of whether you met *your* goals for the meeting, not just some vague idea of how it went. Chances are, if you accomplished what you wanted to, it improved the quality of the entire interview. As you continue to interview, you will want to revise your goals to continue improving your interview skills.

Now, add to the concept of the significant conversation the idea of a beginning, a middle, and a closing and you will have two thoughts that will give your interview a distinctive character. Be sure to make your introduction warm and cordial. Say your full name (and if it's a difficult-to-pronounce name, help the interviewer to pronounce it) and make certain you know your interviewer's name and how to pronounce it. Most interviews begin with some "soft talk" about the weather, chat about the candidate's trip to the interview site, or national events. This is done as a courtesy to relax both you and the interviewer, to get you talking, and to generally try to defuse the atmosphere of excessive tension. Try to be yourself, engage in the conversation, and don't try to second-guess the interviewer. This is simply what it appears to be— casual conversation.

Once you and the interviewer move on to exchange more serious information in the middle part of the interview, the two most important concerns become your ability to handle challenging questions and your success at asking meaningful ones. Interviewer questions will probably fall into one of three categories: personal assessment and career direction, academic assessment, and knowledge of the employer. The following are some examples of questions in each category:

Personal Assessment and Career Direction

1. How would you describe yourself?

2. What motivates you to put forth your best effort?

3. In what kind of work environment are you most comfortable?

4. What do you consider to be your greatest strengths and weaknesses?

5. How well do you work under pressure?

6. What qualifications do you have that make you think you will be successful in this career?

7. Will you relocate? What do you feel would be the most difficult aspect of relocating?

8. Are you willing to travel?

9. Why should I hire you?

Academic Assessment

1. Why did you select your college or university?

2. What changes would you make at your alma mater?

3. What led you to choose your major?

4. What subjects did you like best and least? Why?

5. If you could, how would you plan your academic study differently? Why?

6. Describe your most rewarding college experience.

7. How has your college experience prepared you for this career?

8. Do you think that your grades are a good indication of your ability to succeed with this organization?

9. Do you have plans for continued study?

Knowledge of the Employer

1. If you were hiring a graduate of your school for this position, what qualities would you look for?

2. What do you think it takes to be successful in an organization like ours?

3. In what ways do you think you can make a contribution to our organization?

4. Why did you choose to seek a position with this organization?

The interviewer wants a response to each question but is also gauging your enthusiasm, preparedness, and willingness to communicate. In each response you should provide some information about yourself that can be related to the employer's needs. A common mistake is to give too much information. Answer each question completely, but be careful not to run on too long with extensive details or examples.

Questions About Underdeveloped Skills

Most employers interview people who have met some minimum criteria of education and experience. They interview candidates to see who they are, to learn what kind of personality they exhibit, and to get some sense of how this person might fit into the existing organization. It may be that you are asked about skills the employer hopes to find and that you have not documented. Maybe it's grant-writing experience, knowledge of the European political system, or a knowledge of the film world.

To questions about skills and experiences you don't have, answer honestly and forthrightly and try to offer some additional information about skills you do have. For example, perhaps the employer is disappointed you have no grant-writing experience. An honest answer may be as follows:

No, unfortunately, I was never in a position to acquire those skills. I do understand something of the complexities of the grant-writing process and feel confident that my attention to detail, careful reading skills, and strong writing would make grants a wonderful challenge in a new job. I think I could get up on the learning curve quickly.

The employer hears an honest admission of lack of experience but is reassured by some specific skill details that do relate to grant writing and a confident manner that suggests enthusiasm and interest in a challenge.

For many students, questions about their possible contribution to an employer's organization can prove challenging. Because your education has probably not included specific training for a job, you need to review your academic record and select capabilities you have developed in your major that an employer can appreciate. For example, perhaps you read well and can analyze and condense what you've read into smaller, more focused pieces. That could be valuable. Or maybe you did some serious research and you know you have valuable investigative skills. Your public speaking might be highly developed and you might use visual aids appropriately and effectively. Or maybe your skill at correspondence, memos, and messages is effective. Whatever it is, you must take it out of the academic context and put it into a new, employer-friendly context so your interviewer can best judge how you could help the organization.

Exhibiting knowledge of the organization will, without a doubt, show the interviewer that you are interested enough in the available position to have done some legwork in preparation for the interview. Remember, it is not necessary to know every detail of the organization's history but rather to have a general knowledge about why it is in business and how the industry is faring.

Sometime during the interview, generally after the midway point, you'll be asked if you have any questions for the interviewer. Your questions will tell the employer much about your attitude and your desire to understand the organization's expectations so you can compare it to your own strengths. The following are some selected questions you might want to ask:

1. What are the main responsibilities of the position?

2. What are the opportunities and challenges associated with this position?

3. Could you outline some possible career paths beginning with this position?

4. How regularly do performance evaluations occur?

5. What is the communication style of the organization? (meetings, memos, and so forth)

6. What would a typical day in this position be like for me?

7. What kinds of opportunities might exist for me to improve my professional skills within the organization?

8. What have been some of the interesting challenges and opportunities your organization has recently faced?

Most interviews draw to a natural closing point, so be careful not to prolong the discussion. At a signal from the interviewer, wind up your presentation, express your appreciation for the opportunity, and be sure to ask what the next stage in the process will be. When can you expect to hear from them? Will they be conducting second-tier interviews? If you are interested and haven't heard, would they mind a phone call? Be sure to collect a business card with the name and phone number of your interviewer. On your way out, you might have an opportunity to pick up organizational literature you haven't seen before.

With the right preparation—a thorough self-assessment, professional clothing, and employer information—you'll be able to set and achieve the goals you have established for the interview process.

CHAPTER SIX

NETWORKING OR INTERVIEW FOLLOW-UP

Quite often there is a considerable time lag between interviewing for a position and being hired or, in the case of the networker, between your phone call or letter to a possible contact and the opportunity of a meeting. This can be frustrating. "Why aren't they contacting me?" "I thought I'd get another interview, but no one has telephoned." "Am I out of the running?" You don't know what is happening.

CONSIDER THE DIFFERING PERSPECTIVES

Of course, there is another perspective—that of the networker or hiring organization. Organizations are complex, with multiple tasks that need to be accomplished each day. Hiring is a discrete activity that does not occur as frequently as other job assignments. The hiring process might have to take second place to other, more immediate organizational needs. Although it may be very important to you, and it is certainly ultimately significant to the employer, other issues such as fiscal management, planning and product development, employer vacation periods, or financial constraints may prevent an organization or individual within that organization from acting on your employment or your request for information as quickly as you or they would prefer.

USE YOUR COMMUNICATION SKILLS

Good communication is essential here to resolve any anxieties, and the responsibility is on you, the job or information seeker. Too many job seekers and networkers offer as an excuse that they don't want to "bother" the organization by writing letters or calling. Let us assure you here and now, once and for all, that if you are troubling an organization by over-communicating, someone will indicate that situation to you quite clearly. If not, you can only assume you are a worthwhile prospect and the employer appreciates being reminded of your availability and interest. Let's look at follow-up practices in the job interview process and the networking situation separately.

FOLLOWING UP ON THE EMPLOYMENT INTERVIEW

A brief thank-you note following an interview is an excellent and polite way to begin a series of follow-up communications with a potential employer with whom you have interviewed and want to remain in touch. It should be just that—a thank-you for a good meeting. If you failed to mention some fact or experience during your interview that you think might add to your candidacy, you may use this note to do that. However, this should be essentially a note whose overall tone is appreciative and, if appropriate, indicative of a continuing interest in pursuing any opportunity that may exist with that organization. It is one of the few pieces of business correspondence that may be handwritten, but always use plain, good-quality, standard-size paper.

If, however, at this point you are no longer interested in the employer, the thank-you note is an appropriate time to indicate that. You are under no obligation to identify any reason for not continuing to pursue employment with that organization, but if you are so inclined to indicate your professional reasons (pursuing other employers more akin to your interests, looking for greater income production than this employer can provide, a different geographic location), you certainly may. It should not be written with an eye to negotiation, for it will not be interpreted as such.

As part of your interview closing, you should have taken the initiative to establish lines of communication for continuing information about your candidacy. If you asked permission to telephone, wait a week following your thank-you note, then telephone your contact simply to inquire how things are progressing on your employment status. The feedback you receive here should be taken at face value. If your interviewer simply has no information, he or she will tell you so and indicate whether you should call again and when. Don't be discouraged if this should continue over some period of time.

If during this time something occurs that you think improves or changes your candidacy (some new qualification or experience you may have had), including any offers from other organizations, by all means telephone or write to inform the employer about this. In the case of an offer from a competing but less desirable or equally desirable organization, telephone your contact, explain what has happened, express your real interest in the organization, and inquire whether some determination on your employment might be made before you must respond to this other offer. An organization that is truly interested in you may be moved to make a decision about your candidacy. Equally possible is the scenario in which they are not yet ready to make a decision and so advise you to take the offer that has been presented. Again, you have no ethical alternative but to deal with the information presented in a straightforward manner.

When accepting other employment, be sure to contact any employers still actively considering you and inform them of your new job. Thank them graciously for their consideration. There are many other job seekers out there just like you who will benefit from having their candidacy improved when others bow out of the race. Who knows, you might at some future time have occasion to interact professionally with one of the organizations with which you sought employment. How embarrassing it would be to have someone remember you as the candidate who failed to notify them that you were taking a job elsewhere!

In all of your follow-up communications, keep good notes of whom you spoke with, when you called, and any instructions that were given about return communications. This will prevent any misunderstandings and provide you with good records of what has transpired.

FOLLOWING UP ON THE NETWORK CONTACT

Far more common than the forgotten follow-up after an interview is the situation where a good network contact is allowed to lapse. Good communications are the essence of a network, and follow-up is not so much a matter of courtesy here as it is a necessity. In networking for job information and contacts, you are the active network link. Without you, and without continual contact from you, there is no network. You and your need for employment are often the only shared elements among members of the network. Because network contacts were made regardless of the availability of any particular employment, it is incumbent upon the job seeker, if not simple common sense, to stay in regular communication with the network if you want to be considered for any future job opportunities.

This brings up the issue of responsibility, which is likewise very clear. The job seeker initiates network contacts and is responsible for maintaining those contacts; therefore, the entire responsibility for the network belongs with him or her. This becomes patently obvious if the network is left unattended. It very shortly falls out of existence because it cannot survive without careful attention by the networker.

You have many ways to keep the lines of communication open and to attempt to interest the network in you as a possible employee. You are limited only by your own enthusiasm for members of the network and your creativity. However, you as a networker are well advised to keep good records of whom you have met and contacted in each organization. Be sure to send thank-you notes to anyone who has spent any time with you, whether it was an E-mail message containing information or advice, a quick tour of a department, or a sit-down informational interview. All of these thank-you notes should, in addition to their ostensible reason, add some information about you and your particular combination of strengths and attributes.

You can contact your network at any time to convey continued interest, to comment on some recent article you came across concerning an organization, to add information about your training or changes in your qualifications, to ask advice or seek guidance in your job search, or to request referrals to other possible network opportunities. Sometimes just a simple note to network members reminding them of your job search, indicating that you have been using their advice, and noting that you are still actively pursuing leads and hope to continue to interact with them is enough to keep communications alive.

The Internet has opened up the world of networking. You may be able to find networkers who graduated from your high school or from the college you're attending, who live in a geographic region where you hope to work, or who are employed in a given industry. The Internet makes it easy to reach out to many people, but don't let this perceived ease lull you into complacency. Internet networking demands the same level of preparation as the more traditional forms of networking.

Because networks have been abused in the past, it's important that your conduct be above reproach. Networks are exploratory options; they are not backdoor access to employers. The network works best for someone who is exploring a new industry or making a transition into a new area of employment and who needs to find information or to alert people to his or her search activity. Always be candid and direct with contacts in expressing the purpose of your E-mail, call, or letter and your interest in their help or information about their organization. In follow-up contacts keep the tone professional and direct. Your honesty will be appreciated, and people will respond as best they can if your qualifications appear to meet their forthcoming needs. The network does not owe you anything, and that tone should be clear to each person you meet.

FEEDBACK FROM FOLLOW-UPS

A network contact may prove to be miscalculated. Perhaps you were referred to someone and it became clear that your goals and his or her particular needs did not make a good match. Or the network contact may simply not be in a position to provide you with the information you are seeking. Or in some unfortunate situations, the party may become annoyed by being contacted for this purpose. In such a situation, many job seekers simply say "Thank you" and move on.

If the contact is simply not the right connection, but the individual you are speaking with is not annoyed by the call, it might be a better tactic to express regret that the contact was misplaced and then tell the person what you are seeking and ask for his or her advice or possible suggestions as to a next step. The more people who are aware that you are seeking employment, the better your chances of connecting, and that is the purpose of a network. Most people in a profession have excellent knowledge of their field and varying amounts of expertise in areas tangent to their own. Use their expertise and seek some guidance before you dissolve the contact. You may be pleasantly surprised.

Occasionally, networkers will express the feeling that they have done as much as they can or provided all the information that is available to them. This may be a cue that they would like to be released from your network. Be alert to such attempts to terminate, graciously thank the individual by letter, and move on in your network development. A network is always changing, adding, and losing members, and you want the network to be composed only of those who are actively interested in supporting you.

A FINAL POINT ON NETWORKING

In any of the fields that you might consider as a potential career path, networkers and interviewers will be evaluating all of your written and oral communications. This should serve to emphasize the importance of the quality of your interactions with people in a position to help you in your job search.

In your telephone communications, interview presentations, and follow-up correspondence, your spoken and written use of English will be part of the impressions you create in those you meet along the way.

CHAPTER SEVEN

JOB OFFER CONSIDERATIONS

For many recent college graduates, the thrill of their first job and, for some, the most substantial regular income they have ever earned seems an excess of good fortune coming at once. To question that first income or to be critical in any way of the conditions of employment at the time of the initial offer seems like looking a gift horse in the mouth. It doesn't seem to occur to many new hires even to attempt to negotiate any aspect of their first job. And, as many employers who deal with entry-level jobs for recent college graduates will readily confirm, the reality is that there simply isn't much movement in salary available to these new college recruits. The entry-level hire generally does not have an employment track record on a professional level to provide any leverage for negotiation. Real negotiations on salary, benefits, retirement provisions, and so forth come to those with significant employment records at higher income levels.

Of course, the job offer is more than just money. It can be composed of geographic assignment, duties and responsibilities, training, benefits, health and medical insurance, educational assistance, car allowance or company vehicle, and a host of other items. All of this is generally detailed in the formal letter that presents the final job offer. In most cases this is a follow-up to a personal phone call from the employer representative who has been principally responsible for your hiring process.

That initial telephone offer is certainly binding as a verbal agreement, but most firms follow up with a detailed letter outlining the most significant parts of your employment contract. You may, of course, choose to respond immediately at the time of the telephone offer (which would be considered a binding oral contract), but you will also be required to formally answer the letter of offer with a letter of acceptance, restating the salient elements of the employer's description of your position, salary, and benefits. This ensures that both parties are clear on the terms and conditions of employment and remuneration and any other outstanding aspects of the job offer.

IS THIS THE JOB YOU WANT?

Most new employees will respond affirmatively in writing, glad to be in the position to accept employment. If you've worked hard to get the offer and the job market is tight, other offers may not be in sight, so you will say, "Yes, I accept!" What is important here is that the job offer you accept be one that does fit your particular needs, values, and interests as you've outlined them in your self-assessment process. Moreover, it should be a job that will not only use your skills and education but also challenge you to develop new skills and talents.

Jobs are sometimes accepted too hastily, for the wrong reasons, and without proper scrutiny by the applicant. For example, an individual might readily accept a sales job only to find the continual rejection by potential clients unendurable. An office worker might realize within weeks the constraints of a desk job and yearn for more activity. Employment is an important part of our lives. It is, for most of our adult lives, our most continuous productive activity. We want to make good choices based on the right criteria.

If you have a low tolerance for risk, a job based on commission will certainly be very anxiety-provoking. If being near your family is important, issues of relocation could present a decision crisis for you. If you're an adventurous person, a job with frequent travel would provide needed excitement and be very desirable. The importance of income, the need to continue your education, your personal health situation—all of these have an impact on whether the job you are considering will ultimately meet your needs. Unless you've spent some time understanding and thinking about these issues, it will be difficult to evaluate offers you do receive.

More important, if you make a decision that you cannot tolerate and feel you must leave that job, you will then have both unemployment and self-esteem issues to contend with. These will combine to make the next job search tough going, indeed. So make your acceptance a carefully considered decision.

NEGOTIATING YOUR OFFER

It may be that there is some aspect of your job offer that is not particularly attractive to you. Perhaps there is no relocation allotment to help you move your possessions, and this presents some financial hardship for you. It may be that the health insurance is less than you had hoped. Your initial assignment may be different from what you expected, either in its location or in the duties and responsibilities that comprise it. Or it may simply be that the salary is less than you anticipated. Other considerations may be your official starting date of employment, vacation time, evening hours, dates of training programs or schools, and other concerns.

If you are considering not accepting the job because of some item or items in the job offer "package" that do not meet your needs, you should know that most employers emphatically wish that you would bring that issue to their attention. It may be that the employer can alter it to make the offer more agreeable for you. In some cases it cannot be changed. In any event the employer would generally like to have the opportunity to try to remedy a difficulty rather than risk losing a good potential employee over an issue that might have been resolved. After all, they have spent time and funds in securing your services, and they certainly deserve an opportunity to resolve any possible differences.

Honesty is the best approach in discussing any objections or uneasiness you might have over the employer's offer. Having received your formal offer in writing, contact your employer representative and indicate your particular dissatisfaction in a straightforward manner. For example, you might explain that while you are very interested in being employed by this organization, the salary (or any other benefit) is less than you have determined you require. State the terms you need, and listen to the response. You may be asked to put this in writing, or you may be asked to hold off until the firm can decide on a response. If you are dealing with a senior representative of the organization, one who has been involved in hiring for some time, you may get an immediate response or a solid indication of possible outcomes.

Perhaps the issue is one of relocation. Your initial assignment is in the Midwest, and because you had indicated a strong West Coast preference, you are surprised at the actual assignment. You might simply indicate that while you understand the need for the company to assign you based on its needs, you are disappointed and had hoped to be placed on the West Coast. You could inquire if that were still possible and, if not, would it be reasonable to expect a West Coast relocation in the future.

If your request is presented in a reasonable way, most employers will not see this as jeopardizing your offer. If they can agree to your proposal, they will. If not, they will simply tell you so, and you may choose to continue your candidacy with them or remove yourself from consideration. The choice will be up to you.

Some firms will adjust benefits within their parameters to meet the candidate's need if at all possible. If a candidate requires a relocation cost allowance, he or she may be asked to forego tuition benefits for the first year to accomplish this adjustment. An increase in life insurance may be adjusted by some other benefit trade-off; perhaps a family dental plan is not needed. In these decisions you are called upon, sometimes under time pressure, to know how you value these issues and how important each is to you.

Many employers find they are more comfortable negotiating for candidates who have unique qualifications or who bring especially needed expertise to the organization. Employers hiring large numbers of entry-level college graduates may be far more reluctant to accommodate any changes in offer conditions. They are well supplied with candidates with similar education and experience so that if rejected by one candidate, they can draw new candidates from an ample labor pool.

COMPARING OFFERS

The condition of the economy, the job seekers' academic major and particular geographic job market, and individual needs and demands for certain employment conditions may not provide more than one job offer at a time. Some job seekers may feel that no reasonable offer should go unaccepted for the simple fear there won't be another.

In a tough job market, or if the job you seek is not widely available, or when your job search goes on too long and becomes difficult to sustain financially and emotionally, it may be necessary to accept an inferior offer. The alternative is continued unemployment. Even here, when you feel you don't have a choice, you can at least understand that in accepting this particular offer, there may be limitations and conditions you don't appreciate. At the time of acceptance, there were no other alternatives, but you can begin to use that position to gain the experience and talent to move toward a more attractive position.

Sometimes, however, more than one offer is received, and the candidate has the luxury of choice. If the job seeker knows what he or she wants and has done the necessary self-assessment honestly and thoroughly, it may be clear that one of the offers conforms more closely to those expressed wants and needs.

However, if, as so often happens, the offers are similar in terms of conditions and salary, the question then becomes which organization might provide the necessary climate, opportunities, and advantages for your professional development and growth. This is the time when solid employer research and astute questioning during the interviews really pays off. How much did you learn about the employer through your own research and skillful questioning? When the interviewer asked during the interview "Do you have any questions?" did you ask the kinds of questions that would help resolve a choice between one organization and another? Just as an employer must decide among numerous applicants, so must the applicant learn to assess the potential employer. Both are partners in the job search.

RENEGING ON AN OFFER

An especially disturbing occurrence for employers and career counseling professionals is when a job seeker formally (either orally or by written contract) accepts employment with one organization and later reneges on the agreement and goes with another employer.

There are all kinds of rationalizations offered for this unethical behavior. None of them satisfies. The sad irony is that what the job seeker is willing to do to the employer—make a promise and then break it—he or she would be outraged to have done to him- or herself: have the job offer pulled. It is a very bad way to begin a career. It suggests the individual has not taken the time to do the necessary self-assessment and self-awareness exercises to think and judge critically. The new offer taken may, in fact, be no better or worse than the one refused. You should be aware that there have been incidents of legal action following job candidates' reneging on an offer. This adds a very sour note to what should be a harmonious beginning of a lifelong adventure.

CHAPTER EIGHT

THE GRADUATE SCHOOL CHOICE

The reasons for furthering one's education in graduate school can be as varied and unique as the individuals electing this course of action. Many continue their studies at an advanced level because they simply find it difficult to end the educational process. They love what they are learning and want to learn more and broaden their academic exploration.

••••••••••••••••••••••••••••••••••••

Studying a particular subject in great depth, such as theories and patterns of intercultural communication or language acquisition, and thinking, researching, and writing critically on what others have discovered can provide excitement, challenge, and serious work. Some liberal arts majors have loved this aspect of their academic work and want to continue that activity.

Others go on to graduate school for purely practical reasons; they have examined employment prospects in their field of study, and all indications are that a graduate degree is requisite. If you have earned a B.A. in political science as a stepping stone to a career in law or the foreign service, going on for further training becomes mandatory. As a B.A.-level psychology major, you realize you cannot become state certified without a master's or Ph.D. A review of jobs in different areas will suggest that you need at least a master's degree to be competitive.

Alumni who are working in a variety of fields can be a good source of what degree level the fields are hiring. Ask your college career office for some alumni names, and give them a telephone call. Prepare some questions on specific job prospects in their field at each degree level. A thorough examination of the marketplace and talking to employers and professors will give you a sense of the scope of employment for a bachelor's degree, master's degree, or doctorate.

College teaching will require an advanced degree. Advertising might demand specialization in an additional field (computers, graphic design, and so forth). Editing and publishing and other fields may well put a premium on the advanced degree because the market is oversupplied and the employer can afford to make this demand, or because the additional knowledge and training is essential to function on the job.

CONSIDER YOUR MOTIVES

The answer to the question of "Why graduate school?" is a personal one for each applicant. Nevertheless, it is important to consider your motives carefully. Graduate school involves additional time out of the employment market, a high level of critical evaluation, significant autonomy as you pursue your studies, and considerable financial expenditure. For some students in doctoral programs, there may be additional life choice issues, such as relationships, marriage, and parenthood, that may present real challenges while in a program of study. You would be well advised to consider the following questions as you think about your decision to continue your studies.

Are You Postponing Some Tough Decisions by Going to School?

Graduate school is not a place to go to avoid life's problems. There is intense competition for graduate school slots and for the fellowships, scholarships, and financial aid available. This competition means extensive interviewing, resume submission, and essay writing that rivals corporate recruitment. Likewise, the graduate school process is a mentored one in which faculty stay aware of and involved in the academic progress of their students and continually challenge the quality of their work. Many graduate students are called upon to participate in teaching and professional writing and research as well.

In other words, this is no place to hide from the spotlight. Graduate students work very hard and much is demanded of them individually. If you elect to go to graduate school to avoid the stresses and strains of the "real world," you will find no safe place in higher academics. Vivid accounts, both fictional and nonfictional, have depicted quite accurately the personal and professional demands of graduate school work.

The selection of graduate studies as a career option should be a positive choice—something you *want* to do. It shouldn't be selected as an escape from other, less attractive or more challenging options, nor should it be selected as the option of last resort (i.e., "I can't do anything else; I'd better just stay in school."). If you're in some doubt about the strength of your reasoning about continuing in school, discuss the issues with a career counselor. Together you can clarify your reasoning, and you'll get some sound feedback on what you're about to undertake.

On the other hand, staying on in graduate school because of a particularly poor employment market and a lack of jobs at entry-level positions has proven to be an effective "stalling" strategy. If you can afford it, pursuing a graduate degree immediately after your undergraduate education gives you a year or two to "wait out" a difficult economic climate, while at the same time acquiring a potentially valuable credential.

Have You Done Some "Hands-On" Reality Testing?

There are experiential options available to give some reality to your decision-making process about graduate school. Internships or work in the field can give you a good idea about employment demands, conditions, and atmosphere.

....

Perhaps, as a liberal arts major, you're considering going on to law school or a career in university-level teaching. An internship or summer job in a law firm will put you in contact with practicing attorneys and may help to define for you exactly what attorneys actually do. Or, you can begin with your own college professors and ask them about their educational backgrounds and career paths. They can also talk to you about the time they spend outside the classroom, in research activities or in meetings. Even with the experience of only one law firm or by talking to one professor, you have a stronger concept of the pace of the job, interaction with colleagues, subject matter, and opportunities for specialization.

For liberal arts majors especially, the opportunity to do this kind of reality testing is important. It authoritatively demonstrates what your real-world skills are, how they can be put to use, and what aspects of your academic preparation you must rely on. It has been well documented that liberal arts majors do well in occupations once they identify them. Internships and co-op experiences speed that process up and prevent the frustrating and expensive process of investigation many graduates begin only after graduation.

Do You Need an Advanced Degree to Work in Your Field?

Certainly there are fields such as law, psychiatry, medicine, and college teaching that demand advanced degrees. Is the field of employment you're considering one that also puts a premium on an advanced degree? You may be surprised. Read job ads on the Internet and in a number of major Sunday newspapers for positions you would enjoy. How many of those require an advanced degree?

Retailing, for example, has always put a premium on what people can do rather than how much education they have had. Successful people in retailing come from all academic preparations. A Ph.D. in your field may bring more prestige to a job, but it may not bring a more senior position or better pay. In fact, it may disqualify you for some jobs because an employer might believe you will be unhappy to be overqualified for a particular position. Or your motives in applying for the work may be misconstrued, and the employer might think you will only be working at this level until something better comes along. None of this may be true for you, but it comes about because you are working outside of the usual territory for that degree level.

When economic times are especially difficult, we tend to see stories featured about individuals with advanced degrees doing what is considered unsuitable work, such as the Ph.D. in French driving a cab or the Ph.D. in chemistry waiting tables. Actually, this is not particularly surprising when you consider that as your degree level advances, the job market narrows appreciably. At any one time, regardless of economic circumstances, there are only so many jobs for your particular level of expertise. If you cannot find employment for your advanced degree level, chances are you will be considered suspect for many other kinds of employment and may be forced into temporary work far removed from your original intention.

Before making an important decision such as graduate study, learn your options and carefully consider what you want to do with your advanced degree. Ask yourself whether it is reasonable to think you can achieve your goals. Will there be jobs when you graduate? Where will they be? What will they pay? How competitive will the market be at that time, based on current predictions?

If you're uncertain about the degree requirements for the fields you're interested in, you should check a publication such as the U.S. Department of Labor's *Occupational Outlook Handbook* (www.bls.gov). Each entry on the *OOH* includes a section on training and other qualifications that will indicate clearly what the minimum educational requirement is for employment, what degree is the standard, and what employment may be possible without the required credential.

For example, for physicists and astronomers a doctoral degree in physics or a closely related field is essential. Certainly this is the degree of choice in academic institutions. However, the *Occupational Outlook Handbook* also indicates what kinds of employment may be available to individuals holding a master's or even a bachelor's degree in physics.

Have You Compared Your Expectations of What Graduate School Will Do for You with What It Has Done for Alumni of the Program You're Considering?

Most colleges and universities perform some kind of postgraduate survey of their students to ascertain where they are employed, what additional education they have received, and what levels of salary they are enjoying. Ask to see this information either from the university you are considering applying to or from your own alma mater, especially if it has a similar graduate program. Such surveys often reveal surprises about occupational decisions, salaries, and work satisfaction. This information may affect your decision.

The value of self-assessment (the process of examining and making decisions about your own hierarchy of values and goals) is especially important in analyzing the desirability of possible career paths involving graduate education. Sometimes a job requiring advanced education seems to hold real promise but is disappointing in salary potential or number of opportunities available. Certainly it is better to research this information before embarking on a program of graduate studies. It may not change your mind about your decision, but by becoming better informed about your choice, you become better prepared for your future.

Have You Talked with People in Your Field to Explore What You Might Be Doing After Graduate School?

In pursuing your undergraduate degree, you will have come into contact with many individuals trained in the field you are considering. You might also have the opportunity to attend professional conferences, workshops, seminars, and job fairs where you can expand your network of contacts. Talk to them all! Find out about their individual career paths, discuss your own plans and hopes, get their feedback on the reality of your expectations, and heed their advice about your prospects. Each will have a unique tale to tell, and each will bring a different perspective on the current marketplace for the credentials you are seeking. Talking to enough people will make you an expert on what's out there.

Are You Excited by the Idea of Studying the Particular Field You Have in Mind?

This question may be the most important one of all. If you are going to spend several years in advanced study, perhaps engendering some debt or postponing some lifestyle decisions for an advanced degree, you simply ought to enjoy what you're doing. Examine your work in the discipline so far. Has it been fun? Have you found yourself exploring various paths of thought? Do you read in your area for fun? Do you enjoy talking about it, thinking about it, and sharing it with others? Advanced degrees often are the beginning of a lifetime's involvement with a particular subject. Choose carefully a field that will hold your interest and your enthusiasm.

If nothing else, do the following:

- Talk and question (remember to listen!)

- Reality test

- Soul-search by yourself or with a person you trust

FINDING THE RIGHT PROGRAM FOR YOU: SOME CONSIDERATIONS

There are several important factors in coming to a sound decision about the right graduate program for you. You'll want to begin by locating institutions that offer appropriate programs, examining each of these programs and their requirements, undertaking the application process by reviewing catalogs and obtaining application materials, visiting campuses if possible, arranging for letters of recommendation, writing your application statement, and, finally, following up on your applications.

Locate Institutions with Appropriate Programs

Once you decide on a particular advanced degree, it's important to develop a list of schools offering such a degree program. Perhaps the best source of graduate program information is Peterson's. The website (www.petersons .com) and the printed *Guides to Graduate Study* allow you to search for information by institution name, location, or academic area. The website also allows you to do a keyword search. Use the website and guides to build your list. In addition, you may want to consult the College Board's *Index of Majors and Graduate Degrees*, which will help you find graduate programs offering the degree you seek. It is indexed by academic major and then categorized by state.

Now, this may be a considerable list. You may want to narrow the choices down further by a number of criteria: tuition, availability of financial aid, public versus private institutions, United States versus international institutions, size of student body, size of faculty, application fee, and geographic location. This is only a partial list; you will have your own important considerations. Perhaps you are an avid scuba diver and you find it unrealistic to think you could pursue graduate study for a number of years without being able to ocean dive from time to time. Good! That's a decision and it's honest. Now, how far from the ocean is too far, and what schools meet your other needs? In any case, and according to your own criteria, begin to put together a reasonable list of graduate schools that you are willing to spend time investigating.

Examine the Degree Programs and Their Requirements

Once you've determined the criteria by which you want to develop a list of graduate schools, you can begin to examine the degree program requirements, faculty composition, and institutional research orientation. Again, using resources such as Peterson's website or guides can reveal an amazingly rich level of material by which to judge your possible selections.

In addition to degree programs and degree requirements, entries will include information about application fees, entrance test requirements, tuition, percentage of applicants accepted, numbers of applicants receiving financial aid, gender breakdown of students, numbers of full- and part-time faculty, and often gender breakdown of faculty as well. Numbers graduating in each program and research orientations of departments are also included in some entries. There is information on graduate housing; student services; and library, research, and computer facilities. A contact person, phone number, and address are also standard information in these listings.

It can be helpful to draw up a chart and enter relevant information about each school you are considering in order to have a ready reference on points of information that are important to you.

Undertake the Application Process

Program Information. Once you've decided on a selection of schools, obtain program information and applications. Nearly every school has a website that contains most of the detailed information you need to narrow your choices. In addition, applications can be printed from the site. If, however, you don't want to print out lots of information, you can request that a copy of the catalog and application materials be sent to you.

When you have your information in hand, give it all a careful reading and make notes of issues you might want to discuss via E-mail, on the telephone, or in a personal interview.

••••••••••••••••••••••••••••••••••••••

Remember to look for courses that are *indirectly* related to the field you want to study, too. For example, if you want to study social anthropology, you might also look for classes in sociology, religion, social psychology, and political science.

••••••••••••••••••••••••••••••••••••••

What is the ratio of faculty to the required number of courses for your degree? How often will you encounter the same faculty member as an instructor?

If the program offers a practicum or off-campus experience, who arranges this? Does the graduate school select a site and place you there, or is it your responsibility? What are the professional affiliations of the faculty? Does the program merit any outside professional endorsement or accreditation?

Critically evaluate the catalogs of each of the programs you are considering. List any questions you have and ask current or former teachers and colleagues for their impressions as well.

The Application. Preview each application thoroughly to determine what you need to provide in the way of letters of recommendation, transcripts from undergraduate schools or any previous graduate work, and personal essays. Make a notation for each application of what you will need to complete that document.

Additionally, you'll want to determine entrance testing requirements for each institution and immediately arrange to register for appropriate tests. Information can be obtained from associated websites, including www.ets.org (GRE, GMAT, TOEFL, PRAXIS, SLS, Higher Education Assessment), www. lsat.org (LSAT), and www.tpcweb.com/mat (MAT). Your college career office should also be able to provide you with advice and additional information.

Visit the Campus if Possible

If time and finances allow, a visit, interview, and tour can help make your decision easier. You can develop a sense of the student body, meet some of the faculty, and hear up-to-date information on resources and the curriculum. You will have a brief opportunity to "try out" the surroundings to see if they fit your needs. After all, it will be home for a while. If a visit is not possible but you have questions, don't hesitate to call and speak with the dean of the graduate school. Most are more than happy to talk to candidates and want them to have the answers they seek. Graduate school admission is a very personal and individual process.

Arrange for Letters of Recommendation

This is also the time to begin to assemble a group of individuals who will support your candidacy as a graduate student by writing letters of recommendation or completing recommendation forms. Some schools will ask you to provide letters of recommendation to be included with your application or sent directly to the school by the recommender. Other graduate programs will provide a recommendation form that must be completed by the recommender. These graduate school forms vary greatly in the amount of space provided for a written recommendation. So that you can use letters as you need to, ask your recommenders to address their letters "To Whom It May Concern," unless one of your recommenders has a particular connection to one of your graduate schools or knows an official at the school.

Choose recommenders who can speak authoritatively about the criteria important to selection officials at your graduate school. In other words, choose recommenders who can write about your grasp of the literature in your field of study, your ability to write and speak effectively, your class performance, and your demonstrated interest in the field outside of class. Other characteristics that graduate schools are interested in assessing include your emotional maturity, leadership ability, breadth of general knowledge, intellectual ability, motivation, perseverance, and ability to engage in independent inquiry.

When requesting recommendations, it's especially helpful to put the request in writing. Explain your graduate school intentions and express some of your thoughts about graduate school and your appreciation for their support. Don't be shy about "prompting" your recommenders with some suggestions of what you would appreciate being included in their comments. Most recommenders will find this direction helpful and will want to produce a statement of support that you can both stand behind. Consequently, if your interaction with one recommender was especially focused on research projects, he or she might be best able to speak of those skills and your critical thinking ability. Another recommender may have good comments to make about your public presentation skills.

Give your recommenders plenty of lead time in which to complete your recommendation, and set a date by which they should respond. If they fail to meet your deadline, be prepared to make a polite call or visit to inquire if they need more information or if there is anything you can do to move the process along.

Whether or not you are providing a graduate school form or asking for an original letter to be mailed, be sure to provide an envelope and postage if the recommender must mail the form or letter directly to the graduate school.

Each recommendation you request should provide a different piece of information about you for the selection committee. It might be pleasant for letters of recommendation to say that you are a fine, upstanding individual, but a selection committee for graduate school will require specific information. Each recommender has had a unique relationship with you, and his or her letter should reflect that. Think of each letter as helping to build a more complete portrait of you as a potential graduate student.

Write Your Application Statement

• •

Many graduate applications for liberal arts programs require a written personal statement. For the liberal arts major, the personal essay should be a welcome opportunity to express your deep interest in pursuing graduate study. Your understanding of the challenges ahead, your commitment to the work involved, and your expressed self-awareness will weigh heavily in the decision process of the graduate school admissions committee.

• •

An excellent source to help in writing this essay is *How to Write a Winning Personal Statement for Graduate and Professional School*, by Richard J. Stelzer. It has been written from the perspective of what graduate school selection committees are looking for when they read these essays. It provides helpful tips to keep your essay targeted on the kinds of issues and criteria that are important to selection committees and that provide them with the kind of information they can best utilize in making their decision.

Follow Up on Your Applications

After you have finished each application and mailed it along with your transcript requests and letters of recommendation, be sure to follow up on the progress of your file. For example, call the graduate school administrative staff to see whether your transcripts have arrived. If the school required your recommenders to fill out a specific recommendation form that had to be mailed directly to the school, you will want to ensure that they have all arrived in good time for the processing of your application. It is your responsibility to make certain that all required information is received by the institution.

RESEARCHING FINANCIAL AID SOURCES, SCHOLARSHIPS, AND FELLOWSHIPS

Financial aid information is available from each graduate school. You may be eligible for federal, state, and/or institutional support. There are lengthy forms to complete, and some of these will vary by school, type of school (public versus private), and state. Be sure to note the deadline dates on each form.

There are many excellent resources available to help you explore all of your financial aid options. Visit your college career office or local public library to find out about the range of materials available. Two excellent resources are Peterson's website (www.petersons.com) and its book *Peterson's Grants for Graduate and Post Doctoral Study*. Another good reference is the Foundation Center's *Foundation Grants to Individuals*. These types of resources generally contain information that can be accessed by indexes including field of study, specific eligibility requirements, administering agency, and geographic focus.

EVALUATING ACCEPTANCES

If you apply to and are accepted at more than one school, it is time to return to your initial research and self-assessment to evaluate your options and select the program that will best help you achieve the goals you set for pursuing graduate study. You'll want to choose a program that will allow you to complete your studies in a timely and cost-effective way. This may be a good time to get additional feedback from professors and career professionals who are familiar with your interests and plans. Ultimately, the decision is yours, so be sure you get answers to all the questions you can think of.

SOME NOTES ABOUT REJECTION

Each graduate school is searching for applicants who appear to have the qualifications necessary to succeed in its program. Applications are evaluated on a combination of undergraduate grade point average, strength of letters of recommendation, standardized test scores, and personal statements written for the application.

A carelessly completed application is one reason many applicants are denied admission to a graduate program. To avoid this type of needless rejection, be sure to carefully and completely answer all appropriate questions on the application form, focus your personal statement given the instructions provided, and submit your materials well in advance of the deadline. Remember that your test scores and recommendations are considered a part of your application, so they must also be received by the deadline.

If you are rejected by a school that especially interests you, you may want to contact the dean of graduate studies to discuss the strengths and weaknesses of your application. Information provided by the dean will be useful in reapplying to the program later or applying to other, similar programs.

PART TWO

THE
CAREER PATHS

CHAPTER NINE

INTRODUCTION TO LIBERAL ARTS CAREER PATHS

I n the introduction to this book we discussed the prejudices against liberal arts degrees—that even though they provide a well-rounded education, they leave the new graduate virtually unemployable. As most prejudices are, this notion is based solely upon ignorance. In reality, a liberal arts degree, with all its various subject areas, opens more employment doors than any other area of professional study.

The ability to think creatively, solve problems, and communicate effectively—both verbally and through the written word—are skills liberal arts graduates acquire. And these skills are highly sought by employers in a variety of fields.

THE CAREER PATHS

The actual career paths open to liberal arts majors are too numerous in scope to include all in one book on the subject. Within this book, six major career paths have been identified and examined:

1. Teaching

2. Corporate communications

3. Media

4. Advertising, marketing, and sales

5. The helping professions

6. Law

Within some of these paths are employment opportunities for graduates with *any* major; others prefer more specific specialization; and still others require graduate school or other additional training.

Furthermore, within these paths, other related career paths and job settings are discussed:

Government

Employment opportunities are almost limitless within the various government agencies and departments. Some are identified in the chapters on the helping professions (working for social service agencies), law (working for appellate courts or other government employers), and corporate communications (government functions to a great extent in a fashion similar to most corporations.)

Other settings to consider are government security agencies, such as the FBI or CIA. Even government at the local city or county level offer positions to bachelor's and master's level liberal arts majors.

Business

The category of business is wide open to liberal arts majors and is so broad that it has been broken down into the areas of corporate communications (which also covers public relations) and advertising, marketing, and sales. Job settings described range from your standard corporation or advertising agency to the foreign service and nonprofit associations.

ADDITIONAL PATHS

Some other paths, not specifically or extensively approached in this book, but equally deserving of consideration for liberal arts majors, are:

Nonprofit Agencies

Nonprofits can be the biggest surprise for liberal arts majors. It is a very broad area requiring much of the same expertise as its "for profit" cousins. The nonprofit world needs communication specialists in all areas including advertising and marketing specialists, public relations and publicity personnel, and administrators at all levels.

The Sciences

The sciences are one of those gray areas. Some people study chemistry or biology and graduate with a bachelor's of arts degree. Others pursue a B.S. in the various science and science-related fields. To be realistic, the liberal arts major can rule out all the high tech and hard sciences, but there are still science-related opportunities for liberal arts majors.

Social Sciences

The field of psychology is covered in this book under the helping professions. Two other main areas of the social sciences are also open to liberal arts majors: sociology and anthropology and all their various subspecialties.

Music and Art

This is another one of those gray areas: humanities, yes, liberal arts, maybe. Paths open to liberal arts majors in these two fields include teaching, performing, museum work, studio art, and commercial art, among others.

Languages

For the liberal arts major specializing in one or more languages, opportunities include teaching; translating; government work; educational administration; and business, industry, and commerce.

History

The history major has many paths to pursue and job settings within which to work, from museums to nonprofits, from government to business.

For further help in defining your career path options, other books in the Great Jobs series will lead you to employment possibilities in a variety of fields. They include:

- Great Jobs for Anthropology Majors

- Great Jobs for Art Majors

- Great Jobs for Biology Majors

- Great Jobs for Business Majors

- Great Jobs for Communications Majors

- Great Jobs for Economics Majors

- Great Jobs for Engineering Majors

- Great Jobs for English Majors

- Great Jobs for Foreign Language Majors

- Great Jobs for History Majors

- Great Jobs for Psychology Majors

New titles are regularly added to the list.

CHAPTER TEN

PATH 1: TEACHING

Teaching is a natural path for a graduate with a liberal arts education. For every liberal arts subject area, there is a continuing need for teachers at almost every educational level.

However, while many teaching situations allow entry- to bachelor's-level job candidates, more and more require advanced degrees, occasionally a master's, and more often a doctorate.

For the liberal arts major with a well-rounded education, the love of a particular subject area is not enough to guarantee success in this extremely important field. The love of teaching and the ability to instruct and share knowledge is even more vital. Most teachers will tell you that the process of teaching is give and take. Good teachers learn as much from their students as they impart to them.

DEFINITION OF THE CAREER PATH

An educator can take many career paths, work with many different age groups and in many different settings. For the purposes of this chapter, we will look at the two most traditional teaching paths: kindergarten through secondary school (K–12) and college and university teaching. Alternative suggestions are given later in this chapter under Possible Job Settings.

K–12

The role of a teacher is changing from that of a lecturer or presenter to one of a facilitator or coach. Interactive discussions and hands-on learning are replacing rote memorization. For example, rather than merely telling students about history, mathematics, or psychology, a teacher might ask students to help solve a mathematical problem or perform a laboratory experiment and discuss how these apply to the real world. Similarly, a teacher might arrange to bring three- and four-year-olds into the classroom to demonstrate certain concepts of child psychology.

As teachers move away from the traditional repetitive-drill approaches, they are using more props or manipulative tools to help children understand abstract concepts, solve problems, and develop critical thought processes. For example, young students may be taught the concept of numbers or adding and subtracting by playing board games. As children get older, they may use more sophisticated materials such as tape recorders, science apparatuses, or cameras.

Classes are becoming less structured, and students are working in groups to discuss and solve problems. Preparing students for the future work force is the major stimulus generating the changes in education. To be prepared, students must be able to interact with others, adapt to new technology, and logically think through problems. Teachers provide the tools and environment for their students to develop these skills.

Kindergarten and elementary school teachers play a vital role in the development of children. What children learn and experience during their early years can shape their views of themselves and the world and affect later success or failure in school, work, and their personal lives. Kindergarten and elementary school teachers introduce children to numbers, language, science, and social studies. They may use games, music, artwork, films, slides, computers, and other instructional technology to teach basic skills.

Most elementary school teachers oversee one class of children in several subjects. In some schools, two or more teachers instruct as a team and are jointly responsible for a group of students in at least one subject. In other schools, a teacher may teach one special subject—usually music, art, reading, science, arithmetic, or physical education to a number of classes. A small but growing number of teachers instruct multilevel classrooms, those with students at several different learning levels.

Secondary school teachers help students delve more deeply into subjects introduced in elementary school and learn more about the world and themselves. They specialize in a specific subject, such as English, Spanish, mathematics, history, or biology. They may teach a variety of related courses for example, American history, contemporary American problems, and world geography.

Teachers might use films, slides, overhead projectors, and the latest technology in teaching, such as computers, telecommunication systems, and video discs. Telecommunication technology can bring the real world into the classroom. Through telecommunications, American students can communicate with students in other countries to share personal experiences or research projects of interest to both groups. Computers are used in many classroom activities, from helping students solve math problems to learning English as a second language. Teachers must continually update their skills to use the latest technology.

Teachers design their classroom presentations to meet student needs and abilities. They also may work with students individually. Teachers assign lessons, give tests, hear oral presentations, and maintain classroom discipline. They observe and evaluate a student's performance and potential. Teachers increasingly are using new assessment methods, such as examining a portfolio of a student's artwork or writing, to measure student achievement. Teachers assess the portfolio at the end of a learning period to judge a student's overall progress. They may then provide additional assistance in areas where a student may need help.

In addition to classroom activities, teachers plan and evaluate lessons, sometimes in collaboration with teachers of related subjects. They also prepare tests, grade papers, prepare report cards, oversee study halls and homerooms, supervise extracurricular activities, and meet with parents and school staff to discuss a student's academic progress or personal problems.

Secondary school teachers may assist a student in choosing courses, colleges, and careers.

College and University Teaching

College and university faculty teach and advise more than fourteen million full- and part-time college students and perform a significant part of our nation's research. They also study and meet with colleagues to keep up with developments in their field and consult with government, business, nonprofit, and community organizations.

Faculty generally are organized into departments or divisions, based on subject or field. They usually teach several different courses in their department: introduction to, developmental, and educational psychology, for example. They may instruct undergraduate or graduate students, or both.

College and university faculty may give lectures to several hundred students in large halls, lead small seminars, and supervise students in laboratories. They also prepare lectures, exercises, and laboratory experiments; grade exams and papers; and advise and work with students individually. In universities, they counsel, advise, teach, and supervise graduate student research. They may use closed-circuit and cable television, computers, videotapes, and other teaching aids.

Faculty keep abreast of developments in their field by reading current literature; talking with colleagues; and participating in professional conferences, symposia, and seminars. They also do their own research to expand knowledge in their field and write about their findings in scholarly journals and books.

Most faculty members serve on academic or administrative committees that deal with the policies of their institution, departmental matters, academic issues, curricula, budgets, equipment purchases, and hiring. Some work with student organizations. Department heads generally have heavier administrative responsibilities.

The amount of time spent on each of these activities varies by individual circumstance and type of institution. Faculty members at universities generally spend a significant part of their time doing research; those in four-year colleges, somewhat less; and those in two-year colleges, relatively little. However, the teaching load usually is heavier in two-year colleges.

POSSIBLE JOB SETTINGS

Teachers can be found in almost every sector of society. In addition to the traditional school or college environment, the following list provides alternative settings where those wanting to teach can search for employment.

Each setting has its own requirements of and expectations for its teachers, but each provides an environment where liberal arts majors dedicated to teaching can practice their art.

- Adult-education centers
- Alternative schools
- Community centers
- Community colleges
- Computer on-line services
- Day-care centers
- Four-year colleges and universities
- Military bases
- Nursery schools
- Overseas language centers
- Overseas schools
- Overseas universities
- Peace Corps
- Prisons and jails
- Private schools
- Public schools
- Recreational centers
- Rehabilitation centers
- Religious organizations
- Vocational and technical schools

WORKING CONDITIONS

K-12

Seeing students develop new skills and the appreciation of the joy of learning can be very rewarding. However, teaching may be frustrating when dealing with unmotivated or disrespectful students.

Including school duties performed outside the classroom, many teachers work more than forty hours a week. Most teachers work the traditional ten-month school year with a two-month vacation during the summer. Teachers on the ten-month schedule may teach in summer sessions, take other jobs, travel, or pursue other personal interests. Many enroll in college courses or workshops in order to continue their education. Teachers in districts with a year-round schedule typically work eight weeks, are on vacation for one week, and have a five-week midwinter break.

Most states have tenure laws that prevent teachers from being fired without just cause and due process. Teachers may obtain *tenure* after they have satisfactorily completed a probationary period of teaching, normally three years. Tenure is not a guarantee of a job, but it does provide some security.

College and University Teaching

College faculty generally have flexible schedules. They must be present for classes, usually twelve to sixteen hours a week, and for faculty and committee meetings. Most establish regular office hours for student consultations, usually three to six hours per week. Otherwise, they are relatively free to decide when and where they will work and how much time to devote to course preparation, the evaluation of papers and exams, study, research, and other activities. They may work staggered hours and teach classes at night and on weekends, particularly those faculty who teach older students who may have full-time jobs or family responsibilities on weekdays. They have even greater flexibility during the summer and school holidays, when they may teach or do research, travel, or pursue nonacademic interests. Most colleges and universities have funds used to support faculty research or other professional development needs, including travel to conferences and research sites.

Part-time faculty generally spend little time on campus because they usually don't have an office. In addition, they may teach at more than one college, requiring travel between their various places of employment.

Faculty may experience a conflict between their responsibilities to teach students and the pressure to do research. This may be a particular problem for young faculty members seeking advancement. Increasing emphasis on undergraduate teaching performance, particularly at small liberal arts colleges, in tenure decisions may alleviate some of this pressure, however.

FIRST-HAND ACCOUNTS FROM TWO EDUCATORS

CAROL BEHAN, HIGH SCHOOL ENGLISH TEACHER

Carol Behan has been teaching for more than thirty years. She's been at Edmeston Central School in Edmeston, New York since 1982. Currently, she teaches English to ninth- and tenth-graders. The school holds 580 students, K–12 all in one building.

Carol talks about her job:

"We have a small school and my department has just three teachers. The three of us have a lot of input and freedom in developing our own program. I teach two grades with anywhere from twelve to twenty-eight students in a class at a time. For the most part, I get to see some growth from one year to the next.

"We're on a rotating schedule, not a traditional Monday through Friday schedule. It's a six-day cycle and I have each class four hours out of the six-day cycle. Each day is different. It's very similar to a college schedule. We do a literature strand, a writing strand, and public speaking. I'm allowed to decide which textbooks I'll use, and over the last ten years or so I have developed the program just as I like it.

"One of the downsides of any teaching job is that you constantly run into administrators or people with authority above you who are often inept or unaware of what the students' needs are. You end up having to work around them.

"As much as I love teaching, I know it can definitely be a burnout profession if you put a lot of your heart into it. Even in a small school, you see that the kids' attitudes are worsening; there are discipline problems and violence. One student brought a shotgun into the school a couple of years ago and aimed it at a teacher he'd had a personality conflict with. These problems aren't just in urban schools. They're everywhere.

"It's sad because I love doing what I'm doing. Teaching is a performance art. I love communicating the literature. I teach a real snazzy Shakespeare unit, for example, and I watch the kids really come alive. That's what I went into teaching for."

Carol Behan's Background

"I have a B.A. in liberal arts with a concentration in English from SUNY Potsdam. I got my master's from SUNY Cortland. I chose to major in reading because it would give me more job options.

"When I went to college I had no intention of teaching. My mother was a teacher, a wonderful teacher, very dedicated. But I never thought when I was growing up that I could do it half as well as she, so I chose a completely different direction at first. My dad had died of cancer when I was sixteen so I was on a personal mission to cure cancer; I thought I'd pursue a career as a research scientist. But that really was the wrong way to choose a career.

"Subsequently, remembering that I had been inspired by several of my high school teachers, I decided to get my teaching degree and see what I could do. I always felt that if I put my mind to something I could do it well.

"It was a bad time to find a teaching job, back in the early 1970s, but I persevered and found one."

Advice from Carol Behan

"You have to love your subject matter and see its value in people's lives. You can't be convincing if you don't.

"Teachers are role models, we always will be. But our idealism has to be tempered with reality. Some people come in and they bruise so easily—the kids' attitudes can be very tough. Most of it is just for show, testing us, but we have to remember that we do have a lot of influence on their lives.

"I think teaching is more important than it's ever been, even though it's harder now than it's ever been."

MARSHALL J. COOK, AUTHOR AND PROFESSOR, UNIVERSITY OF WISCONSIN, MADISON

Marshall J. Cook is a full professor in the department of communication programs within the division of continuing studies at the University of Wisconsin, Madison. He is also a writer with hundreds of articles to his credit, a couple of dozen short stories, and numerous books including *Writing for the Joy of It*; *Freeing Your Creativity*; *How to Write with the Skill of a Master and the Genius of a Child*; *Slow Down and Get More Done, Leads and Conclusions*; and *Hometown Wisconsin*.

Before coming to Wisconsin, Marshall Cook was an instructor at Solano Community College in Suisun City, California for eight years.

Marshall J. Cook discusses his job:

"My job is really wonderful and different from the traditional campus teacher. The division of continuing studies is a separate division within the university and our primary mission is adult education. I do a lot of workshops and some consulting and some on-site training of newspaper people, corporate communicators, and others. For example, I run a media workshop for police officers called 'Preparing to be Interviewed by the Press' and one on newsletters that I've done for sixteen years. Another workshop is on stress management and it follows the title of my book, *Slow Down and Get More Done*.

"Basically, I offer anything we can sell to the public. We're an income generating unit, unlike campus teaching, and we're responsible for paying our own way.

"I develop the workshops and help publicize them and teach them, too. I'll personally teach maybe sixty to seventy of these a year along with guest speaking and helping out at other conferences.

"I teach much more than the average professor in a university, but there's no research component to my job. My research is all practical and my publications are all mass media because that's what I teach.

"It's diverse—one of those rare opportunities to combine writing with another career that feeds the writing rather than detracting from it. The writing helps me teach and the teaching helps me write.

"It's very stimulating, but it can be enormously tiring. I do a lot of traveling, mostly within the state, bringing the workshops to where the people are. Sometimes I have to do three workshops in a week. I have to be careful not to overschedule myself."

Marshall J. Cook's Background

"I have a B.A. in creative writing from Stanford University and an M.A. in communications/print journalism, also from Stanford. I went to law school for about four months and I taught one English class at the University of Santa Clara in California. I realized I didn't want to be a lawyer—I liked studying the law, but was not interested in the actual day-to-day work.

"At about that time, one of the teachers at Santa Clara died and I got his job; they hired me full-time. I worked there for four years in the English department.

"It was like an old dream had been reborn. Ever since I was a kid the only two things I really wanted to do was to be a teacher and a writer. And now I've found something that lets me do both—which is really nice. I got the class at Santa Clara basically just to make some money to put myself through law school and I discovered I liked it. I don't think I was actually that good at it at first, but it really appealed to me.

"I came to the University of Wisconsin in 1979 as a member of the academic staff as a program coordinator. I'm probably the last person in the system who came in this way, but at that time you could move from the academic staff track to what they call a tenure track. So I moved into being an assistant professor, which is a professor without tenure. Then I put in my requisite five to six years, and applied for tenure at the associate professor level. Once you achieve that rank it's with tenure. Another three years after that I applied and then became a full professor."

Advice from Marshall J. Cook

"These days to become a full professor on a tenure track you'd need to get your Ph.D. and it should be in a field you have some passion for.

"It's a wonderful thing to do if you get the chance to do it—you not only study and discuss interesting ideas, but you get to share them and watch them grow as you interact with young minds that aren't nearly as trained as yours, but are flexible and hungry for the knowledge you have."

TRAINING AND QUALIFICATIONS

K-12

All fifty states and the District of Columbia require public school teachers to be certified. Certification is generally for one or several related subjects. Usually, certification is granted by the state board of education or a certification advisory committee.

Teachers may be certified to teach the early childhood grades (usually nursery school through grade 3); the elementary grades (grades 1 through 6 or 8); or a special subject, such as reading or music.

In most states, special education teachers receive a credential to teach kindergarten through grade 12. These teachers train in the specialty that they want, for example, teaching children with learning disabilities or behavioral disorders.

Requirements for regular certificates vary by state. However, all states require a bachelor's degree and completion of an approved teacher training program with a prescribed number of subject and education credits and supervised practice teaching.

Traditional education programs for kindergarten and elementary school teachers include courses designed specifically for those preparing to teach in mathematics, physical science, social science, music, art, and literature, as well as prescribed professional education courses, such as philosophy of education, psychology of learning, and teaching methods.

Aspiring secondary school teachers either major in the subject they plan to teach while also taking education courses or major in education and take subject courses. Some states require specific grade point averages for teacher certification.

Many states offer alternative teacher certification programs for people who have college training in the subject they will teach but do not have the necessary education courses required for a regular certificate. Alternative certification programs were designed originally to ease teacher shortages in certain subjects, such as mathematics and science. The programs have expanded to attract other people into teaching, including recent college graduates and midcareer changers. In some programs, individuals begin teaching immediately under provisional certification. After working under the close supervision of experienced educators for one or two years while taking education courses outside school hours, they receive regular certification if they have progressed satisfactorily. Under other programs, college graduates who do not meet certification requirements take only those courses that they lack, and then become certified. This may take one or two semesters of full-time study.

Aspiring teachers who need certification may also enter programs that grant a master's degree in education, as well as certification. States also issue emergency certificates to individuals who do not meet all requirements for a regular certificate when schools cannot hire enough teachers with regular certificates.

Almost all states require applicants for teacher certification to be tested for competency in basic skills such as reading and writing, teaching skills, or subject matter proficiency. Almost all require continuing education for renewal of the teacher's certificate; some require a master's degree.

Many states have reciprocity agreements that make it easier for teachers certified in one state to become certified in another. Teachers may become board certified by successfully completing the National Board for Professional Teaching Standards certification process. This certification is voluntary, but may result in a higher salary.

In addition to being knowledgeable in their subject, teachers must have the ability to communicate, inspire trust and confidence, and motivate students, as well as understand their educational and emotional needs. They also should be organized, dependable, patient, and creative.

College and University Teaching

Most college and university faculty are in four academic ranks: professor, associate professor, assistant professor, and instructor. A small number are lecturers. Most faculty members are hired as instructors or assistant professors. Four-year colleges and universities generally hire doctoral degree holders for full-time, tenure-track positions, but may hire master's degree holders or doctoral candidates for certain disciplines, such as the arts, or for part-time and temporary jobs. In two-year colleges, master's degree holders often qualify for full-time positions.

Doctoral programs usually take four to seven years of full-time study beyond the bachelor's degree. Candidates usually specialize in a subfield of a discipline, for example, American literature, counseling psychology, or European history, and also take courses covering the whole discipline. Programs include twenty or more increasingly specialized courses and seminars plus comprehensive examinations on all major areas of the field. They also include a *dissertation*, which is a report on original research to answer some significant question in the field; it sets forth an original hypothesis or proposes a model and tests it.

A major step in the traditional academic career is attaining tenure. Newly hired faculty serve a certain period (usually seven years) under term contracts. Then, their record of teaching, research, and overall contribution to the institution is reviewed; tenure is granted if the review is favorable and positions are available. With tenure, a professor cannot be fired without just cause and due process. Those denied tenure usually must leave the institution. Tenure protects the faculty's academic freedom—the ability to teach and conduct research without fear of being fired for advocating unpopular ideas. It also gives both faculty and institutions the stability needed for effective research and teaching and provides financial stability for faculty members. About 60 percent of full-time faculty are tenured, and many others are in the probationary period.

College faculty need intelligence, inquisitive and analytical minds, and a strong desire to pursue and disseminate knowledge. They must be able to communicate clearly and logically, both orally and in writing. They should be able to establish a rapport with students and, as models for them, be dedicated to the principles of academic integrity and intellectual honesty. Finally, they must be able to work in an environment where they receive little direct supervision.

CAREER OUTLOOK

K-12

Overall employment of kindergarten, elementary, and secondary school teachers is expected to increase about as fast as the average for all occupations through the year 2008. The expected retirement of a large number of teachers currently in their forties and fifties should open up many additional jobs. However, projected employment growth varies among individual teaching occupations.

Employment of secondary school teachers is expected to grow faster than the average for all occupations through the year 2008, while average employment growth is projected for kindergarten and elementary school teachers. Assuming relatively little change in average class size, employment growth of teachers depends on population growth rates and corresponding student enrollments. Enrollments of secondary school students are expected to grow throughout most of the projection period. On the other hand, elementary school enrollment is projected to decline after 2001.

The number of teachers employed also depends on state and local expenditures for education. Pressures from taxpayers to limit spending could result in fewer teachers than projected; pressures to spend more to improve the quality of education could increase the teacher workforce.

In anticipation of growing student enrollments at the secondary school level, many states are implementing policies that will encourage more students to become teachers. Some are giving large signing bonuses that are distributed over the teacher's first few years of teaching. Some are expanding state scholarships; issuing loans for moving expenses; and implementing loan-forgiveness programs, allowing education majors with at least a B average to receive state-paid tuition, as long as they agree to teach in the state for four years.

The supply of teachers is expected to increase in response to reports of improved job prospects, more teacher involvement in school policy, and greater public interest in education. In recent years, the total number of bachelor's and master's degrees granted in education has steadily increased.

In addition, more teachers will be drawn from a reserve pool of career changers; substitute teachers; and teachers completing alternative certification programs, relocating to different schools, and reentering the workforce.

College and University

Employment of college and university faculty is expected to increase faster than the average for all occupations through 2008 as enrollments in higher education increase. Many additional openings will arise as faculty members retire. Nevertheless, prospective job applicants should expect to face competition, particularly for full-time, tenure-track positions at four-year institutions.

Between 1998 and 2008, the traditional college-age (eighteen to twenty-four) population will grow again after several years of decline. This population increase; a higher proportion of eighteen to twenty-four-year-olds attending college; and a growing number of part-time, female, minority, and older students will spur college enrollments. Enrollment is projected to rise from 14.6 million in 1998 to 16.1 million in 2008, an increase of about 10 percent.

Growing numbers of students will necessitate the hiring of more faculty to teach. At the same time, many faculty will be retiring, opening up even more positions. Also, the number of doctorates is expected to grow more slowly than in the past, somewhat easing the competition for some faculty positions.

Despite expected job growth and the need to replace retiring faculty, many in the academic community are concerned that institutions will increasingly favor the hiring of adjunct faculty over full-time, tenure-track faculty. For many years, keen competition for faculty jobs forced some applicants to accept part-time academic appointments that offered little hope of tenure and others to seek nonacademic positions. Many colleges, faced with reduced state funding for higher education and growing numbers of part-time and older students, increased the hiring of part-time faculty to save money on pay and benefits and to accommodate the needs of nontraditional-age students. If funding remains tight over the projection period, this trend of hiring adjunct or part-time faculty is likely to continue. Because of uncertainty about future funding sources, some colleges and universities are also controlling costs by changing the mix of academic programs offered, eliminating some programs altogether and increasing class size.

Even if the proportion of full-time positions does not shrink, job competition will remain keen for coveted tenure-track jobs. Some institutions are expected to increasingly hire full-time faculty on limited-term contracts, reducing the number of tenure-track positions available. Overall, job prospects will continue to be better in certain fields—business, engineering, health science, and computer science, for example—that offer attractive, nonacademic job opportunities and attract fewer applicants for academic positions.

Also, excellent job prospects in a field—for example, computer science—result in higher student enrollments, increasing faculty needs in that field. On the other hand, poor job prospects in a field, such as history and other liberal arts majors in recent years, discourages students and reduces demand for faculty.

EARNINGS

K-12

According to the American Federation of Teachers, the average salary for 2.8 million teachers in 1999 (the most recent figures available) was $40,574. This is approximately $15,000 a year higher than two years before this—but tens of thousands of dollars less per year than professionals earn in other professions.

Salaries, of course, vary depending upon the area of the country. States in New England, and the east coast and west coast report the highest salaries. States in the southwest and southeast report the lowest.

New Jersey reports the highest average salary—$51,692. South Dakota reports the lowest at $28,386.

Many states are now offering incentives to teachers: signing bonuses, moving allowances, and extra allowances for teaching in rural or inner-city school districts. To see the entire salary report, visit the American Federation of Teachers website at www.aft.org.

College and University

Median annual earnings of college and university faculty in 1998 (the most recent figures currently available) were $46,630. The middle 50 percent earned between $33,390 and $71,360. The lowest 10 percent earned less than $23,100; the highest 10 percent, more than $90,360.

Earnings vary according to faculty rank and type of institution, geographic area, and field. According to the 1999 survey by the American Association of University Professors, salaries for full-time faculty averaged $56,300. By rank, the average for professors was $72,700; associate professors, $53,200; assistant professors, $43,800; instructors, $33,400; and lecturers, $37,200. Faculty in four-year institutions earn higher salaries, on the average, than those in two-year schools. Average salaries for faculty in public institutions— $55,900—were lower in 1998–99 than those for private independent institutions—$63,500—but higher than those for religiously affiliated private colleges and universities—$49,400.

In fields with high-paying, nonacademic alternatives—notably medicine and law but also engineering and business, among others—earnings exceed these averages. In others—such as the humanities and education—they are lower.

Most faculty members have significant earnings in addition to their base salary, from consulting, teaching additional courses, researching, writing for publication, or other employment.

Most college and university faculty enjoy some unique benefits, including access to campus facilities, tuition waivers for dependents, housing and travel allowances, and paid sabbatical leaves. Part-time faculty usually have fewer benefits, including health insurance, retirement benefits, and sabbatical leave, than full-time faculty.

The American Association of University Professors conducts an annual salary survey. The results of the most recent survey can be ordered from their website at www.aaup.org/indexfcs.htm for $66.50.

STRATEGIES FOR FINDING THE JOBS

How you go about your job hunt depends, in part, on the type of job and setting you are seeking. Here are some general suggestions.

Scan Relevant Newspapers

Many employers still rely on the old, faithful method of advertising job openings. If you plan on relocating, you can find out-of-town newspapers at any major library.

The Chronicle of Higher Education. *The Chronicle of Higher Education* is a weekly publication in which employers advertise job openings at community colleges and four-year colleges and universities. It is available by subscription or at your library or university career placement office.

Register at Your Career Placement Office

College career placement offices are often the first place an employer contacts with a new job opening. Some placement offices will allow you to open a file with your resume and references. This file is then made available to prospective employers.

Contact the Employer Directly

This method is still one of the best for jobs with colleges or school boards. Many have job hot lines with recorded announcements of current openings.

Attend Job Fairs and Conferences

Recruiters, especially for overseas schools, attend job fairs and conferences in the hopes of finding qualified staff for yearly job openings. Your career placement office can give you an idea of the different job fairs available. Professional associations will tell you when their annual conferences are held. Attend these events equipped with a stack of your resumes. Some overseas employers appreciate it if you can provide them with a small, passport-sized photo they can attach to your resume. This helps jog memories when they are back in their home country.

Surf the Web

Most public and private schools, as well as colleges and universities, have web pages and list current openings. Use any search engine with keywords such as "education," "university," or "jobs." You can narrow your search by including the state or city in which you prefer to work.

What follows is a list of helpful websites that post teaching and teaching-related job opportunities:

Academic Employment Network. Educational employment opportunities for teachers and other school-related positions at all academic levels are listed on this site. www.academploy.com

Academic360.com. Search through listings of educational institutions, faculty positions by discipline, and/or administrative positions by function. www.academic360.com

American Association of Community Colleges Careerline. Positions for two-year community colleges are listed here, from president and dean through faculty to administration. www.aacc.nche.edu/careerline

The Chronicle of Higher Education. Find job announcements for both faculty and staff positions from *The Chronicle*'s job listings, news and information about the academic community, and excellent lists of links to other academic job resources on-line. http://chronicle.com/jobs

Education Canada. This website is focused on jobs in the field of education in Canada. Search all locations by specialty or by province. http://educationcanada.com

Ed-U-Link. This site has national and international job openings for teachers, from kindergarten through high school, plus a fee-based "Online Teacher Registry" for teachers looking for jobs as well as an "Online Job Registry" for schools to post their job openings. www.edulink.com

Higher Education and Career Information Network. This is a collection of websites for college graduates and undergraduates looking for employment opportunities. www.educareer.com

HigherEdJobs. Search for a faculty or staff position by category (such as administrative, executive, faculty) or location. www.higheredjobs.com

Job-Hunt.Org. Search here for links to dozens of teaching and teaching-related job hunting sites. www.job-hunt.org/academia.html

National Adjunct Faculty Guild. Adjunct, part-time, visiting, or full-time faculty positions are listed by discipline. http://adjunctadvocate.com

National Educators' Employment Review. This publication features elementary, secondary, and college positions for both public and private schools. www.teacherjobs.com

National Teacher Recruitment Clearinghouse. This site provides links to each state's teacher certification/accreditation authority, alternative licensure programs, and financial aid. Select the "Find a Job" link for a page with salary information, information on conducting a job search (with links to teacher job banks by state), and other helpful information. www.recruiting teachers.org

NationJob. Jobs are listed in education, from kindergarten through college. www.nationjob.com/education

RELATED OCCUPATIONS

K-12

Kindergarten, elementary, and secondary school teaching requires a wide variety of skills and aptitudes, including a talent for working with children; organizational, administrative, and record-keeping abilities; research and communication skills; the power to influence, motivate, and train others; patience; and creativity. Workers in other occupations requiring some of these aptitudes include college and university faculty, counselors, education administrators, employment interviewers, librarians, preschool workers, public relations specialists, sales representatives, social workers, and trainers and employee development specialists.

College and University

College and university faculty function both as teachers and researchers. They communicate information and ideas. Related occupations include elementary and secondary school teachers, librarians, writers, consultants, lobbyists, trainers and employee development specialists, and policy analysts.

Faculty research activities often are similar to those of scientists, project managers, and administrators in industry, government, and nonprofit research organizations.

PROFESSIONAL ASSOCIATIONS

K-12

Information on teachers' unions and education-related issues may be obtained from the following two organizations:

American Federation of Teachers
555 New Jersey Ave. NW
Washington, DC 20001
E-mail: online@aft.org
www.aft.org

National Education Association
1201 16th St. NW
Washington, DC 20036
www.nea.org

For information on national teacher certification, contact:

National Board for Professional Teaching Standards
26555 Evergreen Rd., Ste. 400
Southfield, MI 48076
www.nbpts.org

A list of institutions with accredited teacher education programs can be obtained from:

National Council for Accreditation of Teacher Education
2010 Massachusetts Ave. NW, Ste. 500
Washington, DC 20036
www.ncate.org

For information on becoming a teacher, alternative routes to certification, and teacher education programs, contact:

ERIC Clearinghouse on Teacher Education
1307 New York Ave. NW
Washington, DC 20005-4701
www.ericsp.org

College and University

American Association of Community Colleges
One Dupont Circle NW, Ste. 410
Washington, DC 20036
www.aacc.nche.edu

American Association of University Professors (AAUP)
1012 Fourteenth Street NW, Ste. 500
Washington, DC 20005-3465
E-mail: aaup@aaup.org
www.aaup.org

CHAPTER ELEVEN

PATH 2:
CORPORATE COMMUNICATIONS

E very day we are bombarded with words, messages, and information—oral, written, televised, transmitted, faxed, or phoned. We are informed, kept abreast, persuaded, influenced, motivated, directed, led, counseled, helped, entertained, and, sometimes, annoyed by all the communication with which we are confronted.

But there's no escaping it. Whether in school, at work, or on the home-front, we are constantly receiving and exchanging information. Professors strive to stimulate their students; bosses hope to keep their employees motivated and productive; our mailboxes are crammed full of notices, advertisements, and all sorts of enticements to buy or act; the telephone, television, radio, newspapers, books, and magazines all vie for our attention.

It's been reported that we spend 39 percent of all of the available hours within an entire year devoted to watching television, reading, and talking on the telephone. If we discount the time we sleep, we spend 58 percent of our waking hours engaged in these media-oriented activities.

Although many Americans might resent the constant intrusion, to liberal arts majors it's a godsend. Such an all-pervasive focus on communication and information means unlimited opportunities for finding exciting and challenging work.

The information industry outranks any other and in the last four decades has become the central nucleus of the United States economy and its labor force. More workers are now employed in some facet of the information industry than in any other sector. In fact, more than 50 percent of the country's workforce earns its living dealing with information.

DEFINITION OF THE CAREER PATH

If you take the simplest definition of communications as "getting the word out," the corporate community has one of the largest uses of this activity. Some sectors need to get the message out in-house, through newsletters, memos, position papers, letters from the president, corporate training, seminars, and workshops; other sectors need to get the message out to the public or to consumers, through conventions, advertisements, publicity campaigns, community relations, or media contacts.

The process of getting the word out can use the skills of just one person or employ teams of ten, fifty, or a hundred professionals. Their job titles and the roles they play are as varied as the messages they are striving to convey.

Employers, in a trend back to hiring patterns of two or three decades ago, are now looking for graduates with liberal arts backgrounds. They are shunning individuals with technical or job-specific training in favor of those who show themselves to be competent communicators, both in person and on paper. The results of a survey canvassing CEOs based in New York point to the "ability to express ideas verbally" as the most important criteria used to screen and evaluate job candidates. The survey, (conducted by Silverstone, Greenbaum, and MacGregor and presented in their unpublished paper, "The Preferred College Graduate as Seen by the N.Y. Business Community") concluded that "they [CEO's] don't seem to want 'salesmen,' business 'intellectuals,' or 'ready-made' business executives (with an M.B.A. in hand). They do want team players who can express themselves with substance in ideas and thoughts."

These days, this response from the business community can be transferred to just about any field.

The Speech Communication Association has identified the following diverse areas of specialization typically offered in college and university communications departments:

- Advertising

- Education

- Family communication

- Forensics, argumentation, and debate

- Health communication

- Information sciences and human information systems

- Instructional development
- International and intercultural communication
- Interpersonal and small group interaction
- Interpretation and performance studies
- Journalism
- Legal communication
- Mass communication
- Media and communication technologies and policy
- Organizational communication
- Political communication
- Public relations
- Radio, television, and film
- Rhetorical and communication theory
- Speech and language sciences
- Theater

The ideal communications specialist might, in actuality, be a generalist. Today's liberal arts majors learn a wide range of skills with just as wide a range of applications. But a variety of studies shows that the most important skill is still the ability to communicate effectively.

With an understanding of how to penetrate public awareness and mold and respond public opinion, communications can be public relations. With the knowledge of how to reach and influence consumers, communications can be advertising or publicity and promotion. Through the techniques of writing and editing, communications can be journalism. With problem-solving and group management skills, communications can be corporate troubleshooting or training.

POSSIBLE JOB TITLES

The following list has been drawn up to give you an idea of the scope of jobs available in the corporate world. There is much overlap, however, across occupations and job settings. For example, job titles within the field of pub-

lic relations will also be found in health communications, and ,
exist in a corporate setting also find a home within advertising
marketing firms.

For ease in locating particular job titles, the list has been arranged alphabetically. However, this list is by no means exhaustive. During your job
search, you can use this list as a reference, adding to it as you come across
notices for jobs that mention related skills.

Alumni relations coordinator	Group/regional manager
Business development manager	Industrial public relations executive
Civic affairs representative	Intercultural communications specialist
Communications consultant	Intercultural communicator
Communications specialist	Interpersonal communicator
Community affairs coordinator	Investor relations director
Community relations specialist	Management supervisor
Consumer affairs specialist	Patient advocate
Copyeditor	Press secretary
Copywriter	Promotional campaign developer
Corporate communications director	Public information officer
Corporate communicator	Public relations assistant
Director of development	Public relations manager
Editor	Public relations writer
Educational affairs director	Research assistant
Employee publications specialist	Researcher
Event coordinator	Spokesperson
Fundraiser	Staff writer
Government relations	Volunteer coordinator

Modern public relations embraces the following job titles:

- Consultant
- Corporate communicator
- Investor relations specialist
- Public information officer
- Intercultural communicator

- Community liaison
- Government mediator
- Spokesperson
- Media coordinator
- Corporate trainer

What follows is an actual job advertisement for an experienced corporate
communicator.

SENIOR EMPLOYEE: COMMUNICATIONS SPECIALIST

_____, named one of America's ten best employers, is seeking a well-rounded corporate communicator for its_____office. The qualified applicant will be able to plan communication strategies, lead a writing team, edit/write for nationally recognized publications, and serve internal clients. Required is a degree in communications, journalism, or another related liberal arts field and five to ten years corporate agency/newspaper experience to include heavy business writing. Must possess excellent skills in production and project management, communication planning, editing, writing, and interpersonal and client relations. Experience in managing print budgets and desktop publishing would be preferred.

_____offers excellent benefits, competitive salary, and a retirement plan. Salary history and resume should be mailed to . . .

POSSIBLE EMPLOYERS

The International Association of Business Communicators (IABC) conducted a survey of its more than 12,000 members to determine the range of industries and types of businesses or organizations in which member communications professionals were employed. The majority, 40.51 percent, reported working for corporations. Other settings included the following:

Nonprofit associations	12.72%
Consulting firms, communications	8.06%
Self-employed/freelance	5.62%
Utility companies	4.60%
Educational institutions	4.56%
Government/military	4.34%
Consulting firms, management	3.46%
Writing/editing firms	1.15%
State-owned corporations	.99%
Labor unions	.14%
Other	13.85%

The specific industries employing communications professionals included:

Advertising	1.72%	Insurance	5.63%
Aerospace	1.31%	Manufacturing	5.54%
Agriculture	.67%	Medical/health	8.44%
Audiovisual	.70%	Metals/mining	.61%
Automotive	.71%	Petroleum	1.60%
Chemical	1.25%	Pharmaceutical	1.27%
Computers	2.89%	Photography	.37%
Construction	.29%	Professional services	3.27%
Design	1.34%	Public relations	8.06%
Education	5.02%	Publishing	1.99%
Engineering	1.35%	Real estate	.67%
Finance/banking	6.14%	Retail sales	1.23%
Food/beverage	1.82%	Transportation	1.86%
Graphic arts/ printing	1.39%	Utilities (communications)	4.58%
Hotel/lodging	.44%	Other	24.07%

Though the distribution appears to be fairly evenly spread among these specific industries, the medical/health and public relations fields were out in front with an 8.44 and 8.06 percentage.

Corporations

Many large corporations place communication specialists within their personnel departments or human resources programs. Some corporations also have specific communications departments. In addition, communications specialists are commonly found within various other departments such as advertising, publications, public relations, research and development, and sales.

Private Consulting Firms

More and more, private consulting firms are fulfilling a need for those corporations that do not choose, whether because of size or budget, to hire a permanent staff of corporate communicators, trainers, or public relations professionals.

Private consulting firms work with clients on a fee-for-service basis or on a retainer. As a need or problem arises, a corporation can bring in a consulting firm, which will first conduct a needs analysis, then submit a written proposal covering how they plan to proceed and how much it will cost.

Consultants employed by a firm can work on a straight salary basis or salary plus commission.

Private Public Relations Firms

The practice of public relations is a relatively young field, formally founded less than one hundred years ago. Early definitions emphasized public relations as press agentry and publicity. As the profession evolved, those aspects became less the work of the PR professional, falling more into the realm of publicists and advertising and marketing professionals.

Today, public relations is a huge umbrella under which a variety of job titles and professional responsibilities exist. The number of professionals doing public relations work is estimated to be as high as 159,000. Public relations professionals work in every sector, from the corporate world to the sporting world, from government departments to health and medical facilities. And though the settings might vary, their main responsibility usually doesn't. The backbone of every PR professional's job description is his or her role as communicator.

The public relations professional is concerned with how the company is perceived by the various publics. He or she can also help shape a company and the way it performs. The PR practitioner, by research and evaluation, finds out the expectations and concerns of the various publics and reports back to the organization on his or her findings. A good public relations program needs the support of the organization and the publics it is involved with.

Public relations firms function much the way private consulting firms do. They take on a variety of different clients—from large corporations to church groups or government bodies—assess their needs, propose a plan of action, and often implement that plan.

Most PR firms are located in major cities and have a staff size ranging from fewer than a dozen workers to those with one thousand or more. Some offices are generalists, other specialize in specific areas such as government relations, employee communications, or educational and social programs.

Self-Employed or Freelancers

Self-employed or freelance communications consultants work similarly to their counterparts employed by private firms. The advantage is that the money to be made goes directly to the consultant and not into the firm's coffer; the disadvantage is that the independent consultant has to cover all of his or her own expenses and build up a client base from scratch.

Foreign Service

The foreign service is a natural choice for liberal arts majors interested in business and intercultural communications. The foreign service divides the different specialty areas into the following:

Administration. Administrative personnel at overseas posts are responsible for hiring foreign national workers, providing office and residential space, assuring reliable communications with the District of Columbia, supervising computer systems, and providing security for the post's personnel and property.

Consular Services. Consular workers must be excellent communicators and often combine the skills of lawyers, judges, investigators, and social workers. Their duties range from issuing passports and visas to finding a lost child or helping a traveler in trouble.

Economic Officers. Economic officers maintain contact with key business and financial leaders in the host country and report to the District of Columbia on the local economic conditions and their impact on American trade and investment policies. They are concerned with issues such as commercial aviation safety, fishing rights, and international banking.

Political Affairs. Those working in political affairs analyze and report on the political views of the host country. They make contact with labor unions, humanitarian organizations, educators, and cultural leaders.

Information and Cultural Affairs. As part of the foreign service, the United States Information Agency (USIA) promotes U.S. cultural, informational, and public diplomacy programs. An information officer might develop a library open to the public, meet with the press, and oversee English language training programs for the host country.

Commercial and Business Services. In this division, a foreign service officer identifies overseas business connections for American exporters and investors, conducts market research for the success of U.S. products, and organizes trade shows and other promotional events.

Although many foreign service officers are skilled in political science and history, these days candidates are expected to have knowledge in specialized fields such as communications, the environment, computer science, and trade.

Government Agencies

Some readers may not initially associate working for government agencies with corporate communications. In actuality, the services the government needs are similar, if not identical to, those utilized in the business world. Internal employee relations and external public relations are concerns as important in the public sector as they are in the private sector. Although the job titles might vary—public information officer rather than PR specialist—the services they perform are the same.

In addition to the foreign service, scores of government agencies and departments on local, state, and federal levels use the services of professional communicators.

Military

The military use both civilian and noncivilian personnel in a variety of communications activities, from promotion and recruitment to public information and intelligence.

Public information officers (PIOs) will deal with the community, the media, and with internal communications, usually in the form of base newsletters or other military publications. Intelligence agencies, both at home and abroad, employ communications specialists expert in gathering data and channeling it to the appropriate offices.

A stint in military communications is a career in itself or an excellent stepping stone to the corporate world.

Utilities

Utility companies no longer sit quietly in the background going about their business of providing power. Environmentalists (and the PR professionals who work for them) have raised public awareness to the dangers of potential and existing environmental hazards. Public relations professionals employed by utilities keep communication open, instituting programs to work with the community, and documenting and explaining their impact on the environment.

Communications majors in this field need to be skilled negotiators, as comfortable with a computer as a microphone.

Labor Unions

Labor unions recognize the importance of building support for their programs and positions. Major unions and their affiliates operate news and speaker bureaus; publish a variety of newsletters, reports, brochures, and other materials; and offer educational programs to civic groups and schools.

A liberal arts major can find a satisfying lifelong career in this setting.

Nonprofit Associations

The term "nonprofit" is a tax status, exempting some organizations from partial or complete tax payments; it never was intended to mean that a profit couldn't be made. Having said that, it is true that the nonprofit sector often has less money (and more need for it) than the private, profit-making sector. While salaries in these settings might be lower, the work experience can be equally, if not more, rewarding than in the corporate world.

Nonprofit associations number in the hundreds of thousands nationwide. Under this umbrella fall charitable organizations, private foundations, professional associations, and some educational institutions.

Charitable groups such as Easter Seals, the American Red Cross, the American Cancer Society, Big Brothers/Big Sisters, the United Way, YMCA and YWCA, Boy Scouts of America, the American Heart Association, and others all have needs for employees with communications backgrounds.

And for every profession, there is at least one professional association, a membership-supported organization joining together groups of people with common interests and career goals. While most new graduates look upon professional associations as a place to get career support and perhaps help finding a job, communications majors realize that this setting can be the ultimate career goal in itself.

Specialist communicators working for charitable organizations and professional associations perform much the same functions as their counterparts in the corporate world. There are promotional campaigns to be developed, media contacts to be made, and employee and community relations to be maintained. Added to this are the activities of fund-raising and membership drives.

Growth in this sector seems to be on the uprise and more and more rewarding opportunities are becoming available.

Hospitals and Medical Centers

The health care industry—and it is an industry—has a growing need for communications specialists in much the same capacity as needed in the corporate world. With changes in national health care policies, the need for specialists in public relations, community affairs, marketing, and other related areas is on the increase.

Possible settings include:

- Government-funded agencies (such as the Center for Disease Control)

- Health advertising agencies

- Hospitals (both private and community-based)

- Outpatient medical centers

- Pharmaceutical companies

- Professional schools of medicine

- Rehabilitation clinics

- Residential treatment facilities

- Volunteer health organizations

Job titles and responsibilities are similar to those in the corporate world. The main skill being sought is the ability to communicate effectively.

Higher Education

Universities, colleges, and other educational institutions have a great need for liberal arts majors with a variety of backgrounds. Here are just a few departments in which you would be qualified to work:

1. Admissions—communicating the highlights of the institution to attract new students.

2. Alumni relations—maintaining contact with alumni for the purpose of fundraising and community relations.

3. Career placement/service centers—establishing contact with potential employees and providing career counseling and guidance to students.

4. Community affairs/relations—ensuring open communication and cooperation between the institution and neighboring community, and developing outreach programs providing adult and continuing education programs.

5. Cooperative education—maintaining contact with the business community and other fields for student job placement.

6. Development—continuing the ongoing process of fundraising, targeting other groups in addition to alumni.

7. International student affairs—providing orientation, counseling, and help with immigration procedures to foreign students.

8. Publications—working with campus newspapers, magazines, college catalogs, yearbooks, and other print needs of the institution.

WORKING CONDITIONS

Corporations, public relations firms, and most of the possible employers explored in this chapter are usually busy, hectic places. There are deadlines to meet, phones ringing, visitors arriving, and work schedules being interrupted frequently. Public relations people and all the other corporate communicators put in long, sometimes irregular hours. Once a project is under way or a crisis needs to be resolved, the work seldom stops until the job is done.

Employees of nonprofit corporations, associations, and charitable organizations report a calmer work atmosphere, but the pressure is on there, too. These organizations have the same need for effective communicators and a lot less money to accomplish their goals.

Workloads in the different settings will be varied, too. You could be hired to conduct a week's workshop on effective speaking and listening skills designed particularly for the phone company, and when you're finished, there's the company report to work on, letters to write, phone calls to return, meetings to attend, and research to be done. The pace can be exhilarating and challenging to some, stress-producing to others.

TRAINING AND QUALIFICATIONS

For any of the fields covered in this chapter, a bachelor's degree in communications, English, or other related liberal arts major provides a good entry. However, while some positions such as assistant/junior copywriters don't require a four-year degree, as competition for jobs increase, B.A. or even master's degree holders will have an edge. But a degree is not the only criterion an employer sets. The following skills have been identified in an IABC survey as those most commonly used by its membership:

Audience research	Magazine layout
Audiovisual production	Management skills
Budgeting/cost control	Media contact
Communication planning	Newsletter editing
Communication theory	News writing
Event planning	Personnel supervision
Feature writing	Photography
Feedback system design	Print production
Film production	Proposal writing
Government relations	Scriptwriting
Graphic design	Speakers bureaus
Identity programs	Speech writing
Investor relations	Time management

In addition, these other skills and personal qualities become important depending upon the area of business communications you choose to pursue.

The more skills you are able to acquire or nurture, the better your chances of securing the type of job you are seeking.

Bilingual or multilingual abilities	Initiative
Compassion	Integrity
Creativity	Intelligence
Cross-cultural sensitivity	Interpersonal skills
Detail-oriented skills	Organizational skills
Drive	Research skills
Empathy	Verbal skills
Judgment	Writing skills

Some qualities people are born with; others can be learned. Future communications specialists can start while in college. In addition to courses required for the major, a host of other classes will enrich your skill bank and enhance your resume. These days, with more and more businesses and organizations entering the international marketplace, being fluent in one or more foreign languages can work only in your favor. Enroll in classes in economics, finance, management, sociology, psychology, and public speaking.

Get as much practical hands-on experience as you can while in college. Work for the student newspaper or on the yearbook staff. Help organize student activities, volunteer for the speakers bureau, or become a peer counselor. Participate in work-study or cooperative education programs and take advantage of any internships or practicums you are able to line up, even if it means extending your graduation date a semester.

Most university programs cooperate with local, national, and sometimes international businesses to place students in hands-on internships. If your university does not have access to these kinds of placements, you can often arrange them on your own. A phone call or a letter to the right company could be all it takes to open the door to a rewarding experience.

Many successful communications specialists also have a record of volunteer service with civic groups and charities. For those seeking intercultural experiences, find summer employment overseas or after graduation do a stint in the Peace Corps. Teaching English as a foreign language overseas is a rewarding way to acquire cross-cultural experience. While on campus, interact with the international student office or volunteer in the English as a second language (ESL) program. Intercultural sensitivity and experience is difficult to gain just in the classroom.

While the job market is competitive, it is open to newcomers, especially to those who have shown initiative in preparing themselves as much as possible.

CAREER OUTLOOK

Businesses and other organizations spend more than $1 billion dollars annually to communicate with employees or members, with even more money going to fund communication with external audiences such as customers, community residents, alumni, opinion leaders, and the public at large.

According to predictions made in the *Occupational Outlook Handbook* (published by the U.S. Department of Labor, Bureau of Labor Statistics), employment of corporate communications managers is expected to increase faster than the average for all occupations through the year 2008. Employment in the field for public relations specialists other than managers is expected to increase fast or faster than the average for all jobs through the year 2008.

Employment in public relations firms is expected to grow more than in any other setting as corporations, trying to keep costs down, hire contractors to provide PR services rather than support full-time staff.

Keen competition for these jobs, however, will likely continue among recent college graduates with degrees in communications and related fields because the number of applicants is expected to exceed the number of job openings.

EARNINGS

According to a recent salary survey conducted by the Public Relations Society of America, the overall median salary in public relations is about $53,000 per year. Salaries in public relations range from less than $22,800 to more than $142,000. There is little difference among the median salaries for account executives in public relations firms, corporations, government, health care, or nonprofit organizations—all ranged from $32,000 to $34,000.

Median annual earnings in the industries employing the largest numbers of public relations specialists are:

General managers and top executives	$94,702
Advertising, marketing, promotions, public relations, and sales managers	$57,300
Federal government	$56,700
Management and public relations	$35,100
Advertising supervisors	$33,644
Advertising sales agents	$32,614
State government, except education and hospitals	$32,100
Colleges and universities	$30,600

Median annual earnings in the industries employing the largest number of advertising, marketing, promotions, public relations, and sales managers are as follows:

Professional and commercial equipment	$69,800
Telephone communications	$64,100
Computer and data processing services	$60,800

Advertising $54,300

Management and public relations $51,100

According to a recent National Association of Colleges and Employers survey, starting salaries for new marketing major graduates average about $31,900; advertising majors, about $26,600.

Salary levels vary substantially depending upon the level of managerial responsibility, length of service, education, firm size, location, and industry. For example, manufacturing firms usually pay advertising, marketing, and public relations managers higher salaries than nonmanufacturing firms do. For sales managers, the size of their sales territory is another important determinant of salary. Many managers earn bonuses equal to 10 percent or more of their salaries.

The Public Relations Society of America conducts an annual salary survey, which can be ordered at their website www.prsa.org/salserv/enterplate.html for $50.

STRATEGIES FOR FINDING THE JOBS

There are an estimated 3.6 million active corporations in the United States. While not every one of them provides a setting in which communications major would prefer to work, enough do.

Scan the Help-Wanted Ads

The traditional job-hunting method—reviewing help-wanted ads—seldom reaps rewards for the new, inexperienced grad. Most job advertisements are for specialists with time and experience under their belts, or for pre-entry-level, clerical jobs that might not offer enough exposure to lead to promotion. However, the want ads should not be ignored. The plum job you are perfect for could suddenly appear in next Sunday's paper.

Knock on Doors

Knocking on doors is what experts advise. Find the firm for which you would like to work and become a familiar face in the personnel department or front reception area.

Join Professional Associations

Professional associations often maintain job banks. The journals and newsletters they publish usually feature job advertisements. The regional or national conferences they hold usually have job clearinghouses with recruiters in attendance.

Find a Mentor

Your alumni association can put you in touch with professionals who might be able to give you leads.

Check with Your College Department

Don't forget to inquire at your communications department office. It is not unusual for a corporation to call a university and ask for a list of graduating seniors. The jobs they are seeking to fill might also be announced on department bulletin boards.

Register with Your College Placement Office

College placement offices or college career service centers can also provide good leads for your job search. While some employers contact individual departments directly, others send their job openings to the placement office or career counselor.

RELATED OCCUPATIONS

The skills that liberal arts majors possess are valued in a number of related professions. The following is a small sampling of occupations that draw on similar skills to a greater or lesser degree.

Biocommunications	In-house legal counsel
Development specialist	Lobbyist
Financial manager	Medical writer
Health science communications	Technical writer
Industrial psychologist	Volunteer coordinator

HELP IN LOCATING EMPLOYERS

Search the Internet! There are almost countless websites that help locate job opportunities. In particular, check out the Careers in Public Relations page produced by the Public Relations Society of America. In addition to an overview of public relations careers, you'll find places to post your resume or classified ad. The page also provides links to PRSA chapter job search placement services. www.prsa.org/resume2.html.

Visit the library! There are directories galore that list professional associations, public relations firms, and corporations by industry. Make friends with your reference librarian and bring plenty of change for the copy machine.

The following contacts, journals, and directories only begin to scratch the surface:

Communication World
International Association of Business Communicators
One Hallidie Plaza, Ste. 600
San Francisco, CA 94102
www.iabc.com/homepage.htm

Encyclopedia of Associations
Gale Research, Inc.
P.O. Box 33477
Detroit, MI 48232

Foreign Service Recruitment Officer
Office of Personnel
United States Information Agency (USIA)
301 4th St. SW
Washington, DC 20547

O'Dwyer's Directory of Corporate Communications
O'Dwyer's Directory of Public Relations Firms
J.R. O'Dwyer Company, Inc.
271 Madison Ave.
New York, NY 10016

Investor Relations Newsletter
Enterprise Publications
20 N. Wacker Dr.
Chicago, IL 60606

Journal of Communication
Annenberg School Press
P.O. Box 13358
Philadelphia, PA 19101

Peace Corps Recruiting Office
1111 20th St. NW
Washington, D.C. 20526

PR Reporter
P.O. Box 600
Exeter, NH 03833

Public Relations Journal
Public Relations Career Opportunities
Public Relations Society of America
33 Irving Pl.
New York, NY 10003
www.prsa.org

Public Relations News
127 E. 80th St.
New York, NY 10021

Public Relations Quarterly
44 W. Market St.
Rhinebeck, NY 12572

Public Relations Review
7338 Baltimore Blvd., #101A
College Park, MD 20740

Speechwriter's Newsletter
Ragan Communications
407 S. Dearborn St.
Chicago, IL 60605

Training
50 S. 9th St.
Minneapolis, MN 55402

PROFESSIONAL ASSOCIATIONS

A glance through the list will show the variety of professional associations active in the world of business communications. Most offer booklets and pamphlets free of charge or for a nominal one or two dollar charge. Many of the associations listed below provide job placement services and publish career-oriented journals and magazines. Visit their websites or drop them an E-mail or note for more information.

American Advertising Federation
Education Services Department
1101 Vermont Ave. NW, Ste. 500
Washington, DC 20005
www.aaf.org
Services: training, internships, conferences, awards, competitions

American Association of Advertising Agencies
405 Lexington Ave.
New York, NY 10174-1801
www.aaaa.org
Services: job locating, conferences, training

American Business Association
292 Madison Ave., 7th Fl.
New York, NY 10017
Services: financial, publications

American Business Women's Association
9100 Ward Pkwy.
P.O. Box 8728
Kansas City, MO 64114-0728
E-mail: abwa@abwa.org
www.abwahq.org
Services: conferences, awards

American Society of Hospital Marketing and Public Relations
840 N. Lake Shore Dr.
Chicago, IL 60611
Services: annual conference, publications

American Society for Training and Development
Box 1443 1640 King St.
Alexandria, VA 22313
www.astd.org
Services: job bank, career info, training, seminars, workshops, publications

Associated Business Writers of America
1450 S. Havana, Ste. 424
Aurora, CO 80012
Services: publications

Association for Business Communication
Box G-1326 Baruch College
17 Lexington Ave.
New York, NY 10010
www.theabc.org
Services: publications, conventions, awards

The Association for Women in Communications
780 Ritchie Hwy., Ste. 28S
Severna Park, MD 21146
www.womcom.org
Services: publications, annual conference, placement service, career information

Health Sciences Communications Association
One Wedgewood Dr., Ste. 28
Jewett City, CT 06351-2428
E-mail: hesca@hesca.org
www.hesca.org
Services: annual conference, local and regional meetings, publications, job placement services

Institute for Public Relations
Research and Education
University of Florida
P.O. Box 118400
Gainesville, FL 32611-8400
www.instituteforpr.com
Services: research, annual lectures, competitions, publications

International Association of Business Communicators (IABC)
One Hallidie Plaza, Ste. 600
San Francisco, CA 94102
E-mail: service_centre@iabc.com
www.iabc.com/homepage.htm
Services: career and job postings, publications, conferences

International Communication Association (ICA)
P.O. Box 9589
Austin, TX 78766 USA
E-mail: ica@icahdq.org
www.icahdq.org
Services: conferences, publications

International Labor Communications Association
815 16th St. NW, Rm. 509
Washington, DC 20006
Services: publications

The International Listening Association
E-mail: ilistening@aol.com
www.listen.org
Services: conventions, publications

National Business Association
P.O. Box 700728
Dallas, TX 75370
www.nationalbusiness.org
Services: publications, scholarships

National Communication Association (NCA)
1765 N. St. NW
Washington, DC 20036
www.natcom.org
Services: annual convention, conferences, publications, awards, job placement

National Council for Marketing and Public Relations
4602 W. 21st St.
Greely, CO 80634
www.ncmpr.org
Services: annual conference, publications

Public Relations Society of America (PRSA)
33 Irving Pl.
New York, NY 10003-2376
E-mail: hq@prsa.org
www.prsa.org
Services: training, publications, job listings (in journal)

Religious Communication Association
Weber State University
3750 Harrison Blvd.
Ogden, UT 84408
http://gcc.bradley.edu/com/faculty/lamoureux/rsca/index.html
Services: conferences, workshops, seminars, publications

Sales and Marketing Executives International
P.O. Box 1390
Sumas, WA 98295-1390 USA
www.smei.org
Services: job listings, conferences, training, publications, business services

CHAPTER TWELVE

PATH 3: MEDIA

he United States supports the largest mass media system of any country in the world, which in turn has generated millions of jobs for us. The choices for liberal arts majors in search of great jobs could almost be daunting if it weren't so exciting.

The field of journalism is perhaps the most traditional path open to English and communications majors within liberal arts or general studies programs. No longer does the "fourth estate" refer to only newspapers. It includes syndicates and wire services, television and radio, and consumer and trade publications. And while these outlets provide a home for journalists to report and interpret the news, they also furnish niches for creative writers with a vast array of specialties, as well as editors, agents, entertainers, broadcasters, producers, photographers, computer experts, and other important front-line and support positions.

DEFINITION OF THE CAREER PATH

Because there is such a vast range of jobs within the media, and many of those same positions are found in several different outlets, it is more efficient here to examine each outlet as its own career path. While the role of editor, for example, will vary to some degree, depending upon the setting, many of the same functions and skills are used in newspapers as well as magazines. The definitive question is not whether to become an editor, but in which milieu will the future editor be most satisfied working.

Similarly, a liberal arts major with hopes of becoming a writer will benefit from knowing the types of assignments and working conditions involved at the different job settings or whether a career as a freelancer is a viable alternative.

For every interest a liberal arts major has, there is a job and a setting to satisfy it.

POSSIBLE JOB TITLES

Job titles within the media cover the gamut of writers, editors, entertainers, production people, and a host of other professionals working in departments not covered in this chapter. This list is not meant to be exhaustive. You will

---

PRINT MEDIA

Acquisitions editor	Freelance editor
Art director	Freelance writer
Assignment editor	Internal publications editor
Assistant editor	Investigative reporter
Associate editor	Journalist
Author	Literary agent
Book editor	Managing editor
Bureau chief	News editor
Bureau reporter	Newspaper editor
City editor	News writer
Columnist	Photojournalist
Contracts Assistant	President
Copyeditor	Production editor
Copywriter	Publisher
Correspondent	Reporter
Critic	Researcher
Desk assistant	Section editor
Dramatic agent	Senior editor
Editor	Senior writer
Editorial assistant	Staff writer
Editorial writer	Story editor
Editor in chief	Stringer
Electronic publishing specialist	Syndicated columnist
Executive editor	Technical editor
External publications editor	Wire editor
Feature writer	Writer

RADIO AND TELEVISION

Announcer	News announcer
Associate news director	News director
Audiovisual manager/director	News editor
Audiovisual producer	News writer
Audiovisual technician	Operations manager
Audiovisual writer	Production assistant
Broadcast engineers	Production manager
Broadcast technicians	Production sound mixer
CAD Specialist	Program manager
Correspondent	Public services director
Director	Radio/TV traffic assistant
Disc jockey	Radio/TV traffic supervisor
Filmmaker	Scriptwriter
First assistant director	Station manager
Graphics coordinator	TV director
Media resource director	TV managing editor
Mixer	TV producer
Music director	TV production assistant
Music librarian	TV tape-film manager
Newscaster	Video specialist

find additional related job titles and descriptions in other chapters in this book; *The Dictionary of Occupational Titles* (U.S. Department of Labor) gives a comprehensive list with generic descriptions.

Newspapers

Current figures show that there are approximately 10,500 newspapers in the United States; 1,483 are dailies; about half are evening newspapers, and the remainder are weeklies. The number of major dailies has declined in recent years; there are only about 39 newspapers with a circulation of more than 250,000. Despite declining numbers, newspapers rank as the third largest industry in the United States and employ 450,000 people.

Newspapers are usually organized around the following departments: news, editorial, advertising, production, and circulation. All provide job opportunities for communications majors. For the purpose of this chapter, however, we will focus on the news and editorial sections.

The News Department. Within the news section we will examine careers for reporters and photojournalists.

Reporters. A job as a reporter is viewed as a glamorous and exciting Clark Kent/Lois Lane type of existence and probably attracts more applicants than any other spot on a newspaper staff. As a result, competition is stiff; reporters make up less than one fourth of a newspaper's roster.

Reporting work is challenging and fast paced with the pressures of deadlines and space allotments always looming overhead. For those who like to be one step ahead of the general public in knowing what's going on, it's the ideal job.

Whatever the size or location of the newspaper, the job of a reporter is to cover local, state, national, and international events and put all this news together to keep the reading public informed. News reporters could be assigned to a variety of stories, from covering a major world event, monitoring the actions of public figures, or writing about a current political campaign.

Photojournalists. Photojournalism is the telling of a story through pictures. And though it's a form of journalism in which photographs dominate over written copy, photojournalists need to have a strong journalism background, too. To accurately report the news, whether through photographs or copy, you need to be aware of what's happening in the world and why.

Being a jack-of-all-trades is the main requirement. Most photojournalists who work for both major and minor newspapers are expected to cover the exciting as well as the tame. The gamut runs from food to fashion, to spot news, to sports, to a wide range of human interest features.

The Editorial Department. The editorial sections within newspapers vary with size and location, but most include at least some, if not all of, the following sections:

Art	Finance
Books	Food
Business	Foreign affairs
Consumer affairs	Health
Court system	International news
Crime desk	Lifestyles/features
Education	Local news
Entertainment	National news
Fashion	Religion

Science	State news
Social events	Travel
Sports	Weather

Within the editorial department we will look at the key positions of staff writers and section editors.

Staff Writers. Staff or feature writers function in much the same way as news reporters but are generally assigned a regular "beat," such as health and medicine, sports, travel, or consumer affairs. Working in these specialized fields, staff writers keep the public informed about important trends or breakthroughs in a variety of areas.

Contrary to some misconceptions, feature writers are not assigned to only fluff pieces. While a fashion writer might not do in depth investigative pieces, a health and medicine writer can. Nancy McVicar, for example, is a senior writer at the *Sun-Sentinel*, a newspaper in Fort Lauderdale, Florida with a circulation of about one million. She works for the lifestyle section, which has a health page every Thursday and her work has been nominated for the Pulitzer Prize seven times. Several of her stories have won other prestigious national awards.

McVicar was the first to break the story "Are Your Cellular Telephones Safe?" She produced two or three articles on the topic, which went out over the wire and also ended up on the television programs "20/20" and "60 Minutes." The GAO (The General Accounting Office of the U.S. Government, which is also the investigative arm of Congress) was asked to do an in-depth report on whether or not cellular phones are safe, based on the stories she wrote.

Writers in every section of a newspaper can find a way to make an impact.

Section Editors. A job as a section editor is considered by many to be a plum position. Although there are exceptions, section editors have usually paid their dues as reporters or staff writers and only after a few year's of experience would be eligible for consideration.

The duties involved depend in part on the section, but there are many responsibilities in common. Editors write articles or supervise the work of staff writers, making assignments, reviewing copy, and making sure attention is paid to space requirements. They also attend editorial meetings and correspond with freelance writers.

Many perks are associated with some of the sections; travel writers get to travel, book editors get free books in the mail to read and review, sports editors get to go to a lot of the games, food editors get to eat, society page editors get invited to a myriad of social events, and so on.

Working Conditions. Reporters and photojournalists always have deadlines hanging over their heads. Unlike fiction writers, who can work at their own pace, reporters do not have the luxury of waiting for their creative juices to begin to flow. A news reporter has to file a story, or maybe even two, every day by a certain time. A staff writer or section editor with a weekly column has more leeway, but still, everything must be in on time to go to press.

Reporters gather information by visiting the scene, interviewing people, following leads and news tips, and examining documents. While some reporters might rely on their memory, most take notes or use a tape recorder while collecting facts. Back in the office, they organize their material, decide what the focus or emphasis should be, and then write their stories, generally using a computer. Because of deadlines, while away from the office, many reporters use portable computers to file the story, which is then sent by telephone modem directly to the newspaper's computer system.

Some newspapers have modern, state-of-the-art equipment; others do not have the financing they need to update. A reporter could work in a comfortable, private office, or in a room filled with the noise of computer printers or coworkers talking on the telephone.

Working hours vary. Some writers and editors could work Monday through Friday, nine to five, while others cover evenings, nights, and weekends. On some occasions, reporters work longer than normal hours to cover an important ongoing story or to follow late-breaking developments.

Although some desk work is involved, newspaper reporting is definitely not a desk job. Reporters need excellent interviewing and research skills, and the ability to juggle several assignments at once. Computer and typing skills are very important, too.

A reporter also must know how to "write tight." While feature writers can be more creative, news reporters must make sure they get all the facts in within a certain amount of space. The editor might allocate only a column inch or two for your story, leaving room for just the who, what, when, where, why, and how.

Training and Qualifications. A college degree is a must; most employers prefer a B.A. in journalism or communications, while others would accept a degree in a related field such as political science or English.

The courses you should take in college should include introductory mass media, basic reporting and copy editing, history of journalism, and press law and ethics.

Previous work on a school paper or an internship at a newspaper will help to enhance your resume. Experience as a stringer—a part-time reporter who is paid only for stories printed—is also helpful.

Photojournalism is a highly competitive field, so having a good portfolio is very important. Most photojournalists have at least a bachelor's degree, many, especially those with management inclinations, have a master's.

Career Outlook. Overall employment of news analysts, reporters, and correspondents is expected to grow little through the year 2008, the result of mergers, consolidations, and closures of newspapers; decreased circulation; increased expenses; and a decline in advertising profits. In spite of little change in overall employment, some job growth is expected in radio and television stations, whereas more rapid growth is expected in new media areas, such as on-line newspapers and magazines.

Competition will continue to be keen for jobs on large metropolitan newspapers, broadcast stations, and national magazines. Talented writers who can handle highly specialized scientific or technical subjects have an advantage. Also, more newspapers than before are hiring stringers and freelancers.

Most entry-level openings arise on small publications, as reporters and correspondents become editors or reporters on larger publications or leave the field. Small town and suburban newspapers will continue to offer the most opportunities for persons seeking to enter this field.

Turnover is relatively high in this occupation. Some find the work too stressful and hectic, or they do not like the lifestyle and transfer to other occupations. Journalism graduates have the background for work in closely related fields such as advertising and public relations, and many take jobs in these fields. Other graduates accept sales, managerial, or other nonmedia positions, because of the difficulty in finding media jobs.

The newspaper and broadcasting industries are sensitive to economic ups and downs, because these industries depend on advertising revenue. During recessions, few new reporters are hired; and some reporters lose their jobs.

Earnings. Salaries for news analysts (newscasters), reporters, and correspondents vary widely but, in general, are relatively high, except at small stations and small publications where salaries are often very low. Median annual earnings of news analysts are approximately $26,470. The middle 50 percent earn between $19,210 and $40,930. The lowest 10 percent earn less than $14,100 and the highest 10 percent earn more than $70,140. Median annual earnings of news analysts in radio and television broadcasting are about $28,500.

Median annual earnings of reporters and correspondents are about $23,400. The middle 50 percent earn between $17,500 and $35,600. The lowest 10 percent earn less than $12,900 and the highest 10 percent earn more than $55,100.

Median annual earnings for writers and editors, including technical writers, are about $36,480. The middle 50 percent earn between $27,030 and $49,380 a year. The lowest 10 percent earn less than $20,920 and the highest 10 percent earn more than $76,660. Median annual earnings in the industries employing the largest numbers of writers and editors of nontechnical material are as follows:

Advertising	$38,100
Periodicals	35,900
Books	35,200
Newspapers	28,500
Radio and television broadcasting	26,300

Magazines

Visit any bookstore or newsstand and you will see hundreds of magazines covering a variety of topics—from sports and cars to fashion and parenting. There are also many you won't see there, the hundreds of trade journals and magazines written for businesses, industries, and professional workers in as many different careers.

These publications all offer information on diverse subjects to their equally diverse readership. They are filled with articles and profiles, interviews and editorials, letters and advice, as well as pages and pages of advertisements.

Whether you work for a magazine full-time or as an independent freelancer, you will discover that there is no shortage of markets where you can find work or sell your articles.

Positions within magazines are very similar to those found in newspapers.

Freelance Writing

A freelance writer works independently, in rented office space or in a home office. Most freelance writers plan and write articles and columns on their own and actively seek out new markets in which to place them.

Staff writers for newspapers and magazines might have less freedom in what they choose to write, but they generally have more job security and always know when their next paycheck will arrive. Freelancers trade job security and regular pay for their independence.

Both freelancers and those permanently employed have to produce high quality work. They have editors to report to and deadlines to meet.

More and more magazines are open to working with freelancers these days. With budget cuts and staff layoffs, and because magazines don't have syndicated material to fall back on, it is generally less expensive to pay several different freelance writers by the piece, rather than employ a full-time staff writer or two.

Some freelancers are generalists; they will write about anything they think they can sell. Others are specialists, choosing to write only in a particular field such as travel, or health and medicine. Successful freelancers have a lot of market savvy, meaning they are familiar with all the different publications they could market their work to and know how to approach those publications.

Training. While many writers hone their writing craft in college, the business of freelancing is generally self-taught. There are, however, adult education classes throughout the country, as well as writers' associations, that can provide new freelancers with some guidance and marketing strategies.

Before starting, read as many magazines as you can, and in particular, those you would like to write for. It's never a good idea to send an article to a magazine you have never seen before. Familiarity with different magazines will also help you to come up with future article ideas.

Once you have decided what you want to write about, there are two ways you can proceed. You can write the entire article on spec, send it off to appropriate editors, and hope they like your topic. Or, you can write a query letter, a mini-proposal, to see if there is any interest in your idea first. Query letters will save you the time of writing articles you might have difficulty selling. Only once you're given a definite assignment do you then proceed.

You can find out about different magazines and the kind of material they prefer to publish in the market guides listed at the end of this chapter.

Earnings. Getting a check for an article can be rewarding, but sadly, for new freelancers, the checks might not come often enough and are not always large enough to live on.

While staff writers are paid a regular salary (though generally not a very high one), a freelancer gets paid only when he or she sells an article. Fees could range from as low as $5 to $1,000 or more, depending upon the publication. But even with a high-paying magazine, writers often have to wait until their story is published before they are paid. Because publishers work so far ahead, planning issues six months or more in advance, payment could be delayed from three months to a year or more.

To the freelancers' advantage, sometimes the same article can be sold to more than one magazine or newspaper. These resales help to increase income. You can also be paid additional money if you can provide your own photographs to illustrate your articles.

Freelance writers don't need a long, impressive resume to sell their first article. The writing will speak for itself.

Publishing Houses and Literary Agencies

The world of publishing is a busy and exciting place, filled with risks, surprises, and sometimes disappointments. Without the publishing world, writers would never see their words in print; there would be no magazines, newspapers, or books for the public to enjoy; no textbooks for students and teachers to work with; and no written sources for information on any subject.

Those in the publishing industry wield a great deal of power. They determine which books and stories will see print, and to some extent, help to shape the tastes of the reading public.

It's a competitive business, with financial concerns often determining which books will get published. Editors and agents have to be able to recognize good writing and know what topics are popular and what will sell.

For editors and agents, as well as writers, nothing is more exciting than seeing a book you worked on, whether as a writer, editor, or negotiator, finally see print and land in the bookstores. The hope is always there that the book will take off and find its way to the bestseller list and into the homes of thousands of readers. Then everyone is happy, from bookstore owners to the sales team and distributors.

But there are only ten to fifteen slots on the various bestseller lists, and with thousands of books published each year, the odds are against producing a "blockbuster."

Although some books have steady sales and can stay on the publishers' backlist for years, others don't do as well and can disappear from bookstore shelves after only a month or so.

Every book is a gamble; no one can ever predict what will happen. But successful editors and agents thrive on the excitement. In the publishing world, anything is possible.

Literary agents act as go-betweens for writers and editors. These days most of the big New York publishing houses refuse to consider manuscripts unless they are sent to them by an agent. Many publishers credit agents with the ability to screen out inappropriate submissions. An agent is expected to be familiar with the different kinds of books publishers prefer to take on.

An agent spends his or her time reading manuscripts, choosing which ones to work with, and then trying to sell them to publishers. Agents free a writer to concentrate on writing instead of marketing. The agent's job is to find the right house for his or her client's work and, once successful, to negotiate the best financial deal for the writer. Agents also handle film rights for feature or TV movies and foreign rights, selling books to publishers overseas.

How Publishing Houses Are Structured. A small press that puts out only three or four books a year might operate with a staff of only two or three. Each person has to wear many hats: as acquisitions editor, finding new projects to publish; as typesetter and proofreader; as sales manager; as promoter and publicist; as clerk and secretary.

The large publishing houses, which for the most part are located in New York City, can have hundreds of employees and are separated into different departments such as editorial, contracts, legal, sales and marketing, and publicity and promotion.

Within each department there are a number of different job titles. These are some of the different positions within the editorial department, although often the duties can overlap: editorial assistant, assistant/associate editor, editor, senior editor, acquisitions editor, managing editor, production editor, executive editor, editor in chief, publisher, and president.

Editors. Editors work in book-producing publishing houses or for magazines and newspapers. Editors read manuscripts, talk with writers, and decide which books or stories and articles they will publish. Editors also have to read what other houses or publications are printing, to know what's out there and what's selling.

Once a manuscript is selected for publication, an editor oversees the various steps to produce the finished product, from line editing for mistakes, to the book or magazine cover art and copy. Editors also regularly attend editorial meetings and occasionally travel to writer's conferences to speak to aspiring writers and to find new talent.

How Literary Agencies Are Structured. Some literary agents choose to work on their own, with little more than secretarial assistance. They can rent space in an office building or work from a home office.

Other agents prefer to work within a literary agency, either as the owner, or as one of the associates. They can still function independently, choosing the writers and book projects they want to work with.

Usually in an agency, agents must contribute a percentage of their income to cover the office's operating expenses.

Training for Editors and Agents. Most editors and agents have at least a bachelor's degree in communications, English, journalism, or any relevant liberal arts or humanities major. It is helpful to also be familiar with publishing law and contracts, and to know how to type or word process.

In publishing it's rare for someone to start out as an editor or agent without any prior experience. Many agents work for publishing houses first, becoming familiar with the editorial process and contracts, before moving into a literary agency.

And within a publishing house there is a distinct ladder most editors climb as they gain experience and develop a successful track record. They usually start out as editorial assistants, answering the phone, opening and distributing the mail, and preparing correspondence. Some editorial assistants are first readers for their editors; they'll read a manuscript then write a reader's report. If it's a good report then the editor will take a look at the manuscript.

Most editorial assistants learn the editing process from the editor they work for, and over time move up into editorial positions with more and more responsibility.

Earnings for Editors and Agents. Editors are generally paid a set salary. Although their salary is not dependent week to week on the sales success of the books they choose to publish, an editor with a good track record is likely to be promoted and given raises. Starting pay, however, is not particularly glamorous.

Agents, on the other hand, must sell their clients' manuscripts to publishers in order to earn any income. Agents generally work on a commission basis, 10 to 15 percent of the money the writer earns. If an agent has a lot of market savvy, carefully chooses which manuscripts to represent, and has success bargaining for big advances and royalty percentages, then he or she can make a very good living, often much more than the editors to whom he or she is selling.

The downside for agents is that the marketplace is fickle, fads come and go, and publishing houses merge with each other and often decrease the number of books they will let see print. In a bad year, an agent often has to struggle to make a living.

Radio and Television Stations

Although the golden age of radio passed five or six decades ago, it is still considered one of the most effective of the mass media, especially for quickly disseminating information to a large number of people. In the United States alone, more than 10,000 radio stations are on the air with an estimated 500 million radios in use.

Television is as equally effective. Elizabeth Kolbert, writing about television in the *New York Times*, noted that "Television has created not so much a global village as a global front stoop. Instead of gossiping about our neighbors, about whom we know less and less, we gossip about national figures, about whom we know more and more. The color set in the den has so successfully replaced the sewing circle and the hamburger joint that we are now trying to get from television that which television has caused us to give up."

Radio and television stations provide a wide range of jobs for communications majors. Several positions such as announcers and news directors exist in both settings and some jobs at radio stations will open otherwise closed doors at television stations.

The jobs communications majors most qualify for are announcer/disk jockey, music director, program director/production manager/public service director, news writer/editor, and scriptwriter. The duties of each job will vary, depending on the format and the size of the station. Radio stations, for example, can offer specialized programming such as country music, oldies, all-talk shows, all-news, religious broadcasts, or a combination of programming. An all music program would require less scheduling than an all news station. Similarly, a disk jockey (DJ) working for a music format station will have less preparation to do than a talk show host would.

Announcer/DJ. This is the most visible and the most competitive position. Successful DJs build a rapport with their audience and can come to be well-known personalities. Talk show DJs are able to articulate and defend opinions on both side of any topic. They also have an entertainer's instinct for performing.

Music Director. The music director selects and organizes prerecorded music that fits the station's format. Ideally, the music director would be a fan of and knowledgeable about the station's particular area of programming and shares the taste of the listening audience. Some music directors also double as announcers.

Program Director/Production Manager/Public Service Director. In small stations one person might handle the duties of all three job titles; in larger market stations each position will have its own director. Program directors manage a staff of announcers, writers, and producers and schedule broadcasts on a day-to-day basis. A production manager makes sure that programs are aired on schedule and a public service director determines which public service announcements best serve the needs of the community and deserve air time.

News Writer/Editor/Director. Personnel in the news department of both radio and TV stations must keep on top of breaking news such as political events, natural disasters, and social issues. Weather and traffic reports are sometimes originated from this department.

News specialists must have good written and oral skills and be adept at interviewing people and conducting research.

Scriptwriter. Scriptwriters prepare copy for commercials, public service announcements, and for slots between programming. The number of openings in this area are small; the most active employers of scriptwriters are radio stations that program on-air dramas and talk shows.

Earnings. According to a survey conducted by the National Association of Broadcasters and the Broadcast Cable Financial Management Association, the annual average salary, including bonuses, for television news reporters is $33,200 and $32,300 for radio news reporters. Sportscasters average $52,600 in television broadcasting and $57,600 in radio broadcasting. Weathercasters earned an average of $55,000.

STRATEGIES FOR FINDING THE JOBS

Get a Foot in the Door

In the world of newspapers, magazines, and book publishing, some experts advise that you should take *any* job you can to get your foot in the door. If you wanted to be an editor, for example, you could start out as a contract assistant, then move into an editorial position, and up the ladder to senior editor or higher. If you get yourself in the door and get to know the people in the department for which you prefer to work, your chances are better than an unknown candidate wanting to advance immediately into an editorial position.

The same holds true for radio and television stations. Production assistants with a proven track record, for example, will move into higher level positions than job candidates off the street.

Prepare a Portfolio/Audition Tape

For photojournalists, there are a few different routes to take in the job hunting process, but they all include putting together a professional portfolio.

Some photojournalists identify the papers they would like to work for and, at their own expense, fly out on spec to talk to the different editors—even when they know there are currently no openings. This approach, though a bit costly for someone just starting out, can often work. The job applicant makes himself known, and when an opening does occur, potential employers will remember your top-quality portfolio.

Job hunting through the mail can be just as effective. Send out your portfolio with a good cover letter, and don't be afraid to mention any story ideas you might have. Newspapers aren't looking for robots. They appreciate a photojournalist who does more than stand behind the camera and click his or her shutter.

Then follow up a week or so later as a reminder. You can make up your own picture postcards, using your best work. This helps to jog the editor's memory—and shows how creative you are.

Potential DJs/announcers, once they have a foot in the door, should be prepared to take any air-time slot they are offered, even if it's six o'clock on a Sunday morning. This will give you the opportunity to tape yourself. You can constantly update your tape and use it for auditions for more critical time slots.

Internships

Another successful method is to take more than the one required college internship. If you can get involved in two or even three internships, you'll make more contacts and have a better chance of lining up full-time employment when you graduate. At the same time you'll be adding to your portfolio and creating impressive specifics to include on your resume.

RELATED OCCUPATIONS

Liberal arts majors acquire skills that can be transferred to a number of related occupations. Here is a representative list of the job titles in a few similar career paths; no doubt further investigation will reveal more.

Actor	Feature film producer
Comedian	Ghostwriter
Documentary maker	Lyricist
Drama/music teacher	Musician
Educational film/video maker	Performing artist
Entertainer	Playwright
Feature film director	Poet
Feature filmmaker	Visual artist

HELP IN LOCATING EMPLOYERS

The following listings, directories, magazines, and resource books can help you in your job search. Most are available in the reference section of your library.

Broadcasting and Cable Marketplace
R.R. Bowker
121 Chanlon Rd.
New Providence, NJ 07974

Broadcasting Yearbook
Contains a listing of television stations.

Encyclopedia of Associations
Gale Research, Inc.
P.O. Box 33477
Detroit, MI 48232

Gale Directory of Publications and Broadcast Media
Gale Research, Inc.
P.O. Box 33477
Detroit, MI 48232-5477

Guide to Literary Agents, Photographer's Market, Writer's Market
Writer's Digest Books
F & W Publications
1507 Dana Ave.
Cincinnati, OH 45207

The Literary Marketplace
R.R. Bowker
121 Chanlon Rd.
New Providence, NJ 07974

National Directory of Weekly Newspapers National Public Radio
2025 M St. NW
Washington, DC 20036

Newspapers Career Directories Publishers Weekly
P.O. Box 1979
Marion, OH 43306

Writer's Digest Magazine
Writer's Digest Books
1507 Dana Ave.
Cincinnati, OH 45207

PROFESSIONAL ASSOCIATIONS

Deciding in what area of the media you would like to work and contacting
a few of the related professional associations will help with your job search
as well as your professional development. Professional associations offer conferences, seminars and workshops, a variety of publications, and job placement services.

**The Accrediting Council on Education in Journalism and Mass
Communications**
University of Kansas School of Journalism
Stauffer-Flint Hall
Lawrence, KS 66045
www.ukans.edu/~acejmc
Services: For a list of schools with accredited programs in journalism send a
stamped, self-addressed envelope.

American Society of Journalists and Authors (ASJA)
1501 Broadway, Ste. 302
New York, NY 10036
www.asja.org
Services: publications, market search, conferences, information on contract
negotiations, copyright, intellectual property, and similar issues

American Society of Magazine Editors
919 Third Ave.
New York, NY 10022
Services: career information, conferences

American Society of Media Photographers
150 N. Second St.
Philadelphia, PA 19106
www.asmp.org
Services: educational programs and seminars, publications

American Society of Newspaper Editors
P.O. Box 4090
Reston, VA 22090-1700
www.asne.org
Services: convention, publications, grants for school newspapers

Association for International Broadcasting
P.O. Box 4440
Walton CO14 8BX
United Kingdom
www.aibcast.demon.co.uk/index.html
Service: publications

Association of American Publishers
71 Fifth Ave.
New York, NY 10010
www.publishers.org
Services: seminars and workshops, book fairs, publications

Association of Authors' Representatives (AAR)
P.O. Box 237201
Ansonia Station
New York, NY 10003
www.publishersweekly.com/aar
Services: publications, including Canon of Ethics, agent membership directory

Association of Independent TV Stations
1320 19th St. NW, Ste. 300
Washington, DC 20015
Service: publications

Author's League of America
330 W. 42nd St., 29th Fl.
New York, NY 10036
Service: publications

Association of Independent Video & Filmmakers
(also the Foundation for Independent Video and Film)
304 Hudson St., 6th Fl.
New York, NY 10013
www.aivf.org/index_basic.html
Services: training seminars, journals, resources guides, work referrals

Broadcast Education Association
1771 N St. NW
Washington, DC 20036
www.beaweb.org
Services: training, educational materials, annual convention, publications, job placement

Canadian Magazine Publishers Association
130 Spadina Ave., Ste. 202
Toronto, ON M5V2L4
Canada
www.cmpa.ca
Services: training, publications

The Dow Jones Newspaper Fund, Inc.
P.O. Box 300
Princeton, NJ 08543-0300
www.dowjones.com
Services: information on careers in journalism, colleges and universities offering degree programs in journalism or communications, and journalism scholarships and internships

Education Writers Association
1331 H St. NW, #307
Washington, DC 20005
www.ewa.org
Services: publications, job bank, seminars, fellowships, contests

Magazine Publishers Association
919 Third Ave., 22nd Fl.
New York, NY 10022
Services: annual conference, seminars, publications

National Academy of Television Arts and Sciences
111 W. 57th St., Ste. 1050
New York, NY 10019
www.emmyonline.org
Services: workshops, seminars, publications, awards, job bank

National Association of Broadcast Employees and Technicians
Communications Workers of American (NABET/CWA), International
501 Third St. NW
Washington, DC 20001
http://union.nabetcwa.org/nabet
Service: career information

National Association of Broadcasters, Career Center
1771 N St. NW
Washington, DC 20036
www.nab.org
Services: publications, career information

National Association of Broadcasters, Research
and Planning Department
1771 N St. NW
Washington, DC 20036
www.nab.org
Services: employment and salary information

National Association of Independent Publishers Representatives
111 E. 14th St.
New York, NY 10003
www.naipr.org
Services: publications, conferences, job listings

National Cable Television Association
1724 Massachusetts Ave. NW
Washington, DC 20036
www.ncta.com
Services: publications, career information

National Newspaper Association
1525 Wilson Blvd., Ste. 550
Arlington, VA 22209

Services: publications, career information, including a pamphlet titled *Newspaper Careers and Challenges for the Next Century*

National Press Photographers Association (NPPA)
3200 Cloasdaile Dr., Ste. 306
Durham, NC 27705
http://metalab.unc.edu/nppa
Services: annual television-newsfilm workshop, publications, job bank, membership directory

Newsletter & Electronic Publishers Association
1501 Wilson Blvd., Ste. 509
Arlington, VA 22209
www.newsletters.org
Services: publications, conferences, professional development

The Newspaper Guild
Research and Information Department
501 3rd St. NW, Ste. 250
Washington, DC 20001
www.newsguild.org
Services: information on union wage rates for newspaper and magazine reporters

Newspaper Association of America
1921 Gallows Rd., Ste. 600
Vienna, VA 22182
www.naa.org
Services: publications, including pamphlets titled *Newspaper Career Guide* and *Newspaper: What's in It for Me?*

Radio and Television News Directors Foundation
1000 Connecticut Ave. NW
Washington, DC 20036
www.rtndf.org
Services: publications, career information, job placement, scholarships, internships

Society for Technical Communication, Inc.
901 N. Stuart St., Ste. 904
Arlington, VA 22203
www.stc.org
Service: career information

Society of National Association Publications
1150 Connecticut Ave. NW, Ste. 1050
Washington, DC 20036
www.snaponline.org
Services: seminars and resource networks, publications, job listings

Writers Guild of America (East)
555 W. 57th St., Ste. 1230
New York, NY 10019
www.wgaeast.org
Services: resources for writers, seminars, script registration

Writers Guild of America (West)
7000 W. Third St.
Los Angeles, CA 90048
www.wga.org

CHAPTER THIRTEEN

PATH 4: ADVERTISING, MARKETING, AND SALES

B ecause we have progressed from an agrarian way of life to a complex society filled with an abundance of commercial activity, competing for the consumer dollar has become a necessity for business survival and economic well-being in general.

We are a country of choices. Just go into any American supermarket and walk down the cereal or soap aisles. How many ways do we have to start off our mornings or wash our clothes, dishes, floors, and bodies? Some would say too many, but that's not the point. In a free enterprise system, competition is the name of the game and to succeed, or just stay afloat, businesses have to attract the consumer with the biggest, tastiest, most colorful, most convenient, most healthful, and most efficient product or service.

Like it or not, methods of reaching the consumer and getting a share of that dollar have permeated every aspect of our lives. Advertising is all around us, through print and film, broadcasting and public appearances, and a host of other devices and campaigns.

Consumers might sometimes see this bombardment as an intrusion; for liberal arts majors, it has opened the door to a wide range of employment possibilities.

DEFINITION OF THE CAREER PATH

While some of the careers explored in this chapter are, indeed, entered by graduates with field-specific majors (e.g., advertising majors go into advertising, marketing majors go into marketing, and so forth), graduates of liberal arts programs are blazing new trails as well as following well-established ones through a variety of these terrains. University communications depart-ments now cover areas that were once the realm of different and separate departments. They offer programs that successfully compete with the depart-ments of business, advertising, marketing, public relations, journalism, broad-casting, and other fields.

The skills students acquire ignore career boundaries that, these days, are becoming more and more ill-defined. Not wanting to limit the potential tal-ent they could attract, many employers and personnel directors shy away from specifying particular majors when advertising an opening.

Here is a sample job advertisement within this career path that stresses skills and responsibilities rather than majors.

ACCOUNT EXECUTIVE

Expanding advertising agency seeks customer-service oriented professional to provide strategic guidance and advertising expertise to a growing list of clients. Minimum requirements: bachelor's degree and three years experience as a human resource generalist. Must have ability to establish and maintain long-standing relationships with major corporate clients, work independently, listen, and analyze client needs. Outgoing, poised individual with strong communication skills a must. Send resume to . . .

Not only is a major not specified in the sample ad, the employer is seek-ing a generalist, someone who has not been pigeonholed by his or her work experience or university program.

If you isolate the skills mentioned as requirements, you will see that all could belong to a liberal arts major.

Advertising and Marketing Goals

Although advertising and marketing are distinct fields, they are often linked together. In simple terms, advertisers create a package to sell a product, ser-vice, or idea; marketing experts help decide toward which audiences the adver-tisement should be aimed.

The goal of advertising and marketing is to reach the consumer—to moti-vate or persuade a potential buyer; to sell a product, service, idea, or cause; to gain political support; or to influence public opinion. In the words of the American Association of Advertising Agencies (known as the *4 As*):

Advertising is an indispensable part of our economic system. It is the vital link between businesses and consumers. The business of advertising involves marketing objectives and artistic ingenuity. It applies quantitative and qualitative research to the creative process. It is the marriage of analysis and imagination, of marketing professional and artist. Advertising is art and science, show business and just plain business, all rolled into one. And it employs some of the brightest and most creative economists, researchers, artists, producers, writers, and business people in the country today.

To aid in the advertising endeavor, marketing professionals poll public opinion or analyze the demographics and buying patterns of specific audiences. They play the role of researcher, statistician, social psychologist, and sociologist.

With an idea of the specific audience to target, advertising professionals assess the competition, set goals and a budget, and design an advertisement—whether a simple three-line ad or a full-blown campaign—and determine what vehicle is best used to reach that audience.

Most advertising agencies are organized into the following departments (although within smaller agencies, departments can be combined or services contracted out to independent subcontractors): agency management, account management, creative services, traffic control and production, media services, publicity and public relations, sales promotion, direct response, television production, and personnel.

To work within these departments, advertising agencies employ a number of professionals to perform a variety of duties.

A FIRST-HAND LOOK AT A MARKETING MANAGER'S JOB

CHRIS FULLER, GENERAL MANAGER, FOOD SERVICES

Chris Fuller has worked in food services for more than thirty years. He worked his way up through a variety of responsible positions at Colgate Palmolive, Pepsi Cola, and Thomas J. Lipton, retiring in 1988.

Chris talks about his job:

"Food service is a secondary business within the framework of a retail business in most food companies, e.g., General Foods, Nabisco, or Proctor and Gamble. It is usually a much smaller and less profitable part of their business.

"The purpose of the food service industry, at least at Thomas J. Lipton, was to sell company products, such as tea bags, and try and get them into restaurants and cafeterias—wherever food was sold throughout the United States. The retail end deals with supermarkets and smaller Mom and Pop stores. Food service is designed to sell products to restaurants.

"The most important function in a food service business is to take the product that a retail business is selling and get it designed in the right size and package to sell to restaurants. You don't necessarily sell the same product to a restaurant that you would to a consumer through a food store.

"You have to take the entire line of products you want to sell to restaurants and have them redesigned for the restaurant trade. When I was there, the major product happened to be tea bags. A tea bag that you sell to a consumer is for one cup of tea. The tea bag you'd sell to a restaurant might be for a whole jug of tea.

"Another function in a food service business is marketing. Marketing is pricing, packaging, and the development of the particular product you're going to advertise, promote, and sell. You advertise in the trade journals to let customers know you're going to be offering a particular product.

"Marketing also includes sales. We worked as part of a team. The salespeople, although responsible for sales volume and reaching a quota every week, do not have any profit responsibility and they are always asking for lower prices, more advertising, and more promotion. The marketing person says 'You can't have that much, because if we spend that much and price the product ten cents a case less, we're going to lose money.' Marketing and sales are often at odds with each other.

"I had many businesses I was responsible for. My particular job encompassed the Good Humor business. The ice cream business is enormous and very important within Lipton.

"I had a person I supervised who managed the day-to-day business of the food service end and his job was to decide what pricing promotions and advertising were needed that month to sell the product. He also decided how many salespeople he needed, what kind of training they should have, where they should be stationed, which accounts those salesmen would call on, and how much time they could give to each account.

"Food service salespeople cover a lot more territory than the retail sales end. The volume is generally lower so you can't afford to have too many salespeople."

The Downsides

"There's a considerable amount of automobile travel and very tough schedules to meet. Sometimes the accounts will see you when you want to see them, sometimes you have to wait and see them another day—after having traveled over three hundred miles! So what are you going to do if you don't have it planned to see other accounts in that area? There's a lot of planning and time away from home; it affects family life very negatively.

"The sales manager has to go out and see his sales reps because they can't afford to take the time to come in to the office and lose sales. Therefore, the sales manager is out in the field with his personnel too, making calls and making sure the reps are using the right techniques and handling each situation the way it should be handled in order to get the maximum sales volume.

"In marketing, a step up from sales, your traveling time would be much shorter. The sales manager would normally report to the vice president of marketing. Sales is part of the marketing mix. Although marketing is a step up, there's also a downside to it. If they're not making the expected profit, they can lose their jobs. They have the same sales volume responsibility that the salespeople have because the salespeople report directly to them.

"They make an agreement with sales—they say for example, 'we're going to sell one hundred units of X to Denny's Restaurants.' However, they only sell ninety units. The salesperson has the first responsibility, but the marketing person also shares that responsibility too. He or she had agreed that product could be sold with a specific advertising, pricing, and quality-promotion campaign. Missing the intended sales quota puts both jobs on the line."

The Pluses

"The upside is that most successful salespeople like their job. If you don't like walking in and talking to people every day, this job isn't for you.

"There's a great deal of socializing in this business. You get to know the purchasing person and if you've been calling on him for a number of years, you get to know who his wife is, who the kids are, when their birthdays are, etc. You may often take him out to dinner. You're not giving expensive presents—that isn't allowed—but little courtesies are fine.

"Money is not much better than it is in retail. I wouldn't say that the money is terrific. It's hard work, you're not going to become wealthy. But you do get a decent pension plan and some bonuses.

"When you're selling food, you're selling the brand name or a recipe. You're not selling what it can do—you're selling recognition. You might cook up a batch of macaroni and cheese for the purchaser to sample, but it's not the same as selling a computer or a car."

Chris Fuller's Background

"I was attracted to this field by the glamour. You had a lot of advertising and promotion. Product managers made good money, the businesses were stable, and you didn't have the big hiring and firing problems we have in the 1990s. You could stay with a company for a long time. They had good programs and they were well respected in the business community all around the United States.

"I got my B.A. in economics and my M.B.A., both at Dartmouth College in the 1950s. I've been in this business for thirty years. I started with Colgate Palmolive in 1956. They weren't a food business, but they were analogous to it; they were in the household products business, which sold products through the same channels as the food companies.

"At General Foods I was manager of marketing analysis and then became a product manager in the frozen potato business. At Pepsi Cola I was vice president of finance and president of Metrop Bottling Company, which sold Pepsi through company-owned franchises in the United States.

"I went to work for Thomas J. Lipton in 1977. 1 was senior vice-president of operations and finance there, then became senior vice-president of general management. That was a marketing job, where I managed a group of businesses including the food service end."

Some Advice from Chris Fuller

"The most important thing is that you don't mind traveling and that you like to meet and talk to people every day. You also have to be able to follow directions. You're going to have a regional manager or a division manager supervise you and they give you directions that you will have to follow explicitly.

"What you do every day is tracked—where you have been, who you have seen, and what you have sold. You work in a fishbowl type of environment. Every salesperson in the United States has his working record somewhere on a computer.

"You need to be a gregarious person, and you have to be thick-skinned and able to take criticism. Frequent customer complaints are not unusual: a shipment didn't come in on time; a man thinks the macaroni and cheese didn't taste the same as the batch you cooked up for him that day; or the wrong product was delivered.

"If you go into food service, in order to advance you might want to transfer over to the retail side at a later date, selling to supermarkets.

"Your eventual aim is to go up the ladder in sales and then into marketing. Many people from sales go over to marketing. You need to start young, when you're in your twenties, then move over to marketing in your early thirties. If you don't move to marketing in your early thirties, it will be too late and you'll get stuck in sales.

"In general, food service is a good career and a stable business. The companies that are in this business are solid, not fly-by-night.

"You have to get up and do something every single day; you can't rest on your laurels. If you like people and competition, you'll be fine."

Sales Goals

Millions of dollars are spent each day on all types of merchandise—everything from sweaters and cosmetics to lumber, office equipment, and plumbing supplies. Sales workers are employed by many types of retailers to assist customers in the selection and purchase of these items.

Whether selling antiques, computer equipment, or automobiles, a sales worker's primary job is to interest customers in the merchandise. This may be done by describing the product's features, demonstrating its use, or showing various models and colors.

For some jobs, particularly those selling expensive and complex items, special knowledge or skills are needed. For example, workers who sell personal computers must be able to explain to customers the features of various brands and models, the meaning of manufacturers' specifications, and the types of software that are available.

The field of sales covers several different areas: retail sales, anything from food to flowers; service sales, from hotel rooms to financial reporting systems; manufacturers' and wholesale sales, anything from books to computer disks; medical sales, from pharmaceuticals to hospital beds; travel sales; real estate sales; and insurance agents and brokers.

POSSIBLE EMPLOYERS

Advertising Agencies

About one third of America's advertising professionals work for ad agencies. There are approximately 9,600 advertising agencies nationwide, employing an estimated 106,000 people. A third are small, one-person offices; another third employ from two to five people; and the remaining third extend up to international megacompanies, such as Young & Rubicam, which has four thousand employees in thirty-five offices across the United States and close to three thousand employees in ninety-one foreign countries.

New York continues to be the advertising hub of the world with, according to *Advertising Age*, sixty-one of the top one hundred agencies ranked by gross income headquartered there. But you don't have to move to New York to find work. As mentioned previously, many agencies have regional and international offices, and almost every major city, and even smaller ones, can claim their share of agencies.

Advertising agencies help clients, the advertisers, to identify potential customers, create effective advertisements, and arrange for the air time or print space to run the advertising.

The large agencies generally have a wide range of clients and can provide a new graduate with varied work experience. Starting your career off in a small agency would allow you to quickly specialize in a particular area of advertising.

Marketing Firms/Departments

Marketers and advertising professionals work hand in hand, and thus many marketing departments are located within corporate advertising departments or within private advertising agencies. Private marketing firms function similarly to advertising agencies and work toward the same goals—identifying and targeting specific audiences that will be receptive to specific products, services, or ideas.

Corporate Advertising Departments

While many corporations use the services of outside advertising agencies and marketing firms, just as many, especially the very large ones, operate their own in-house departments. Here, workers create and develop the company's advertising and sales promotion material. For example, a large department store such as Macy's or Bloomingdale's will have its professional staff create catalogs, brochures, newspaper inserts, flyers, as well as place the regular flow of daily newspaper ads.

Developing this material, especially glossy catalogs, is a big endeavor, requiring the skills of a variety of people—copywriters, art directors, photographers, layout artists, and models.

Corporations that do use the services of an outside agency might also maintain their own advertising department to function as a liaison between the agency and the company. Here the responsibilities include ensuring that the advertising being produced meets the company's objectives and is placed in the appropriate media outlets.

Self-Employed/Freelancers

Freelance "ad men" hire their services to advertising agencies and corporations. They are usually looked to when staffing is not sufficient to handle a new client or there is a sudden overload of work. Freelancers are also successful when working with small businesses that don't have the desire or budget to work with a large, expensive agency.

Freelancers can pick and choose their projects, although that is usually not an option starting out. Once established, though, a freelancer who finds himself with enough clients can open his own office. As the clientload increases, so does the need to have help and this is how many small agencies get their start—an enterprising freelancer builds up enough business to take on employees.

Freelance publicists work with people who, simply put, need publicity. Here are two examples: a former politician wants to get on the university campus speaker circuit; and an independent film company with a small-time budget wants a chance at big-time distribution.

Publishing Companies

Large publishing companies, especially those located in New York City, operate publicity departments to promote their authors and their books. Some of the duties of a publishing house publicist are arranging for point-of-sale material (e.g., printed bookmarks) to be made available at bookstores; organizing book tours, including booking speaking engagements on television and radio shows and setting up book-signing engagements at bookstores and other appropriate outlets; and writing jacket copy.

Bookstores

More and more bookstores, especially the new "super stores," coordinate events to bring in the customers. This calls for a publicist who can book name and local authors for speaking and signing engagements; arrange for cookbook authors to give cooking demonstrations; and find other ways to appeal to the tastes of the book-buying public.

Vacation Resorts/Chambers of Commerce

Promoting a vacation spot or city falls into the realm of a publicist's duties. Publicists working for a vacation resort would produce pamphlets, brochures, press releases, and perhaps video demonstrations of the location's selling points. Their target audience would be travel agents, travel writers and editors, and the vacationing public.

Publicists working for chambers of commerce aim their efforts at potential businesses and new residents as well as vacationers and other visitors.

Other settings include but are not limited to are:

- Retail stores
- Manufacturing companies
- Wholesale firms
- Medical supply houses
- Travel agencies

- Insurance firms
- Real estate brokerage houses

WORKING CONDITIONS

This is a competitive business, with every industry vying for the all-important consumer dollar. While this can make the working atmosphere challenging and exciting, it can also make it hectic and stressful.

A busy ad agency, for example, will have a long list of ongoing projects needing attention at the same time. No matter how large the agency is and how many professionals it employs, the workload often strains available staff. This atmosphere lends itself to employees feeling overworked. It is not uncommon for "burnout" to occur after a few years of constant pressure.

In order to attract clients and beat out the competition, there are campaigns to be developed and ideas and concepts to be presented. If the account managers misjudged the goals of the client, there's the stress of losing an account. If the campaign was successful, there are still pressures to keep that client—not to mention the deadlines to be met and the crises to be resolved when things go wrong.

Hours can be long and disruptive to a personal life. Contributing to this is a substantial amount of travel—to meet with clients or attend conferences—that managers for some agencies might have to do.

Although to many outsiders the life of an ad exec might seem "glamorous," the reality is that the work is less secure than most, with staff layoffs occurring when the workload drops.

TRAINING AND QUALIFICATIONS

The course of study that potential advertising, marketing, and sales specialists should pursue has been the issue of some debate. While many believe firmly that in sales any liberal arts major will suffice, there are those who feel that for some specialty products, such as pharmaceuticals or computers, a specialized degree is preferred.

Some believe that a straight degree in advertising is the best preparation for advertising positions, but they are usually shouted down by those who recognize the importance of a broader curriculum.

To some extent, the answer is determined by the area of this career path you intend to pursue. If you are aiming for a title of account manager, courses in marketing, business and finance, and speech communications are as important as advertising theory. Potential art directors obviously need technical training in drawing, illustration, and graphic design. All are well-served, however, by courses in effective communications.

CAREER OUTLOOK

There are more than 9,600 advertising agencies in the United States, but the "4 As" estimates that the annual number of openings for new grads is only 1,000 to 1,200 each year.

Marketing, advertising, and public relations managers held about 432,000 jobs in virtually every industry. Employment is expected to increase faster than the average for all occupations through the year 2008. According to the *Occupational Outlook Handbook,* increasingly intense domestic and global competition in products and services offered to consumers should require greater marketing, advertising, public relations, and promotional efforts. As businesses increasingly hire contractors for these services rather than support additional full-time staff, private consulting firms and agencies may experience particularly rapid growth.

During recessions, sales volume and the resulting demand for sales workers generally decline. Purchases of costly items such as cars, appliances, and furniture tend to be postponed during difficult economic times. In areas of high unemployment, sales of all types of goods may decline. However, since turnover of sales workers is usually very high, employers often can control employment simply by not replacing all those who leave.

In some geographic areas, employers face a shortage of qualified applicants. As a result, employers can be expected to improve efforts to attract and retain workers by offering higher wages, more generous benefits, and more flexible schedules.

EARNINGS

According to the U.S. Bureau of Labor Statistics, median annual earnings of advertising, marketing, promotions, public relations, and sales managers are approximately $57,300. The middle 50 percent earn between $38,230 and $84,950 a year. The lowest 10 percent earn less than $28,190 and the highest 10 percent earn more than $116,160 a year.

Median annual earnings in the industries employing the largest number of advertising, marketing, promotions, public relations, and sales managers are as follows:

Professional and commercial equipment	$69,800
Telephone communications	$64,100
Computer and data-processing services	$60,800
Advertising	$54,300
Management and public relations	$51,100

According to a National Association of Colleges and Employers survey, starting salaries for marketing majors graduating in 1999 averaged about $31,900; advertising majors, about $26,600.

Salary levels vary substantially, depending upon the level of managerial responsibility, length of service, education, firm size, location, and industry. For example, manufacturing firms usually pay advertising, marketing, and public relations managers higher salaries than nonmanufacturing firms do.

For sales managers, the size of their sales territory is another important determinant of salary. Many managers earn bonuses equal to 10 percent or more of their salaries.

Nonsupervisory workers in advertising average $647 a week—significantly higher than the $442 a week for all nonsupervisory workers in private industry.

The table below shows the median hourly earnings of the largest occupations in advertising, compared to all industries:

Occupation	Advertising	All Industries
General managers and top executives	$45.53	$26.05
Marketing, advertising, and public relations managers	26.11	25.61
Writers and editors	18.31	15.69
Artists and related workers	16.74	14.89
Sales agents, advertising	15.68	14.16
First-line supervisors and managers/supervisors-clerical and administrative support workers	15.17	14.26
Secretaries, except legal and medical	11.89	11.00
Bookkeeping, accounting, and auditing clerks	11.54	10.80
General office clerks	9.23	9.10
Demonstrators and promoters	7.95	7.65

Other surveys show a variation of $25,000 to $250,000 for marketing managers, depending on the level of education, experience, industry, and the number of employees he or she supervises.

Salaries for sales professionals are harder to pin down. Depending upon the setting and the product, workers can earn as low as minimum wage or in the high six figures with commissions and bonuses figured in.

STRATEGIES FOR FINDING THE JOBS

As with the corporate world, it's a good idea for a job seeker to become a familiar fixture inside an advertising agency's reception area. Sending out blind resumes has never been an effective method for finding a job in any profession. The key is having a good portfolio with you, one that you can quickly open and display if the right person walks by. A portfolio should showcase your best work. If you are interested in copywriting, visuals are less important than writing samples and a good marketing sense. Aspiring art directors need samples of their work that show their design ability.

Persistence is a trait valued in this career path; showing the same quality in your job search can help pay off.

The strategies mentioned in Chapter Ten also apply here. Use your university's resources as well as the library's.

Here are some additional tips:

■ Start your job search before you near graduation. Those who arrange internships for themselves have an edge; they've already become familiar faces on-the-job. When an opening comes up, a known commodity (who performed well during the internship) is going to be chosen over an unknown one.

■ Learn as much as you can about the agency or firm you're interested in. In other words, target your prospects.

POSSIBLE JOB TITLES

There is a wide variety of job titles in this field. In addition, within certain job titles there are different rankings. For example, the position of account executive would have entry-level positions called assistant account executive or junior account executive; the next rank up would be associate account executive, moving on to senior account executive and account manager.

Account coordinator	Market research manager
Account director	Media buyer
Account/district manager	Media director
Account executive	Media evaluator
Account representative	Media placement specialist
Account specialist	Media planner
Account supervisor	Media supervisor
Account trainee	Print production manager
Advertising director	Producer
Art buyer	Production assistant
Art director	Production manager
Broadcast production manager	Project director
Consumer affairs specialist	Promotion manager
Copyeditor	Publicist
Copywriter	Research assistant
Creative director	Researcher
Designer	Sales assistant
Editor	Sales planner
Event coordinator	Sales representative
Graphic artist	Spokesperson
Management supervisor	Traffic assistant
Market analyst	Traffic manager

This list will give you an idea of the jobs available. You will be able to add to the list as you investigate all the possibilities.

RELATED OCCUPATIONS

The skills liberal arts majors use in advertising, marketing, sales, publicity, and promotion can also be transferred to different settings. A market analyst, for example, adept at collecting and interpreting data on different pop-

Actuarian	Fundraiser
Advertising photography	Hotel sales
Campaign developer	Membership-services director
Convention sales	Researcher
Demographer	Statistician
Function-sales manager	Travel photography

ulations, could also work for the government as a demographer helping to prepare a census, or with an insurance company as an actuarian.

HELP IN LOCATING EMPLOYERS

The following list includes contacts, journals, and directories that can aid in your job search. Many of the publications are available as reference material at local libraries.

Advertising Age
Crain Communications, Inc.
711 Third Ave.
New York, NY 10017-4036
www.adage.com

Advertising Career Directory
Magazine Publishing Career Directory
Public Relations Career Directory
Gale Research, Inc.
P.O. Box 33477
Detroit, MI 48232-5477

Adweek
Adweek Online
Brandweek
Mediaweek
770 Broadway, 7th Fl.
New York, NY 10003
www.adweek.com

Encyclopedia of Associations
Gale Research, Inc.
P.O. Box 33477
Detroit, MI 48232

Standard Directory of Advertisers (The Advertiser Red Book)
Standard Directory of Advertising Agencies (The Agency Red Book)
Reed Reference Publishing
P.O. Box 31
New Providence, NJ 07974

The *Agency Red Book* lists more than four thousand agencies and includes regional offices, accounts specializations, number of employees and names and titles of key personnel. It is published every February, June, and October.

U.S. Department of Commerce
Maintains a list of approximately eight thousand advertising agencies nationwide.

PROFESSIONAL ASSOCIATIONS

The following list of professional associations will give you an idea of the variety available within this career path. To receive detailed information about each association and the professional area it supports takes only a letter or phone call.

The Advertising Club of New York
235 Park Ave. S, 6th Fl.
New York, NY 10003
www.andyawards.com
Services: annual advertising and marketing course with classes in copywriting, special graphics, verbal communication, advertising production, and others; publications; membership directory

Advertising Council
261 Madison Ave.
New York, NY 10016-2303
Services: conducts public service advertising campaigns, publications

Advertising Photographers of America, Inc.
27 W. 20th St.
New York, NY 10011
Services: lectures, seminars, discussion groups, publications

Advertising Research Foundation
641 Lexington Ave.
New York, NY 10022
www.arfsite.org
Services: annual meeting, regional meetings, workshops, conferences, publications

Advertising Women of New York
153 E. 57th St.
New York, NY 10022
Services: annual career conference for college seniors, publications, job listings

American Advertising Federation
Education Services Department
1101 Vermont Ave. NW, Ste. 500
Washington, DC 20005
www.aaf.org
Services: training, internships, conferences, awards, competitions

American Association of Advertising Agencies
405 Lexington Ave.
New York, NY 10174-1801
www.aaaa.org
Services: job locating, conferences, training

American Council of Highway Advertisers
P.O. Box 809
North Beach, MD 20714
www.penrose-press.com/IDD/org/cards/S3452.html

American Marketing Association
311 S. Wacker Dr., Ste. 5800
Chicago, IL 60606
www.ama.org
Services: seminars, conferences, student marketing clubs, placement service, publications

Association of National Advertisers
708 Third Ave.
New York, NY 10017-4270
www.ana.net
Services: conducts studies, surveys, seminars, and workshops; provides a specialized education program; publishes *The Advertiser*

Council of Sales Promotion Agencies
750 Summer St.
Stamford, CT 06901
Services: intern program, conducts research

National Council For Marketing and Public Relations
1809 74th Ave.
Greeley, CO 80634
www.ncmpr.org
Services: annual conference, national surveys, needs assessment, awards, publications

Point of Purchase Advertising International
1600 L St. NW, 10th Fl.
Washington, DC 20036
www.popai.com
Services: conducts student education programs, publications

Retail Advertising & Marketing Association
333 N. Michigan Ave., Ste. 3000
Chicago, IL 60601
www.rama-nrf.org
Services: conducts annual conference, offers education programs for retail marketers

Sales and Marketing Executives International
P.O. Box 1390
Sumas, WA 98295-1390
E-mail: smei@earthlink.net
www.smei.org
Services: job listings, conferences, training, publications, business services

Specialty Advertising Association International
3125 Skyway Circle N
Irving, TX 75038-3526
Services: speakers bureau; conducts research and organizes executive training and development seminars; publications

CHAPTER FOURTEEN

PATH 5:
THE HELPING PROFESSIONS

T he helping professions career path encompasses a wide range of occupational categories, from clinical psychologist or social worker to rehabilitation and vocational counseling. For some jobs, a B.A. in psychology or a related liberal arts field is sufficient; for others, a graduate degree—a master's or doctorate—is required.

While helping professionals might come to their fields with a variety of backgrounds and training, they usually have a few traits and skills in common. The ability to listen and empathize, a tolerance of and sensitivity to individuals who may be different from themselves, and a sincere desire to help without judging are all qualities they must share.

DEFINITION OF THE CAREER PATH

Within the helping professions you will find the following possible job titles. However, this list is by no means exhaustive. During your job search, you can use this list as a reference, adding to it as you come across notices for jobs that mention related skills.

Each job title requires different levels of training and education. Each has a different set of working conditions and job settings. However, for some there is a great deal of overlap in duties and responsibilities. A counselor working in a mental health clinic might function the same way a therapist would working in a private practice.

Following the list, you will find a more detailed description of three of the major occupational categories with the helping professions: human services workers, mental health counselors, and psychologists.

Academic counselor	Mental health counselor
Alcohol counselor	Mental health technician
Case management aide	Psychiatric nurse
Career counselor	Psychiatrist
Child abuse worker	Psychologist
Child psychiatrist	Psychotherapist
Child psychologist	Rehabilitation counselor
Clinical psychologist	Residential counselor
Clinical social worker	Social service technician
Community outreach worker	Social work assistant
Drug abuse counselor	Social worker
Educational counselor	Special education teacher
Educational therapist	Spiritual counselor
Gerontology aide	Substance abuse counselor
Guidance counselor	Therapist
Marriage and family counselor/therapist	Vocational counselor

Human Services Workers

Human services worker is a generic term for people with various job titles, such as alcohol counselor, case management aide, child abuse worker, community outreach worker, drug abuse counselor, gerontology aide, mental health technician, residential counselor, social service technician, and social work assistant.

They generally work under the direction of social workers or, in some cases, psychologists. The amount of responsibility and supervision they are given varies a great deal. Some are on their own most of the time and have little direct supervision; others work under close direction.

Human services workers help clients obtain benefits or services. They assess the needs and establish the eligibility of clients for services. They examine financial documents, such as rent receipts and tax returns, to determine whether the client is eligible for food stamps, Medicaid, or other welfare programs. They also inform clients on how to obtain services; arrange for transportation and escorts, if necessary; and provide emotional support. Human services workers monitor and keep case records on clients and report progress to supervisors.

Human services workers may transport or accompany clients to group meal sites, adult day-care programs, or doctors' offices; telephone or visit clients' homes to make sure services are being received; or help resolve disagreements, such as those between tenants and landlords.

Human services workers also play a variety of roles in community settings. They may organize and lead group activities, assist clients in need of counseling or crisis intervention, or administer a food bank or emergency fuel program. In halfway houses and group homes, they oversee adult residents who need some supervision or support on a daily basis but do not need to live in an institution. They review clients' records, talk with their families, and confer with medical personnel to gain better insight into their background and needs. Human services workers may teach residents to prepare their own meals and to do other housekeeping activities. They also provide emotional support and lead recreation activities.

In mental hospitals and psychiatric clinics, they may help clients master everyday living skills and teach them how to communicate more effectively and get along better with others. They often assist with music, art, and dance therapy and with individual and group counseling and lead recreational activities.

Working conditions of human services workers vary. Many spend part of their time in an office or group residential facility and the rest in the field visiting clients or taking them on trips or meeting with people who provide services to the clients.

Most work a regular forty-hour week, although some work may be in the evening and on weekends. Human services workers in residential settings generally work in shifts because residents need around-the-clock supervision.

The work, while satisfying, can be emotionally draining. Understaffing and lack of equipment may add to the pressure. Turnover is reported to be high, especially among workers without academic preparation for this field.

Training and Qualifications. While some employers hire high school graduates, most prefer applicants with some college preparation in human services, social work, one of the social or behavioral sciences, or another related liberal arts degree. Some prefer to hire persons with a four-year college degree. The level of formal education of human service workers often influences the kind of work they are assigned and the amount of responsibility entrusted to them. Workers with no more than a high school education are likely to perform clerical duties, while those with a college degree might be assigned to do direct counseling, coordinate program activities, or manage a group home.

Employers may also look for experience in other occupations or leadership experience in school or in a youth group. Some enter the field on the basis of courses in social work, psychology, sociology, rehabilitation, or special education. Most employers provide in-service training such as seminars and workshops.

Because so many human services jobs involve direct contact with people who are vulnerable to exploitation or mistreatment, employers try to select applicants with appropriate personal qualifications. Relevant academic preparation is generally required, and volunteer or work experience is preferred. A strong desire to help others, patience, and understanding are highly valued characteristics. Other important personal traits include communication skills, a strong sense of responsibility, and the ability to manage time effectively. Hiring requirements in group homes tend to be more stringent than in other settings.

Approximately, 375 certificate- and associate-degree programs in human services or mental health are offered at community and junior colleges, vocational-technical institutes, and other postsecondary institutions. In addition, 390 programs offer a bachelor's degree in human services. A small number of programs leading to master's degrees in human services administration are offered as well.

Generally, academic programs in this field educate students for specialized roles. Students are exposed early and often to the kinds of situations they may encounter on the job. Programs typically include courses in psychology, sociology, crisis intervention, social work, family dynamics, therapeutic interviewing, rehabilitation, and gerontology. Through classroom simulation internships, students learn interview, observation, and record-keeping skills; individual and group counseling techniques; and program planning.

Formal education is almost always necessary for advancement. In group homes, completion of a one-year certificate in human services along with several years of experience may suffice for promotion to supervisor. In general, however, advancement requires a bachelor's or master's degree in counseling, rehabilitation, social work, or a related field.

Career Outlook. Human services workers held about 288,000 jobs in 1998. About one fourth were employed by state and local governments, primarily in public welfare agencies and facilities for the mentally retarded and developmentally disabled. Another fourth worked in private social services agencies offering a variety of services, including adult day care, group meals, crisis intervention, and counseling. Still another fourth supervised residents of group homes and halfway houses. Human services workers also held jobs in clinics, community mental health centers, and psychiatric hospitals.

Opportunities for human services workers are expected to be excellent for qualified applicants. The number of human services workers is projected to grow much faster than the average for all occupations between 1998 and 2008—ranking this profession among the most rapidly growing occupations.

The need to replace workers who retire or stop working for other reasons will create additional job opportunities. However, these jobs are not attractive to everyone because the work is responsible and emotionally draining and most offer relatively poor pay, so qualified applicants should have little difficulty finding employment.

Opportunities are expected to be best in job-training programs, residential settings, and private social service agencies, which include such services as adult day care and meal-delivery programs. Demand for these services will expand with the growing number of older people, who are more likely to need services.

In addition, human services workers will be needed to provide services to the mentally impaired and developmentally disabled, those with substance abuse problems, and a wide variety of others.

Faced with rapid growth in the demand for services, but slower growth in resources to provide the services, employers are expected to rely increasingly on human services workers rather than other occupations that command higher pay.

Job training programs are expected to require additional human services workers as the economy grows and businesses change their mode of production and workers need to be retrained. Human services workers help determine workers' eligibility for public assistance programs and help them obtain services while unemployed.

Residential settings should expand also as pressures to respond to the needs of the chronically mentally ill persist. For many years, the mentally ill have been deinstitutionalized and left to their own devices. Now, more community-based programs and group residences are expected to be established to house and assist the homeless and chronically mentally ill, and demand for human services workers will increase accordingly.

Although overall employment in state and local governments will grow only as fast as the average for all industries, jobs for human services workers will grow more rapidly. State and local governments employ most of their human services workers in correctional and public assistance departments. Correctional departments are growing faster than other areas of government, so human services workers should find their job opportunities increasing along with other corrections jobs. Public assistance programs have been relatively stable within governments' budgets, but they have been employing more human services workers in an attempt to employ fewer social workers, who are more educated and higher paid.

Earnings. Median annual earnings of human services workers and assistants are about $21,360. The middle 50 percent earn between $16,620 and

$27,070. The top 10 percent earn more than $33,840, while the lowest 10 percent earn less than $13,540.

Median hourly earnings in the industries employing the largest numbers of human services workers and assistants are as:

State government, except education and hospitals	$25,600
Local government, except education and hospitals	$23,500
Hospitals	$21,200
Health and allied services, not elsewhere classified	$20,600
Social services, not elsewhere classified	$20,200

A FIRST-HAND REPORT FROM A HUMAN SERVICES WORKER

M. ALLEN BROYLES, RESIDENTIAL COUNSELOR

M. Allen Broyles has worked in a group home for the mentally impaired since 1992. He is responsible for teaching independent living skills to the residents. Allen discusses his job:

"Jadwin House, the group home I work in, is owned by Sunderland Family Treatment Services, an outpatient counseling service organization for the community. It houses up to eight residents who have been released from mental institutions and want to learn how to live on their own.

"I teach the residents independent living skills. This includes personal hygiene, money management, time management, cooking skills, etc.—all the skills and tools each individual may need to live on his or her own.

"I work the swing shift—the busiest shift of the day. I am the only staff member on duty from 3:00 to 11:00 P.M. When I get to work I take a few minute's briefing from the day shift regarding any unusual developments during the day—new residents, new procedures, medicine changes, etc. Most of the residents will be gone at that time, tending to their daily routines. Many go to another facility called Wilson House, a day facility that trains our people in working skills; others go to doctors' appointments.

"I make all changes needed at that time in meds and procedures. I may go around and let the residents who are in the house know that I am on duty for their peace of mind. I then check the evening meal sheet to see which resident is assigned cooking duty that evening. Sometimes that resident will be on leave or absent for some reason and I must make alternative plans.

"At around 4:30 P.M. I locate the assigned cook and we begin the evening meal. All items on the menu are brought from the food storage area and the resident is brought up to speed on what is going to be prepared. The resident decides what he or she is going to do in preparation. I then show the resident all the things he or she needs to know to accomplish the tasks. I perform the remainder of the cooking in order to finish the meal. It is my feeling that these residents have very few pleasures in their lives. I make every effort to see that they have a pleasurable dinner each day. The resident sets the table and serves the meal home style. This allows the residents to interact with each other at meal time, compared to cafeteria style.

"After dinner, the cook cleans the kitchen and the other residents are assigned other additional cleaning chores. I see that those chores are accomplished and give instructions as needed.

"At 8:00 P.M. I monitor the medications for the evening. Once this is done the residents settle into their evening routines such as watching TV, listening to the stereo, or going out for walks. From 9:00 to 11:00 P.M. it is usually quiet. That is when I get my paperwork or personal things done, such as working on my own writing. I often go out and watch TV with the residents.

"At 11:00 P.M. my relief arrives. I give him a brief report on the house activities and/or developments and then go home."

The Up- and Downsides of the Profession

"I enjoy being able to help people with their second, third, or even fourth chances in life. The staff has observed some very dramatic turnarounds. For example, when a patient named Henry came to us, he was disheveled and haggard-looking. His schizophrenia made him so delusional it was impossible to talk to him. Paranoia gripped Henry so tightly he was afraid to leave the home.

"Henry stayed with us for three years. He gradually improved and today has his own apartment where he lives alone. He is not working at the present time, but the improvements in his quality of life have been dramatic.

"Another resident, Joanie, came to us so paranoid she isolated herself in her room, coming out only to eat. There were times we felt she might have to return to the hospital. Today she still hears voices from time to time and her paranoia is still present, but over time she has learned to control these problems and lives on her own. She is now a fully working productive citizen.

"The only major downside I've experienced is the hopeless feeling I get when a resident has to be readmitted back to the hospital."

Some Advice from M. Allen Broyles

"First and foremost, you must be the type of person who interacts well with others. Do you want to have an impact on people's lives—sometimes at great cost? Are you willing to put up with all the downsides of mental illness to see the positive effects later? Do you really care about the well-being of those less fortunate than yourself?

"Second, you must educate yourself as much as possible. The higher your education and the more specialized that education is, the more successful you will find yourself within your chosen field."

Mental Health and Rehabilitation Counselors

Counselors assist people with personal, family, social, educational, and career decisions, problems, and concerns. Their duties depend on the individuals they serve and the settings in which they work.

Mental Health Counselors. These individuals emphasize prevention and work with individuals and groups to promote optimum mental health. They help individuals deal with addictions and substance abuse; family, parenting, and marital problems; suicide; stress management; problems with self-esteem; issues associated with aging; job and career concerns; educational decisions; and issues of mental and emotional health.

Mental health counselors work closely with other mental health specialists, including psychiatrists, psychologists, clinical social workers, psychiatric nurses, and school counselors.

Some counselors specialize in a particular social issue or population group, such as marriage and family, grief counseling, multicultural, and gerontological counseling. A gerontological counselor may provide services to elderly persons who face changing lifestyles because of health problems, as well as help families cope with these changes. A multicultural counselor might help employers adjust to an increasingly diverse workforce.

Rehabilitation Counselors. These professionals help people deal with the personal, social, and vocational impact of their disabilities. They evaluate the strengths and limitations of individuals; provide personal and vocational counseling; and may arrange for medical care, vocational training, and job placement. Rehabilitation counselors interview individuals with disabilities and their families; evaluate school and medical reports; and confer and plan with physicians, psychologists, occupational therapists, employers, and others. Conferring with the client, they develop and implement a rehabilitation program, which may include training to help the person become more independent and employable. They also work toward increasing the client's capacity to adjust and live independently.

Self-employed counselors and those working in mental health and community agencies, often work evenings to counsel clients who work during the day. Rehabilitation counselors generally work a standard forty-hour week.

Counselors work in a wide variety of public and private establishments. These include health care facilities; vocational rehabilitation centers; social agencies; correctional institutions; and residential care facilities, such as halfway houses for criminal offenders and group homes for children, the aged, and the disabled.

Counselors also work in organizations engaged in community improvement and social change, as well as drug and alcohol rehabilitation programs and state and local government agencies. A growing number of counselors work in health maintenance organizations, insurance companies, group practice, and private practice, spurred by laws allowing counselors to receive payments from insurance companies, and requiring employers to provide rehabilitation services to injured workers.

Training and Qualifications. Generally, counselors have a master's degree in mental health counseling, counseling psychology, gerontological counseling, marriage and family counseling, substance abuse counseling, rehabilitation counseling, agency or community counseling, or a related field.

Graduate-level counselor education programs in colleges and universities usually are in departments of education or psychology. Courses are grouped into eight core areas:

- Human growth and development

- Social and cultural foundations

- Helping relationships

- Groups

- Lifestyle and career development

- Appraisal

- Research and evaluation

- Professional orientation

In an accredited program, forty-eight to sixty semester hours of graduate study, including a period of supervised clinical experience in counseling, are required for a master's degree. The Council for Accreditation of Counseling and Related Educational Programs (CACREP) accredits graduate counseling programs in counselor education and in community, gerontological, mental health, school, student affairs, and marriage and family counseling.

In 1999, forty-five states and the District of Columbia had some form of counselor credentialing legislation licensure, certification, or registry for practice outside schools. Requirements vary from state to state. In some states, credentialing is mandatory; in others, voluntary.

Many counselors elect to be nationally certified by the National Board for Certified Counselors (NBCC), which grants the general practice credential, National Certified Counselor. In order to be certified, a counselor must hold a master's degree in counseling, have at least two years of professional counseling experience, and pass NBCC's National Counselor Examination. This national certification is voluntary and distinct from state certification. However, in some states those who pass the national exam are exempt from taking a state certification exam. NBCC also offers specialty certification in career, gerontological, school, and clinical mental health counseling.

Mental health counselors generally have a master's degree in mental health counseling, another area of counseling, or in psychology or social work. They are voluntarily certified by the National Board of Certified Clinical Mental Health Counselors. Generally, to receive this certification as a mental health counselor, a counselor must have a master's degree in counseling, two years of post-master's experience, a period of supervised clinical experience, a taped sample of clinical work, and a passing grade on a written examination.

Vocational and related rehabilitation agencies generally require a master's degree in rehabilitation counseling, counseling and guidance, or counseling psychology for rehabilitation counselor jobs. Some, however, may accept applicants with a bachelor's degree in rehabilitation services, counseling, psychology, or related fields.

A bachelor's degree in counseling qualifies a person to work as a counseling aide, rehabilitation aide, or social service worker. Experience in employment counseling, job development, psychology, education, or social work may be helpful.

The Council on Rehabilitation Education (CORE) accredits graduate programs in rehabilitation counseling. A minimum of two years of study including a period of supervised clinical experience are required for the master's degree. Some colleges and universities offer a bachelor's degree in rehabilitation services education.

In most state vocational rehabilitation agencies, applicants must pass a written examination and be evaluated by a board of examiners. Many employers require rehabilitation counselors to be certified. To become certified by the Commission on Rehabilitation Counselor Certification, counselors must graduate from an accredited educational program, complete an internship, and pass a written examination. They are then designated as Certified Rehabilitation Counselors.

Some employers provide training for newly hired counselors. Many have work-study programs so that employed counselors can earn graduate degrees. Counselors must participate in graduate studies, workshops, institutes, and personal studies to maintain their certificates and licenses.

Persons interested in counseling should have a strong interest in helping others and the ability to inspire respect, trust, and confidence. They should be able to work independently or as part of a team.

Mental health and rehabilitation counselors may become supervisors or administrators in their agencies. Some counselors move into research, consulting, or college teaching, or private practice.

Career Outlook. Overall employment of counselors is expected to grow faster than the average for all occupations through the year 2008. In addition, replacement needs should increase significantly by the end of the decade as a large number of counselors reach retirement age.

Mental health and rehabilitation counselors should be in strong demand. Insurance companies increasingly provide for reimbursement of counselors— enabling many counselors to move from schools and government agencies to private practice. The number of people who need rehabilitation services will rise as advances in medical technology continue to save lives that only a few years ago would have been lost.

In addition, legislation requiring equal employment rights for persons with disabilities will spur demand for counselors. Counselors not only will help individuals with disabilities with their transition into the workforce, but also will help companies comply with the law.

More mental health and rehabilitation counselors will be needed as the elderly population grows and as society focuses on ways of developing mental well-being, such as controlling stress associated with job responsibilities.

Similar to other government jobs, the number of employment counselors who work primarily for state and local governments, could be limited by budgetary constraints.

Earnings. Median annual earnings of vocational and educational counselors are about $38,650. The middle 50 percent earn between $28,400 and $49,960. The lowest 10 percent earn less than $21,230 and the highest 10 percent earn more than $73,920. Median annual earnings in the industries employing the largest numbers of vocational and educational counselors are shown here:

Elementary and secondary schools	$42,100
State government, except education and hospitals	$35,800
Colleges and universities	$34,700
Job training and related services	$24,100
Individual and family services	$22,300

School counselors can earn additional income working summers in the school system or in other jobs.

Self-employed counselors who have well-established practices, as well as counselors employed in group practices, usually have the highest earnings, as do some counselors working for private firms, such as insurance companies and private rehabilitation companies.

Psychologists

Psychologists study human behavior and mental processes to understand, explain, and change people's behavior. They may study the way a person thinks, feels, or behaves. Research psychologists investigate the physical, cognitive, emotional, or social aspects of human behavior. Like other social scientists, psychologists formulate hypotheses and collect data to test their validity. Research methods depend on the topic under study. Psychologists may gather information through controlled laboratory experiments; personality, performance, aptitude, and intelligence tests; observation, interviews, and questionnaires; clinical studies; or surveys. Computers are widely used to record and analyze this information.

Psychologists in applied fields counsel and conduct training programs; do market research; apply psychological treatments to a variety of medical and surgical conditions; or provide mental health services in hospitals, clinics, or private settings.

Because psychology deals with human behavior, psychologists apply their knowledge and techniques to a wide range of endeavors, including human services, management, education, law, and sports.

In addition to the variety of work settings, psychologists specialize in many different areas.

Clinical Psychologists. They constitute the largest specialty and generally work in independent or group practice or in hospitals or clinics. They may help the mentally or emotionally disturbed adjust to life and increasingly are helping all kinds of medical and surgical patients deal with their illnesses or injuries. They may work in physical medicine and rehabilitation settings, treating patients with spinal cord injuries, chronic pain or illness, stroke, and arthritis and neurologic conditions, such as multiple sclerosis. Others help people deal with life stresses, such as divorce or aging.

Clinical psychologists interview patients; give diagnostic tests; provide individual, family, and group psychotherapy; and design and implement behavior modification programs. They may collaborate with physicians and other specialists in developing treatment programs and help patients understand and comply with the prescribed treatment.

Some clinical psychologists work in universities, where they train graduate students in the delivery of mental health and behavioral medicine services. Others administer community mental health programs.

Counseling Psychologists. These individuals perform many of the same functions as clinical psychologists and use several different techniques, including interviewing and testing, to advise people on how to deal with the personal, social, educational, or vocational problems of everyday living.

Developmental Psychologists. These professionals study the patterns and causes of behavioral change as people progress through life from infancy to adulthood. Some concern themselves with behavior during infancy, childhood, and adolescence, while others study changes that take place during maturity and old age. The study of developmental disabilities and how they affect a person and others around them is a new area within developmental psychology.

Educational Psychologists. They evaluate student and teacher needs and design and develop programs to enhance the educational setting.

Experimental Psychologists. They study behavior processes and work with human beings and animals such as rats, monkeys, and pigeons. Prominent areas of experimental research include motivation, thinking, attention, learning and retention, sensory and perceptual processes, effects of substance use and abuse, and genetic and neurological factors in behavior.

Industrial and Organizational Psychologists. They apply psychological techniques to personnel administration, management, and marketing problems. They are involved in policy planning, applicant screening, training and development, psychological test research, counseling, and organizational development and analysis. For example, an industrial psychologist may work with management to develop better training programs and to reorganize the work setting to improve worker productivity or quality of worklife.

School Psychologists. These experts work with students, teachers, parents, and administrators to resolve students' learning and behavior problems. Social psychologists examine people's interactions with others and with the social environment. Prominent areas of study include group behavior, leadership, attitudes, and interpersonal perception.

Cognitive Psychologists. These professionals deal with the brain's role in memory, thinking, and perceptions; some are involved with research related to computer programming and artificial intelligence.

Health Psychologists. They promote good health through health maintenance counseling programs that are designed, for example, to help people stop smoking or lose weight.

Neuropsychologists. These individuals study the relation between the brain and behavior. They often work in stroke and head injury programs.

Geropsychologists. They deal with the special problems faced by the elderly.

The emergence and growth of these specialties reflect the increasing participation of psychologists in providing direct services to special patient populations.

Other areas of specialization include psychometrics, psychology and the arts, history of psychology, psychopharmacology, community, comparative, consumer, engineering, environmental, family, forensic, population, military, and rehabilitation psychology.

Besides the jobs described above, many persons hold positions as psychology faculty at colleges and universities, and as high school psychology teachers.

Working Conditions. A psychologist's specialty and place of employment determine working conditions. For example, clinical, school, and counseling psychologists in private practice have pleasant, comfortable offices and set their own hours. However, they often have evening hours to accommodate their clients.

Some employed in hospitals, nursing homes, and other health facilities often work evenings and weekends, while others in schools and clinics work regular hours.

Psychologists employed by academic institutions divide their time among teaching, research, and administrative responsibilities. Some maintain part-time consulting practices as well.

In contrast to the many psychologists who have flexible work schedules, most in government and private industry have more structured schedules.

Reading and writing research reports, they often work alone. Many experience the pressures of deadlines, tight schedules, and overtime work. Their routine may be interrupted frequently. Travel may also be required to attend conferences or conduct research.

After several years of experience, some psychologists (usually those with doctoral degrees) enter private practice or set up their own research or consulting firms. A growing proportion of psychologists are self-employed.

Career Outlook. Psychologists held about 155,000 jobs in 1998. Educational institutions employed nearly four out of ten salaried psychologists in positions involving counseling, testing, special education, research, and administration; hospitals, mental health clinics, rehabilitation centers, nursing homes, and other health facilities employed three out of ten; and government agencies at the federal, state, and local levels employed one-sixth. The Department of Veterans Affairs, the Department of Defense, and the Public Health Service employ the overwhelming majority of psychologists working for federal agencies. Governments employ psychologists in hospitals, clinics, correctional facilities, and other settings. Psychologists also work in social service organizations, research organizations, management consulting firms, marketing research firms, and other businesses.

Employment of psychologists is expected to grow about as fast as the average for all occupations through the year 2008. Largely because of the substantial investment in training required to enter this specialized field, psychologists have a strong attachment to their occupation; only a relatively small proportion leave the profession each year. Nevertheless, replacement needs are expected to account for most job openings, similar to most occupations.

Programs to combat the increase in alcohol abuse, drug dependency, marital strife, family violence, crime, and other problems plaguing society should stimulate employment growth. Other factors spurring demand for psychologists include increased emphasis on mental health maintenance in conjunction with the treatment of physical illness; public concern for the development of human resources, including the growing elderly population; increased testing and counseling of children; and more interest in rehabilitation of prisoners. Changes in the level of government funding for these kinds of services could affect the demand for psychologists.

Job opportunities in health care should remain strong particularly in health care provider networks, such as health maintenance (HMOs) and preferred provider organizations (PPOs), that specialize in mental health, and in nursing homes and alcohol and drug abuse rehabilitation programs. Job opportunities will arise in businesses, nonprofit organizations, and research and computer firms. Companies will use psychologists' expertise in survey design, analysis, and research to provide personnel testing, program evaluation, and statistical analysis. The increase in employee assistance programs in which psychologists help people stop smoking, control weight, or alter other behaviors also should spur job growth. The expected wave of retirements among college faculty, beginning in the late 1990s, should result in job openings for psychologists in colleges and universities.

Other openings are likely to occur as psychologists study the effectiveness of changes in health, education, military, law enforcement, and consumer protection programs. Psychologists also are increasingly studying the effects on people of technological advances in areas such as agriculture, energy, the conservation and use of natural resources, and industrial and office automation.

Opportunities are best for candidates with a doctoral degree. Persons holding doctorates from leading universities in applied areas such as school, clinical, counseling, health, industrial, and educational psychology should have particularly good prospects.

Psychologists with extensive training in quantitative research methods and computer science may have a competitive edge over applicants without this background.

Graduates with a master's degree in psychology may encounter competition for the limited number of jobs for which they qualify. Graduates of master's degree programs in school psychology should have the best job prospects, as schools are expected to increase student counseling and mental health services. Some master's degree holders may find jobs as psychological assistants in community mental health centers these positions often require direct supervision by a licensed psychologist.

Others may find jobs involving research and data collection and analysis in universities, government, or private companies.

Bachelor's degree holders can expect very few opportunities directly related to psychology. Some may find jobs as assistants in rehabilitation centers or in other jobs involving data collection and analysis.

Those who meet state certification requirements may become high school psychology teachers.

Training and Qualifications. A doctoral degree generally is required for employment as a psychologist. Psychologists with a Ph.D. qualify for a wide range of teaching, research, clinical, and counseling positions in universities, elementary and secondary schools, private industry, and government.

Psychologists with a Psy.D., Doctor of Psychology, qualify mainly for clinical positions.

Persons with a master's degree in psychology can administer tests as psychological assistants. Under the supervision of doctoral level psychologists, they can conduct research in laboratories, conduct psychological evaluations, counsel patients, or perform administrative duties. They may also teach in high schools or two-year colleges or work as school psychologists or counselors.

A bachelor's degree in psychology qualifies a person to assist psychologists and other professionals in community mental health centers, vocational rehabilitation offices, and correctional programs; to work as research or administrative assistants; and to take jobs as trainees in government or business. However, without additional academic training, his or her advancement opportunities in psychology are severely limited.

In the federal government, candidates who have at least twenty-four semester hours in psychology and one course in statistics qualify for entry-level positions. Competition for these jobs is keen, however. Clinical psychologists generally must have completed the Ph.D. or Psy.D. requirements and have served an internship; vocational and guidance counselors usually need two years of graduate study in counseling and one year of counseling experience.

In most cases, two years of full-time graduate study are needed to earn a master's degree in psychology. Requirements usually include practical experience in an applied setting or a master's thesis based on a research project. A master's degree in school psychology requires about two years of course work and a one-year internship.

Five to seven years of graduate work usually are required for a doctoral degree. The Ph.D. degree culminates in a dissertation based on original research. Courses in quantitative research methods, which include the use of computers, are an integral part of graduate study and usually necessary to complete the dissertation.

The Psy.D. is usually based on practical work and examinations rather than a dissertation. In clinical or counseling psychology, the requirements for the doctoral degree generally include a year or more of internship or supervised experience.

Competition for admission into most graduate programs is keen. Some universities require an undergraduate major in psychology. Others prefer only basic psychology with courses in the biological, physical, and social sciences, statistics, and mathematics.

Most colleges and universities offer a bachelor's degree program in psychology; several hundred offer a master's and/or a Ph.D. program. A relatively small number of professional schools of psychology some affiliated with colleges or universities offer the Psy.D.

The American Psychological Association (APA) presently accredits doctoral training programs in clinical, counseling, and school psychology. The National Council for Accreditation of Teacher Education, with the assistance of the National Association of School Psychologists, also is involved in the accreditation of advanced degree programs in school psychology. The APA also accredits institutions that provide internships for doctoral students in school, clinical, and counseling psychology.

Although financial aid is difficult to obtain, some universities award fellowships or scholarships or arrange for part-time employment. The Veterans Administration (VA) offers predoctoral traineeships to interns in VA hospitals, clinics, and related training agencies. The National Science Foundation, the Department of Health and Human Services, and many other organizations also provide grants to psychology departments to help fund student stipends.

Psychologists in independent practice or those who offer any type of patient care, including clinical, counseling, and school psychologists, must meet certification or licensing requirements. All states and the District of Columbia have such requirements.

Licensing laws vary by state, but generally require a doctorate in psychology, completion of an approved internship, and one to two years of professional experience. In addition, most states require that applicants pass an examination. Most state boards administer a standardized test and, in many instances, additional oral or essay examinations. Very few states certify those with a master's degree as psychological assistants or associates; some states require continuing education for license renewal.

Most states require that licensed or certified psychologists limit their practice to those areas in which they have developed professional competence through training and experience.

The American Board of Professional Psychology recognizes professional achievement by awarding diplomas primarily in clinical psychology, clinical neuropsychology, counseling, forensic, industrial and organizational, and school psychology. Candidates need a doctorate in psychology, five years of experience, and professional endorsements; they also must pass an examination.

Even more so than in other occupations, aspiring psychologists who are interested in direct patient care must be emotionally stable, mature, and able to deal with people effectively. Sensitivity, compassion, and the ability to lead and inspire others are particularly important for clinical work and counseling. Research psychologists should be able to do detailed work independently and as part of a team. Verbal and writing skills are necessary to communicate treatment and research findings. Patience and perseverance are vital qualities because results from psychological treatment of patients or research often are long in coming.

Earnings. Median annual earnings of salaried psychologists are about $48,000. The middle 50 percent earn between $36,500 and $70,800 a year. The lowest 10 percent earn less than $27,900 and the highest 10 percent earn more than $88,000 a year.

Median annual earnings in the industries employing the largest number of psychologists are as follows:

Offices of other health care practitioners	$54,000
Hospitals	$49,300
Elementary and secondary schools	$47,400
State government, except education and hospitals	$41,600
Health and allied services, not elsewhere classified	$38,900

The federal government recognizes education and experience in certifying applicants for entry-level positions. In general, the starting salary for psychologists having a bachelor's degree was about $20,600 in 1999; those with superior academic records could begin at $25,500.

Psychologists with a master's degree and one year of experience could start at $31,200. Psychologists having a Ph.D. or Psy.D. degree and one year of internship could start at $37,800, and some individuals with experience could start at $45,200.

Beginning salaries are slightly higher in selected areas of the country where the prevailing local pay level is higher. The average annual salary for psychologists in the federal government was $66,800 in early 1999.

STRATEGIES FOR FINDING THE JOBS

For any of the helping professions, there are some tried and true strategies to follow to secure a job in the field. The following steps are offered by clinical psychologist, Gerald Oster.

Mentors

Talk to your professors; they want to help and have placed themselves as models and as valuable resources. Let them know your interests and career goals. From their many years in the field they will have valuable contacts and will be able to steer you in the right direction.

A FIRST-HAND ACCOUNT FROM A MENTAL HEALTH PROFESSIONAL

GERALD D. OSTER, CLINICAL PSYCHOLOGIST

Gerald D. Oster is a licensed psychologist with a private practice. He is also a clinical associate professor of psychiatry at the University of Maryland Medical School in Baltimore.

He earned his B.A. in sociology at the University of South Florida, Tampa in 1971; his M.A. in psychology at Middle Tennessee State University in Murfreesboro in 1976; and his Ph.D. in psychology at Virginia Commonwealth University in Richmond in 1981.

Gerald talks about his job:

"Since I have decided to have several jobs—and this was a conscious decision on my part—my days are filled with variety. For instance, for two hours on Tuesday mornings I'm at a community mental health center in Baltimore's inner city where I work as a child and family therapist. Right now I'm working with two specific patients. One is a sixteen-year-old youth who had trouble with the law. He served time in juvenile delinquent centers and now is trying to make it back into the community. He is also struggling to fit in at school and in his foster care placement.

"The other is a kindergarten child who is very insecure about the world around him. He lives in a dangerous neighborhood with his grandparents as his primary caretakers. His mother, who also lives with him, is a drug addict.

"When I am not attending to these two patients, I am doing the tremendous amount of paperwork required by the various governing agencies that monitor the clinic.

"After catching up at the clinic (I work at home and in my private practice on Mondays), I spend an eight-hour period at the University Counseling Center where I see intelligent and creative individuals who are in various professional schools (law, medicine, social work, etc.). Although quite articulate and resourceful, they, too, have their own struggles and often make good use of the support that our center provides. They come to us for help in coping with school stress and relationship problems, including caretaking of others (many are married or have relatives or children that they are responsible for). After these hours are over, I usually go to my private practice to sort through mail or see an occasional evening patient.

"My other days are similar but involve different demands and different populations each day. Often, I am at the local community hospital interviewing or administering tests to a suicidal patient or out-of-control adolescent. My private practice is divided between seeing children and adults with an assortment of troubles.

"I stay quite busy but always have to seek out new ways to maintain my practice, especially in the context of managed care. For myself and many of my colleagues in a solo private practice, managed care has become a nightmare with confusing paperwork and payment reimbursement problems. This has made life more problematic and anxiety-provoking. It has also affected the hospitals where I work and created uncertainty in many of the health professions. The future depends on adapting to these changes and using different skills to negotiate new expectations."

Gerald D. Oster's Background

"My initial undergraduate years were from 1967–71, a period of great social change, activism, and self-exploration. Although I began as a business major, the courses in sociology were much more appealing and similar to my viewpoints at the time.

"I relished the prospect of studying topics such as social and political theory and how people adapt to environmental and economic change. Also, learning about and helping people in all aspects of life filled a need in myself to go beyond my own boundaries and provide support to people in stress.

"It was not until several years after receiving my undergraduate degree (and owning a bookstore) that I was able to focus my thoughts into a single direction. I am sure this waiting period is not unique. Only a few students have a specific direction regarding careers and go through college with the hope that their degree will get them some type of job. However, a career choice means much more. It is something that you love and want to pursue full-time.

"For me, psychology was that path. And even in psychology, there were many roads to pursue. At first, I wanted to be a criminal psychologist and found courses in personality and psychopathology fascinating. I also found courses in child development extremely interesting and had an outstanding professor that was able to demonstrate the early cognitive and emotional stages of life. My first choice, criminal psychology, led me to my first graduate school and master's degree. For a time, I worked within the juvenile justice system, providing evaluations for the courts on delinquents. However, through the support of my professors and continuing interest in other aspects of psychology, I entered a doctoral program where I was exposed to a greater depth and breadth of psychology.

"While there, I worked in a rat laboratory, was part of a developing center for aging, taught courses in developmental psychology and child development, and was exposed to continuing clinical work through practicums at child development centers and psychiatric units for the aged. I also participated with many research teams on topics of learning theory, intellectual testing, and cognitive changes over the lifespan.

"I started my professional career in 1981 at a private research firm that subcontracted work from NIH. At the time, I was involved with coordinating research projects for a nationwide study on depression. After one year, I decided to return to clinical work and obtained a job in a state hospital as a psychologist on an adolescent unit. During that time, I also consulted to a geriatric unit and continued my learning through weekly seminars and clinical rounds.

"After several years and having obtained my independent professional license I changed locations and jobs. I began working at a residential treatment center for emotionally disturbed children and adolescents. While there I became Director of Psychology Internship Training. I also continued my own training, which included study in family therapy at a well-known institute. I then became interested in expanding my private practice and to continue my writing, which I had begun during this time. So, I resigned and began amassing a series of part-time positions.

"I have co-authored six professional books on psychological testing and therapy. I have also co-written a trade book, entitled *Helping Your Depressed Teenager: A Guide for Parents and Caregivers* (Wiley, 1995). My latest book is *Clinical Uses of Drawings* (Jason Aronson, 1996)."

Some Advice from Gerald Oster

"Learning is a lifelong process. 'Degrees only give you permission to learn.' These were words from an uncle and ring true in today's world. Most people anticipate change and you can expect to change career paths several times during a lifetime. Thus, going to college and possibly to graduate school allows you the exposure to valuable technical skills and other social, intellectual, and educational possibilities."

Attend Professional Conventions

Go to seminars and to conventions. There is no better place to see the kinds of possibilities than at a national convention within a profession. You gain incredible exposure and an awareness of what the field is all about.

Build up Your Resume

Become an assistant, whether it is in teaching or research, or within your college's counseling center. This is an excellent way to discover what your strengths and weaknesses are and whether you could see yourself doing this work on a daily basis. Take as many practicums or internships as possible. And, if possible, work full-time or volunteer during the summers.

RELATED OCCUPATIONS

Human Services Workers

Workers in other occupations that require skills similar to those of human services workers include social workers, community outreach workers, religious workers, occupational therapy assistants, physical therapy assistants and aides, psychiatric aides, and activity leaders.

Mental Health Counselors

Counselors help people evaluate their interests, abilities, and disabilities, and deal with personal, social, academic, and career problems. Others who help people in similar ways include college and student personnel workers, teachers, personnel workers and managers, human services workers, social workers, psychologists, psychiatrists, members of the clergy, occupational therapists, training and employee development specialists, and equal employment opportunity/affirmative action specialists.

Psychologists

Psychologists are trained to conduct research and teach, evaluate, counsel, and advise individuals and groups with special needs. Others who do this kind of work include psychiatrists, social workers, sociologists, clergy, special education teachers, and counselors.

PROFESSIONAL ASSOCIATIONS

Human Service Workers

Council for Standards in Human Services Education
Northern Essex Community College
Haverhill, MA 01830

National Organization for Human Service Education
Brookdale Community College
Lincroft, NJ 07738

Counseling

American Counseling Association
5999 Stevenson Ave.
Alexandria, VA 22304-3300
www.counseling.org

Council for Accreditation of Counseling and Related Educational Programs
American Counseling Association
5999 Stevenson Ave., 4th Fl.
Alexandria, VA 22304
www.counseling.org/cacrep

Commission on Rehabilitation Counselor Certification
1835 Rohlwing Rd., Ste. E
Rolling Meadows, IL 60008

National Board for Certified Counselors, Inc.
3 Terrace Way, Ste. D
Greensboro, NC 27403-3660
www.nbcc.org

State departments of education can supply information on colleges and universities that offer approved guidance and counseling training for state certification and licensure requirements.

State employment service offices have information about job opportunities and entrance requirements for counselors.

Psychology

American Psychological Association
Research Office and Education in Psychology and Accreditation Offices
750 1st St. NE
Washington, DC 20002
www.apa.org

National Association of School Psychologists
4030 East West Hwy., Ste. 402
Bethesda, MD 20814
www.nasponline.org

Information about state licensing requirements is available from:

Association of State and Provincial Psychology Boards
P.O. Box 4389
Montgomery, AL 36103-4389
www.asppb.org

Information on obtaining a job with the federal government may be obtained from the Office of Personnel Management through a telephone-based system. Consult your telephone directory under U.S. Government for a local number or call 912-757-3000 (TDD 912-744-2299). This number is not toll-free and charges may result. Information also is available from their website: www.usajobs.opm.gov.

CHAPTER FIFTEEN

PATH 6: LAW

or many, a liberal arts bachelor's degree is a stepping stone to careers that require additional education and training. The pathways for professional careers beyond the bachelor's level seem almost limitless. Many are discussed in other chapters as well as in the introductory sections to this book. But in this chapter, we focus on law, a wide-open field for which a liberal arts B.A. is the best preparatory background.

Preparation for a career as a lawyer really begins in college. Although there is no recommended prelaw major, the choice of an undergraduate program is important. Certain courses and activities are desirable because they give the student the skills needed to succeed both in law school and in the profession.

Essential skills include proficiency in writing, reading, and analyzing; thinking logically; and communicating verbally. An undergraduate program that cultivates these skills while broadening the student's view of the world is desirable. Courses in English, a foreign language, public speaking, government, philosophy, history, economics, mathematics, and computer science, among others, are useful. Whatever the major, students should not specialize too narrowly.

Students interested in a particular aspect of law may find related courses helpful; for example, many law schools with patent law tracks require bachelor's degrees, or at least several courses, in engineering and science. Future tax lawyers should have a strong undergraduate background in accounting.

DEFINITION OF THE CAREER PATH

Attorneys, also called lawyers, act as both advocates and advisors in our society. As advocates, they represent one of the opposing parties in criminal and civil trials by presenting evidence that supports their client in court. As advisors, lawyers counsel their clients as to their legal rights and obligations and suggest particular courses of action in business and personal matters. Whether acting as advocates or advisors, all attorneys interpret the law and apply it to specific situations. This requires excellent research and communication abilities.

Lawyers perform in-depth research into the purposes behind the applicable laws and into judicial decisions that have been applied to those laws under circumstances similar to those currently faced by the client.

While all lawyers continue to make use of law libraries to prepare cases, some supplement their search of the conventional printed sources with computer software packages that automatically search the legal literature and identify legal texts that may be relevant to a specific subject. In litigation that involves many supporting documents, lawyers may also use computers to organize and index the material.

Tax lawyers also use computers to make tax computations and explore alternative tax strategies for clients.

Lawyers then communicate to others the information obtained by research. They advise what actions clients may take and draw up legal documents, such as wills and contracts.

Lawyers must deal with people in a courteous, efficient manner and not disclose matters discussed in confidence with clients. They hold positions of great responsibility and are obligated to adhere to strict rules of ethics.

POSSIBLE JOB TITLES

While the majority of lawyers are in private practice where they may concentrate on criminal or civil law, there are many specialized areas into which an attorney can enter.

Trial Lawyers

The more detailed aspects of a lawyer's job depend upon his or her field of specialization and position. Even though all lawyers are allowed to represent parties in court, some appear in court more frequently than others. Some lawyers specialize in trial work. These lawyers need an exceptional ability to think quickly and speak with ease and authority and must be thoroughly familiar with courtroom rules and strategy. Trial lawyers still spend most of their time outside the courtroom conducting research, interviewing clients and witnesses, and handling other details in preparation for trial.

Criminal Law

In criminal law, lawyers represent persons who have been charged with crimes and argue their cases in courts of law.

Civil Law

In civil law, attorneys assist clients with litigation, wills, trusts, contracts, mortgages, titles, and leases. Some manage a person's property as trustee or, as executor, see that provisions of a client's will are carried out. Others handle only public interest cases, civil or criminal, that have a potential impact extending well beyond the individual client.

Other lawyers work for legal-aid societies private, nonprofit organizations established to serve disadvantaged people. These lawyers generally handle civil rather than criminal cases.

Some other specializations within civil law include:

- Bankruptcy
- Probate
- International law
- Environmental law
- Intellectual property
- Insurance law
- Family law
- Real estate law
- Public defence

House Counsel

Lawyers sometimes are employed full-time by a single client. If the client is a corporation, the lawyer is known as house counsel and usually advises the company about legal questions that arise from its business activities. These questions might involve patents, government regulations, contracts with other companies, property interests, or collective-bargaining agreements with unions.

Government Attorneys

Attorneys employed at the various levels of government make up still another category. Lawyers that work for state attorneys general, prosecutors, public defenders, and courts play a key role in the criminal justice system. At the federal level, attorneys investigate cases for the Department of Justice or other agencies. Also, lawyers at every government level help develop programs, draft laws, interpret legislation, establish enforcement procedures, and argue civil and criminal cases on behalf of the government.

Law Clerks

Law clerks are fully trained attorneys who choose to work with a judge, either for a one- to two-year stint out of law school or as a full-time, professional career. Their duties involve mainly research and writing reports.

Law Professors

A relatively small number of trained attorneys work in law schools. Most are faculty members who specialize in one or more subjects, and others serve as administrators. Some work full-time in nonacademic settings and teach only part-time.

WORKING CONDITIONS

Lawyers and judges do most of their work in offices, law libraries, and court-rooms. Lawyers sometimes meet in clients' homes or places of business and, when necessary, in hospitals or prisons. They frequently travel to attend meet-ings; to gather evidence; and to appear before courts, legislative bodies, and other authorities.

Salaried lawyers in government and private corporations generally have structured work schedules. Lawyers in private practice may work irregular hours while conducting research, conferring with clients, or preparing briefs during nonoffice hours.

Lawyers often work long hours, and about half regularly work fifty hours or more per week. They are under particularly heavy pressure, for example, when a case is being tried. Preparation for court includes keeping abreast of the latest laws and judicial decisions.

Although work generally is not seasonal, the work of tax lawyers and other specialists may be an exception. Because lawyers in private practice can often

FIRST-HAND ACCOUNTS FROM TWO LAWYERS

M. J. GOODWIN, FAMILY LAW

M. J. Goodwin has a B.A. in modern languages and a minor in business from Clemson University. She received her J.D. from the University of South Carolina in Columbia in 1991.

M. J. discusses her work:

"I am a female solo practitioner, which makes me a minority in my town: Anderson, South Carolina. My firm has two other employees: my husband, who left his job this year to join as my manager/ investigator, and my paralegal. I've been opened for almost two years and have done much better than I ever imagined.

"I prefer being on my own rather than working for a large firm because it gives me more control—I'm fully in charge. The flip side of that, though, is that I'm responsible for everything! If something needs to be done Saturday night, I'm going to be the one to do it.

"I practice in a variety of areas: family law (divorce, custody, adoption, guardian ad litem), personal injury (accidents, workman's compensation, etc.), and miscellaneous legal issues.

"I am essentially a trial lawyer. I don't like to be still or sit in the office too much. I also have a part-time contract as the city prosecutor, which means I handle municipal level crimes for our local public defender, mainly DUI, domestic violence, and shoplifting cases.

"There is no such thing as a typical day in my practice. I am involved with domestic litigation, divorces, child custody, separations, and adoptions. Anything in family court—particularly the break-up of a marriage or a custody dispute—are the most emotionally charged types of cases. These cases are usually worse than murder cases. It's very difficult to deal with people who are thinking with their emotions. They're usually so hurt they can't think straight. And that's what makes it stressful. Even when they do win, and we have a pretty high success rate, they don't feel any better. The legal win doesn't necessarily heal the emotional scars.

"I'm always on the move, meeting with clients and going to court almost every day. I also do a tremendous amount of paperwork—summons and complaints, answers and counterclaims, and affidavits and financial declarations.

"The legal system is very complicated. Helping people get through that system, however their case is going to be resolved, gives me a great deal of satisfaction. Not everyone gets a good verdict, not everyone wins. I also do many pro bono cases. When I left the prosecutor's office I made a public commitment to continue helping battered women. I called the newspapers and told them I would help women who were staying in the local shelter, that I would cut my hourly rate and let them make payments. I think that once someone has gone to the shelter they've made enough of a commitment to get out. I had prosecuted these cases before. I think I can help more now. Many of these women often refuse to prosecute, they just want to get away. I do my part by helping them with their divorces.

"If I had been asked about 'my career choice three years ago when I was at the prosecutor's office, I probably would have said I was really unhappy and wished that I hadn't gone to law school. I was actually thinking that way at the time. I enjoyed the work, especially helping people, but experienced major burnout as a prosecutor. Burnout, for most prosecuting attorneys, is caused by the high volume of pending cases, the nature of the work (dealing with victimized souls and putting up with criminals), and the very low pay (as compared to private practice and larger firms). A prosecutor also has many bosses to please: an immediate supervisor, the judge, the public, the victim, and the police. It's unlikely that you can please all of them at the same time."

M. J. Goodwin's Background

"I was set on getting a master's degree in French when I was suddenly called for jury duty. The experience fascinated and mesmerized me. After that, I made numerous inquiries to law schools for information. Law schools will usually take any major, so I didn't have to change mine.

"Directly out of law school I worked as an assistant prosecutor. For about three years I handled cases involving juveniles, domestic violence, and some sex crimes, particularly those involving children. In September of 1994, I opened my own firm."

Some Advice from M. J. Goodwin

"Don't become a lawyer with the idea that you're going to get rich. It's a huge misconception. The prosecutor jobs in Anderson, for example, pay between $32,000 and $40,000 a year. You can make more money working in a bank. The large firms pay very well, however, but they expect sixty to seventy-five hours a week.

"In my solo practice I get paid dependent upon what type of case I handle. For domestic work I charge by the hour—my fee is $100 an hour—because contingency fees in divorce cases are prohibited by our code of ethics. You wouldn't want an attorney pushing for someone *not* to settle a case so they could get a bigger fee. In some cases, such as car accidents, I work on a contingency fee. And for criminal cases I get a flat fee when I accept the case.

"Think very carefully about a career in law before you set out. Most people borrow money to go to law school. Get a job in a law firm before making the decision to go to law school. Some lawyers are difficult to get along with or work for. Be aware of all the stresses involved before you commit yourself.

"Becoming a lawyer is a big decision. I don't think anyone should impulsively get into this career thinking they're automatically going to get a job to make a lot of money."

GIST FLESHMAN, CLERK OF THE COURT

Gist Fleshman has a bachelor's degree in political science from Illinois State University in Normal, Illinois. After working for a Congressman in Washington D.C. for a couple of years, he went back to school and earned his J.D. from DePaul University in Chicago in 1985. He is Clerk of the Court for the Illinois Appellate Court Third District.

Gist Fleshman talks about his job:

"My official job title is Clerk of the Appellate Court/Attorney. There are also Clerks of the Court who are not attorneys—it's a lower pay grade.

"The Clerk of the Court is the head administrative official in a court. He or she is the person who runs the court's operations on a day-to-day basis. The clerk may or may not answer to the judges, depending on the system.

"In Illinois we have Clerks of the Court at the trial level (circuit court) who are elected. In the appellate and state supreme court, we have appointed clerks. People appeal to this court if they aren't satisfied with their trial results. This court then reviews it.

"My job is about 40 percent legal, 60 percent administrative. I'm the day-to-day operations manager for the court. I deal with the public and press. I still do all the motions that are filed in the court. The court has authorized me to make decisions on the routine ones. We receive thousands of motions, so the judge usually authorizes the staff to handle most of the work. On the more complex issues there is a motions judge and I'll discuss them with him.

"In my administrative capacity, I make sure people show up everyday for work and do their job. I make some policy decisions and take care of the maintenance of the building. I also supervise eighteen people: staff attorneys, the chief deputy clerk and seven deputy clerks, the maintenance and housekeeping staff. There are six judges in the court and each has two law clerks and one secretary.

"I have variety in my work without the stress. In the practice of law in a general firm you get the variety, too, but with a great deal of stress to go along with it. I get to do legal work and I often decide how much I want to do. If I don't have time, I can delegate things to the research department. On the other hand, if it's some particular issue I find interesting, I do the research myself.

"The major downside is the same as for any other administrator: personnel problems. They can often be uncomfortable, but you have to deal with them. One thing I have found out is that 'subtle' doesn't work. In my opinion, when a problem arises you should take the person aside—you don't want to embarrass him or her in front of others—and tell them exactly what the problem is and exactly what you expect. That usually takes care of the situation.

"One of the things I love about my job is that you can make a big difference. You definitely see injustices, where people have gotten a bad deal—people in prison who shouldn't be, or children who were taken away needlessly from their parents. Unlike in other jobs, you can do something about it here. You can pick up the phone and talk to a judge and tell him what's going on. You often become an advocate for a particular party. Nevertheless, the judges listen to me. Wrongs can be righted. I love that aspect. It's very gratifying."

Gist Fleshman's Background

"I got my degree in political science. I enjoyed that, but didn't want to do it for the rest of my life. I took some time off and realized I needed more than a political science degree, something that would allow me to go into a job immediately. I decided to pursue a degree in law.

"Originally, I had planned to practice law, but I came to this courthouse directly out of law school as a staff attorney. There's a central research staff that functions the way law clerks do. I thought I'd stay one year, maybe two, then go into private practice. After a year I went on a few interviews and was offered some jobs, but they didn't interest me. I really enjoyed what I was doing so I thought I'd stay another year—and then another year went by. Then two judges asked me if I'd like to be their personal law clerk, which entailed a $7,000 raise. I thought I'd do that for a year, then I'd definitely move on. But then, after a few months the research director, who is the day-to-day supervisor of the central staff attorneys, resigned and I was offered that position. I did that job for two-and-a-half years. I still thought I'd move on, however, and was preparing for that. But the Clerk of the Court started talking about retirement, I put in my name among the applicants and I was chosen. That was in 1992.

"I started out earning $21,500 and after each promotion I had a raise in salary. My pay went to $26,800 then jumped to $33,800. When I became research director I got my salary moved up to $41,000. I now earn $61,500, yet I'm one of the lowest paid clerks in the country at the appellate court level.

"I've been here ten years now—longer than any judge that's been here. The judges put more trust in me than they would in someone they just hired from the outside."

Advice from Gist Fleshman

"You need to work your way up through the ranks. The courts want someone with experience. Coming in as a staff attorney or law clerk is the best way to do it because you learn how the court works.

"In some ways it's a position you can create for yourself. If you prove yourself you could make the job whatever you want it to be.

"It's a very competitive field. You need to make sure you have excellent reading and writing skills."

determine their own workload and when they will retire, many stay in practice well beyond the usual retirement age.

TRAINING AND QUALIFICATIONS

To practice law in the courts of any state or other jurisdiction, a person must be licensed, or admitted to its bar, under rules established by the jurisdiction's highest court. Nearly all require that applicants for admission to the bar pass a written bar examination. Most jurisdictions also require applicants to pass a separate written ethics examination. Lawyers who have been admitted to the bar in one jurisdiction occasionally may be admitted to the bar in another without taking an examination, if they meet that jurisdiction's standards of good moral character and have a specified period of legal experience.

Federal courts and agencies set their own qualifications for those practicing before them.

To qualify for the bar examination in most states, an applicant must complete at least three years of college and graduate from a law school approved by the American Bar Association (ABA) or the proper state authorities.

ABA approval signifies that the law school, particularly its library and faculty, meets certain standards developed by the Association to promote quality legal education. The American Bar Association currently approves 183 law schools. Others are approved by state authorities only. With certain exceptions, graduates of schools not approved by the ABA are restricted to taking the bar examination and practicing in the state or other jurisdiction in which the school is located; most of these schools are in California.

Seven states accept the study of law in a law office or in combination with study in a law school; only California accepts the study of law by correspondence as qualifying for taking the bar examination. Several states require registration and approval of students by the State Board of Law Examiners, either before they enter law school or during the early years of legal study.

Although there is no nationwide bar examination, forty-seven states, the District of Columbia, Guam, the Northern Mariana Islands, and the Virgin Islands require the six-hour Multistate Bar Examination (MBE) as part of the bar examination; the MBE is not required in Indiana, Iowa, Louisiana, Washington, or Puerto Rico. The MBE, covering issues of broad interest, is given in addition to a locally prepared, six-hour state bar examination. The three-hour Multistate Essay Examination (MEE) is used as part of the state bar examination in a few states. States vary in their use of MBE and MEE scores.

The required college and law school education usually takes seven years of full-time study after high school: four years of undergraduate study, followed by three years in law school. Although some law schools accept a very small number of students after three years of college, most require applicants to have a bachelor's degree. To meet the needs of students who can attend only part-time, a number of law schools have night or part-time divisions that usually require four years of study.

Acceptance by most law schools depends on the applicant's ability to demonstrate an aptitude for the study of law, usually through good undergraduate grades, the Law School Admission Test (LSAT), the quality of the applicant's undergraduate school, any prior work experience, and sometimes a personal interview. However, law schools vary in the weight that they place on each of these factors.

All law schools approved by the American Bar Association require that applicants take the LSAT. Nearly all law schools require that applicants have certified transcripts sent to the Law School Data Assembly Service. This service then sends applicants' LSAT scores and their standardized records of college grades to the law schools of their choice. Both this service and the LSAT are administered by the Law School Admission Services.

Competition for admission to many law schools is intense. Enrollments rose very rapidly during the 1970s, with applicants far outnumbering available seats. Since then, law school enrollments have remained relatively unchanged, and the number of applicants has fluctuated. However, the number of applicants to most law schools still greatly exceeds the number that can be admitted. Enrollments are expected to remain at about their present level through the year 2005, and competition for admission to the more prestigious law schools will remain keen.

During the first year or year and a half of law school, students generally study fundamental courses such as constitutional law, contracts, property law, torts, civil procedure, and legal writing. In the remaining time, they may elect specialized courses in fields such as tax, labor, or corporation law. Law students often acquire practical experience by participation in school-sponsored legal aid or legal clinic activities; in the school's moot court competitions in which students conduct appellate arguments; in practice trials under the supervision of experienced lawyers and judges; and through research and writing on legal issues for the school's law journal.

In 1997, law students in fifty-two states were required to pass the Multistate Professional Responsibility Examination (MPRE), which tests their knowledge of the ABA codes on professional responsibility and judicial conduct. In some states, the MPRE may be taken during law school, usually after completing a course on legal ethics.

A number of law schools have clinical programs where students gain legal experience through practice trials and law school projects under the supervision of practicing lawyers and law school faculty. Law school clinical programs might include work in legal aid clinics, for example, or on the staff of legislative committees. Part-time or summer clerkships in law firms, government agencies, and corporate legal departments also provide experience that can be extremely valuable later on. Such training can provide references or lead directly to a job after graduation and can help students decide what kind of practice best suits them. Clerkships also may be an important source of financial aid.

Graduates receive the degree of juris doctor (J.D.) or bachelor of law (LL.B.) as the first professional degree. Advanced law degrees may be desirable for those planning to specialize, do research, or teach. Some law students pursue joint degree programs, which generally require an additional year. Joint degree programs are offered in a number of areas, including law and business administration and law and public administration.

After graduation, lawyers must keep informed about legal and nonlegal developments that affect their practice. Thirty-seven states and jurisdictions mandate Continuing Legal Education (CLE). Furthermore, many law schools and state and local bar associations provide continuing education courses that help lawyers stay abreast of recent developments.

The practice of law involves a great deal of responsibility. Persons planning careers in law should like to work with people and be able to win the respect and confidence of their clients, associates, and the public. Integrity and honesty are vital personal qualities. Perseverance and reasoning ability are essential to analyze complex cases and reach sound conclusions. Lawyers also need creativity when handling new and unique legal problems.

Most beginning lawyers start in salaried positions. Newly hired salaried attorneys usually act as research assistants to experienced lawyers or judges. After several years of progressively more responsible salaried employment, some lawyers are admitted to partnership in their firm or go into practice for themselves. Some lawyers, after years of practice, become full-time law school faculty or administrators; a growing number have advanced degrees in other fields as well.

Some people use their legal training in administrative or managerial positions in various departments of large corporations. A transfer from a corporation's legal department to another department often is viewed as a way to gain administrative experience and rise in the ranks of management.

CAREER OUTLOOK

Lawyers and judges held about 735,000 jobs in 1994. About three-fourths of the 656,000 lawyers practiced privately, either in law firms or in solo practices. Most of the remaining lawyers held positions in government, the greatest number at the local level.

In the federal government, lawyers are concentrated in the Departments of Justice, Treasury, and Defense, but they work for other federal agencies as well. Other lawyers are employed as house counsel by public utilities, banks, insurance companies, real estate agencies, manufacturing firms, welfare and religious organizations, and other business firms and nonprofit organizations.

Some salaried lawyers also have part-time independent practices; others work as lawyers part-time while working full-time in another occupation.

Persons seeking positions as lawyers or judges will encounter keen competition through the year 2008. Law schools still attract large numbers of applicants and are not expected to decrease their enrollments, so the supply of persons trained as lawyers should continue to exceed job openings.

Employment of lawyers has grown very rapidly since the early 1970s and is expected to continue to grow faster than the average for all occupations through the year 2008. New jobs created by growth should exceed job openings that arise from the need to replace lawyers who stop working or leave the profession. The strong growth in demand for lawyers will result from growth in the population and the general level of business activities. Demand also will be spurred by growth of legal action in such areas as employee benefits, consumer protection, criminal prosecution, the environment, and finance and an anticipated increase in the use of legal services by middle-income groups through legal clinics and prepaid legal service programs.

Even though jobs for lawyers are expected to increase rapidly, competition for job openings should continue to be keen because of the large numbers graduating from law school each year.

During the 1970s, the annual number of law school graduates more than doubled, outpacing the rapid growth of jobs. Growth in the yearly number of law school graduates tapered off during the 1980s, but again increased in the early 1990s. The high number of graduates will strain the economy's capacity to absorb them. Although graduates with superior academic records from well-regarded law schools will continue to enjoy good opportunities, most graduates will encounter competition for jobs. As in the past, some graduates may have to accept positions in areas outside their field of interest or for which they feel they are overqualified. They may have to enter jobs for which legal training is an asset but not normally a requirement.

Due to the competition for jobs, a law graduate's geographic mobility and work experience assume greater importance. The willingness to relocate may be an advantage in getting a job, but to be licensed in a new state, a lawyer may have to take an additional state bar examination. In addition, employers increasingly seek graduates who have advanced law degrees and experience in a particular field such as tax, patent, or admiralty law.

Employment growth of lawyers will continue to be concentrated in salaried jobs, as businesses and all levels of government employ a growing number of staff attorneys, and as employment in the legal services industry is increasingly concentrated in larger law firms.

The number of self-employed lawyers is expected to continue to increase slowly, reflecting the difficulty of establishing a profitable new practice in the face of competition from larger, established law firms. Also, the growing complexity of law, which encourages specialization, and the cost of maintaining up-to-date legal research materials both favor larger firms.

For lawyers who nevertheless wish to work independently, establishing a new practice, probably will continue to be easiest in small towns and expanding suburban areas, as long as an active market for legal services already exists. In such communities, competition from larger established law firms is likely to be less than in big cities, and new lawyers may find it easier to become known to potential clients; also, rent and other business costs are somewhat lower. Nevertheless, starting a new practice will remain an expensive and risky undertaking that should be weighed carefully.

Most salaried positions will remain in urban areas where government agencies, law firms, and big corporations are concentrated.

Some lawyers are adversely affected by cyclical swings in the economy. During recessions, the demand for some discretionary legal services, such as planning estates, drafting wills, and handling real estate transactions, declines. Also, corporations are less likely to litigate cases when declining sales and profits result in budgetary restrictions. Although few lawyers actually lose their jobs during these times, earnings may decline. Some corporations and law firms will not hire new attorneys until business improves. Several factors, however, mitigate the overall impact of recessions on lawyers. During recessions, individuals and corporations face other legal problems, such as bankruptcies, foreclosures, and divorces, that require legal action. Furthermore, new laws and legal interpretations will create new opportunities for lawyers.

EARNINGS

The median annual earnings of all lawyers are $78,170. The middle half of the occupation earns between $51,450 and $114,520. The bottom tenth earns less than $37,310. Median annual earnings in the industries employing the largest numbers of lawyers are shown below:

Legal services	$78,700
Federal government	$78,200
Fire, marine, and casualty insurance	$74,400
State government	$59,400
Local government	$49,200

The National Association for Law Placement reports that the median salaries of lawyers six months after graduation from law school in 1998 varied by type of work, as indicated below:

Private practice	$60,000
Business/industry	$50,000
Academe	$38,000
Judicial clerkship	$37,500
Government	$36,000
Public interest	$31,000

The average salary of all lawyers six months after graduation is $45,000.

Salaries of experienced attorneys vary widely according to the type, size, and location of their employer. Lawyers who own their own practices usually earn less than those who are partners in law firms. Lawyers starting their own practices may need to work part-time in other occupations to supplement their income until their practice is well established.

Earnings among judicial workers also vary significantly. According to the Administrative Office of the U.S. Courts, the Chief Justice of the United States Supreme Court earns $175,400, and the Associate Justices earns $167,900.

Federal district court judges have salaries of approximately $136,700, as do judges in the Court of Federal Claims and the Court of International Trade; circuit court judges earn about $145,000 a year.

Federal judges with limited jurisdiction, such as magistrates and bankruptcy court judges, have salaries of $125,800.

According to a survey by the National Center for State Courts, annual salaries of associate justices of states' highest courts average $105,100 and range from about $77,100 to $137,300.

Salaries of state intermediate appellate court judges average $103,700 and range from $79,400 to $124,200.

Salaries of state judges of general jurisdiction trial courts average $94,000 and range from $72,000 to $115,300.

Most salaried lawyers and judges are provided health and life insurance, and contributions are made on their behalf to retirement plans. Lawyers who practice independently are only covered if they arrange and pay for such benefits themselves.

STRATEGIES FOR FINDING THE JOBS

The following steps are offered by attorney Gist Fleshman. (See his first-hand account earlier in this chapter.)

Work Part-time During Law School

The best way to find a job after law school is to already have a job. Many firms, government agencies, and companies with legal staff hire new attorneys who have worked for the firm part-time or during the summers while attending law school. This gives both sides a chance to try each other out before committing to a long-term relationship. At smaller firms with no set hiring schedule, you may well convince the firm it's time to expand.

Law School Placement Office

Your next best bet is your law school's placement office. Firms and government agencies looking for attorneys with little or no experience often advertise there. Some firms will come onto your campus at a set time to interview prescreened applicants. Talk with a placement advisor about how that works at your school. Other firms simply want applicants to send them a combination of a cover letter, resume, transcript, and writing samples. Most law schools have reciprocity with other schools' placement offices. Check with your placement director, because you may need a letter from him or her to use the other school's office. This is definitely worth your time. Listings at various placement offices often differ markedly.

Ads in Legal Periodicals

You're not likely to find any ads in general newspapers or magazines, though; it's not worth the firm's money when so few readers qualify. Specialized legal periodicals are the place to look for job openings. The smaller the readership, the better your chances. You aren't likely to get one of those jobs listed in *The National Law Journal.* You do have a shot at the jobs listed in your local bar journals. Larger cities have daily legal newspapers that carry numerous ads. Call the local bar association to learn which legal periodicals cover your area.

Networking

Networking may also pay dividends. In fact, some people might place it at the head of the list based on their experiences. On the other hand, "networking" for recent graduates generally amounts to little more than extortion. You know someone with enough clout to pressure a law firm to interview and possibly hire you. Often, the interview is a farce, with the law firm having no intention of hiring you. It just helps to keep your mentor happy. Even if you do get a job, there's a good chance the firm will resent you. You've got enough hurdles as a new attorney without this headache.

The Shotgun Approach

Finally, there's the shotgun approach. You send out hundreds of letters to law firms and government agencies, simply hoping one of them will be so intrigued by you it will set up an interview. Some people have gotten jobs this way. But, the reality is that unless you have a super-specialty, such as an undergraduate degree in engineering and you want to be a patent lawyer, chances are you won't get any significant responses.

One exception is applying to appellate judges. Many interview year-round for upcoming law clerk openings. Judges also tend to be poor advertisers, so the pool of applicants may well be small.

No matter what approach you take, remember these two things:

1. Send the firms and agencies exactly what they asked for. When there are 140 applicants for one opening, the employer may start by automatically rejecting anyone who, for example, didn't include a writing sample of less than ten pages, as requested.

2. During interviews honesty doesn't always pay. Don't lie about important matters, such as your class rank or achievements, but don't be brutally honest, either. A woman who was being interviewed who stated that she wanted to leave her current employer because they made her work too hard. That may well have been true, but the employer wasn't going to hire anyone who lacked the basic common sense to realize how bad that sounded to an interviewer.

PROFESSIONAL ASSOCIATIONS

Information on law schools and a career in law may be obtained from:

American Bar Association
750 N. Lake Shore Dr.
Chicago, IL 60611
www.abanet.org

Information on the LSAT, the Law School Data Assembly Service, applying to law school, and financial aid for law students may be obtained from:

Law School Admission Council
P.O. Box 40
Newtown, PA 18940
www.lsac.org

Information on acquiring a job as a lawyer with the federal government may be obtained from the Office of Personnel Management through a telephone-based system. Consult your telephone directory under U.S. Government for a local number or call 912-757-3000, TDD 912-744-2299. This number is not toll-free and charges may result.

Information also is available from their website: www.usajobs.opm.gov.

The requirements for admission to the bar in a particular state or other jurisdiction may also be obtained at the state capital from the clerk of the Supreme Court or the administrator of the State Board of Bar Examiners.

INDEX

237